Assessing Child Maltreatment Reports: The Problem of False Allegations

THE CHILD & YOUTH SERVICES SERIES:

EDITOR-IN-CHIEF

JEROME BEKER, *Director and Professor, Center for Youth Development and Research, University of Minnesota*

- *Institutional Abuse of Children & Youth*, edited by Ranae Hanson
- *Youth Participation & Experiential Education*, edited by Daniel Conrad and Diane Hedin
- *Legal Reforms Affecting Child & Youth Services*, edited by Gary B. Melton
- *Social Skills Training for Children and Youth*, edited by Craig W. LeCroy
- *Adolescent Substance Abuse: A Guide to Prevention and Treatment*, edited by Richard Isralowitz and Mark Singer
- *Young Girls: A Portrait of Adolescence*, by Gisela Konopka
- *Adolescents, Literature, and Work with Youth*, co-edited by J. Pamela Weiner and Ruth M. Stein
- *Residential Group Care in Community Context: Implications From the Israeli Experience*, edited by Zvi Eisikovits and Jerome Beker
- *Helping Delinquents Change: A Treatment Manual of Social Learning Approaches*, by Jerome Stumphauzer
- *Qualitative Research and Evaluation in Group Care*, edited by Rivka Eisikovits and Yitzhak Kashti
- *The Black Adolescent Parent*, edited by Stanley F. Battle
- *Developmental Group Care of Children and Youth: Concepts and Practice*, by Henry W. Maier
- *Assaultive Youth: Responding to Physical Assaultiveness in Residential, Community and Health Care Settings*, edited by Joel Kupfersmid and Roberta Monkman
- *Family Perspectives in Child and Youth Services*, edited by David H. Olson
- *Transitioning Exceptional Children and Youth into the Community: Research and Practice*, edited by Ennio Cipani
- *Helping the Youthful Offender: Individual and Group Therapies That Work*, by William B. Lewis
- *Specialist Foster Family Care: A Normalizing Experience*, edited by Joe Hudson and Burt Galaway
- *Perspectives in Professional Child and Youth Care*, edited by James P. Anglin, Carey J. Denholm, Roy V. Ferguson and Alan R. Pence
- *Homeless Children: The Watchers and the Waiters,* edited by Nancy A. Boxill
- *Being in Child Care: A Journey into Self,* by Gerry Fewster
- *People Care in Institutions: A Conceptual Schema and Its Application* by Yochanan Wozner
- *Assessing Child Maltreatment Reports: The Problem of False Allegations*, by Michael Robin

Assessing Child Maltreatment Reports: The Problem of False Allegations

Michael Robin
Editor

The Haworth Press
New York • London • Sydney

Assessing Child Maltreatment Reports: The Problem of False Allegations has also been published as *Child & Youth Services*, Volume 15, Number 2 1991.

The Haworth Press, Inc., 10 Alice Street, Binghamton, NY 13904-1580
EUROSPAN/Haworth, 3 Henrietta Street, London WC2E 8LU England
ASTAM/Haworth, 162-168 Parramatta Road, Stanmore, Sydney, N.S.W. 2048 Australia

Library of Congress Cataloging-in-Publication

Assessing child maltreatment reports : the problem of false allegations / Michael Robin, editor.
    p. cm.
    "Has also been published as Child & youth services, volume 15, number 2, 1991"—T.p. verso.
    ISBN 0-86656-931-6 (alk. paper). —ISBN 1-56024-161-6 (pbk. : alk. paper)
    1. Child abuse—United States—Investigation. 2. Child molesting—United States—Investigation. 3. Interviewing in child abuse—United States. 4. False testimony—United States. 5. Malicious accusation—United States. I. Robin, Michael.
    [DNLM: 1. Child Abuse. 2. Child Abuse, Sexual. W1 CH644 v. 15 no. 2]
HV8079.C46A77 1991
363.2'595554—dc20
DNLM/DLC
for Library of Congress
        91-20799
        CIP

Assessing Child Maltreatment Reports: The Problem of False Allegations

CONTENTS

ALLEGATIONS OF MALTREATMENT
IN FAMILY FOSTER HOMES

Assessing Child Maltreatment Reports: The Problem of False Allegations

To Peggy and Sarah

ABOUT THE EDITOR

Michael Robin, ACSW, MPH, a clinical social worker in St. Paul, Minnesota, is currently a doctoral student at the School of Social Work, University of Minnesota. He has worked with children and families in residential care, adoption, foster care, and community mental health. Mr. Robin's research interests include the history of child welfare services. He has also lectured widely and presented many workshops on children, child abuse, and child welfare services in the United States, Canada, Europe, and Mexico.

Preface

The underlying theme of this book is the age-old problem of deciding which verbal or written reports represent truth or falsehood. This issue is as pertinent today when assessing reports of child maltreatment as it was in the Old Testament with respect to the Ninth Commandment: "Thou shall not bear false witness against thy neighbor." The pronouncement "Thou shall not bear false witness" embraces all forms of slander, defamation, and misrepresentation, whether of an individual, a group, a people, a race, or a faith. "Thy neighbor" refers to all our fellow human beings. In regard to the Ten Commandments, it is easier to deal with the prohibitions against killing, as in the Sixth Commandment: "Thou shall not murder" or stealing, as in the Eighth Commandment: "Thou shall not steal." However, when one deals with "words of accusation" in the area of child maltreatment, special problems are posed.

Professionals who hear the words and read the reports of allegations of maltreatment from children, parents and other professionals are confronted with these realities every day. Given the serious consequences of reports of maltreatment, the determination of the accuracy of such reports is of critical importance to all concerned. This book brings home to us the complexity and the seriousness of confronting the need to separate out those reports that are true and those that are false. It deals with the everyday world of assessing the validity and reliability of reports and, more importantly, deals with the professional, philosophical, and religious value — "first, do no harm" (Primum Non Nocere).

The motivation behind this collection of articles is a realization that professionals must remain objective, keep an open mind, and know theory from hypothesis and fact from fiction. This is not an easy task, and it takes a great deal of courage to bring this controversial issue before our professional groups as well as our communities. These articles give us hope for establishing a deeper understanding of the broad system of child protection as well as how to better handle individual cases.

There is always the realization that it is difficult to know absolutely what is "truth." Over the Arc of the Covenant are the words "truth, justice, and peace." Only by striving for truth can we have a system of justice that works and provides peace for the community. We must all be aware of the pitfalls involved in assessing allegations of child maltreatment. A compassionate and understanding approach to these issues will help in providing guideposts for further research and discussion.

Robert W. ten Bensel
University of Minnesota

Acknowledgements

I would like to give special thanks to the authors who contributed their thought-provoking essays to this volume. In addition, I would also like to thank the following individuals: Robert ten Bensel, who as teacher, mentor, and friend, has been a continuing source of support and inspiration to me for many years; Jerry Beker, who as general editor of *Child & Youth Services*, has guided me through the arduous process of editing this book; Richard Cronk, Margaret Gran, David Perrin, David Wilson, Jackie Wiersma, and Norma Jean Akrivos, who each in their own way made a special contribution to this book; Betty Schiefelbein, who patiently and expertly typed the manuscript; and most of all, I wish to thank my wife, Peggy, and my daughter, Sarah, for their patient and loving support. It is to Peggy and Sarah that this book is dedicated.

The Social Construction
of Child Abuse
and "False Allegations"

Michael Robin

ABSTRACT. This essay traces the evolution and development of child abuse and neglect as a serious social problem. It examines how the topic has been brought to public attention, the content of the claims that have been made about the problem, and the practical and political implications of how the problem has been socially constructed. It also examines how current approaches to the problem of child abuse and neglect have led, in the mid 1980's, to the development of "false allegations" as a serious social problem.

I hear so much of people's calling out to punish the guilty, but very few are concerned to clear the innocent.

—Daniel DeFoe

Nothing so offends the moral sensibilities of our society as the maltreatment of children. Child abuse and neglect evokes a range of emotions including shame, disgust, horror and outrage. In recent years, there has been a tremendous outpouring of sentiment and support for protecting children from abuse and neglect. "Child protection" has become well established as a social value and there are few who would question its

Michael Robin is affiliated with the School of Social Work, University of Minnesota, 400 Ford Hall, 224 Church Street SE, Minneapolis, MN 55454.

importance. As Myers (1987) has said, "society has an abiding interest in the welfare of children. It is in the interest of youth itself, and the whole community, that children be safeguarded from abuses and given opportunities for growth into free and independent citizens" (p. 380).

But as society intervenes into families on behalf of children, it must do so with caution and due regard to the needs and rights of both children and their families. This should include the right to due process of law as well as protection from those who might bear false witness. An accusation of child maltreatment can be easy to make but is often difficult to disprove. Because reports of abuse have serious consequences, great care should be taken when assessing whether or not a child has been maltreated.

This essay, which draws on social constructionist theory (Best, 1989; Spector & Kitsuse, 1977) examines the emergence of "child abuse" as a social problem in contemporary society. It will examine the social organization of child protective services, and the role of child protection professionals, who as claims-makers, have played a major role in shaping professional and public attitudes about the nature of the problem. This essay takes for granted that child abuse and neglect is a serious and widespread problem in the United States. It also assumes that false allegations of child abuse and neglect are a problem of significant proportions. While no one knows the true extent of false allegations, the word "significant" implies, according to Webster's dictionary, the problem is "meaningful" and worthy of increased public attention. Throughout, this paper will be guided by the following assumptions:

1. Despite its problems, the child protective system has been successful in identifying, and protecting many children from unnecessary suffering, pain, and even death.
2. That the non-recognition and non-reporting of maltreated children still remains a serious and extensive problem.
3. That over-reporting or "false accusations" are also a serious and extensive problem that causes harm and suffering for children, their families and others.
4. That both the problems of underreporting and overreporting are jeopardizing the integrity of the child protective system.

EMERGENCE OF CHILD ABUSE AS A SOCIAL PROBLEM

While the maltreatment of children dates back to antiquity, "child abuse" as a social construction is a recent concept (Robin, 1982). Child abuse, according to Garbarino (1989), is not a fixed, objective entity, but is essentially a socially mediated conclusion about parent-child relationships that is based on community standards of appropriate and reasonable child care. What is considered "child abuse" or "child neglect" in any particular society is a product of social negotiation between individual values and beliefs, social norms, and professional knowledge about children, child development, and family relationships. "Child abuse" is ultimately what a community, through its representatives (i.e., child protection workers), defines as unreasonable and inappropriate in child care.

The "Rediscovery" of Abuse

Public perceptions about child abuse and neglect have been influenced to a great extent by the work of pediatrician, C. Henry Kempe. In 1962, Kempe and a group of colleagues published an article, "The Battered Child Syndrome" in the prestigious Journal of the American Medical Association (Kempe et al., 1962). Kempe's article, which is often associated with the "rediscovery" of child abuse, brought legitimacy to child abuse as a serious public concern.

"The Battered Child Syndrome" described the clinical manifestations, psychiatric aspects, and techniques of evaluation and management of abused children and their families. Kempe and colleagues wrote that psychiatric factors were of prime importance in the pathogenesis of the Battered Child Syndrome. They argued that most abusive parents had some deficit in character or had been abused themselves as children. Abuse was defined as a "syndrome" rooted in the problem of inadequate parenting.

Following the publication of Kempe's article, whose title was chosen for its evocative appeal, all of the states passed child abuse reporting laws between 1963 and 1967. The passage of child abuse reporting laws represented one of the most rapid adoptions of public law in the history of the country. There was a strong response from every level of society. Discussions of child abuse were held in private homes, public meetings, and in professional forums creating considerable political pressure to strengthen protective services for children. These activities eventually culminated in the passage of the Child Abuse Prevention and Treatment Act of 1973, which created the National Center on Child Abuse and Neglect (Nelson, 1984).

The Child Abuse Prevention and Treatment Act was introduced in the Senate by Walter Mondale of Minnesota. At the senate hearings preceding the passage of the act, Mondale argued that child abuse was not a poverty problem. Mondale feared that the legislation would be blocked if it was viewed as a poverty program, or if the problem was conceived as being confined predominantly to the poor (Nelson, 1984). The hearings were dominated by those who argued from the "psychopathological model" that "the parent who abuses his or her child suffers from some psycholog-

ical disease which must be cured in order to prevent further abuse"
(Gelles, 1973). As metaphor, "abuse" carries the inference that the indi-
vidual parent is solely responsible for the harm brought upon the child
(Pelton, 1989).

The Politics of Individualism

The individualistic premises of child abuse policy are reinforced by
what LeRoy Pelton has called the "myth of classlessness" (Pelton, 1989).
Although there is considerable evidence of a strong relationship between
poverty and child abuse and neglect, many practitioners argue that abuse
cuts across class lines. While not without an element of truth, such an
approach leaves the impression that abuse and neglect is caused primarily
by individual psychological factors. The degree to which economic and
social stresses contribute to child abuse and neglect is acknowledged in
research studies, but tends to be discounted or ignored in clinical practice.
Consequently, most efforts at responding to the problem have focused on
identifying and treating individual abusers and victims with psychological
therapies, rather than remediating the economic and social conditions that
allow abuse to occur (Nelson, 1984; Edelman, 1988).

Defining child abuse as a problem of "troubled persons" is a way of
"depoliticizing" the problem (Gusfield, 1989). The psychologizing of
social phenomena, according to Gusfield, draws attention away from the
institutional or structural aspects of the problem. The term "child abuse"
itself displaces our attention from the context of abuse to the moral and
psychological failings of the individual abuser. By making the individual
abuser the "causal agent," agent, rather than scene becomes the focus of
attention (Gusfield, 1981).

An alternative consciousness might conceive of the problem of child
abuse and neglect from an ecological perspective with multiple levels of
causality and responsibility. There is considerable research that identifies
a series of factors that are associated with child abuse and neglect including economic stress, isolation, and poor social support; cultural values
that justify the use of force in conflict resolution; and personal factors such
as low self-esteem, poor impulse control, and psychological disturbances.
While the psychopathology of "perpetrators" may be only one part of a
complicated picture, the "psychopathological" paradigm, has nonetheless dominated contemporary thinking about child abuse and neglect policy (Dubowitz & Newberger, 1989).

That child abuse and neglect is defined as a form of medical deviance
rather than a poverty problem helps account for its "valence quality."
Valence issues, according to Nelson (1984), are issues that are non-con-
troversial and evoke strong, emotional responses. The valence quality of

child abuse helps to account for the great magnetism of the phenomenon. Child abuse is able to gain considerable public support because it is defined in a manner that is consistent with traditional American approaches to social problems. The problem is rooted in individual behavior, and is described as an illness solvable through "doses of therapeutic conversation" (Nelson, 1984). This construction of child abuse allows the public to sympathize with the plight of abused children without calling into question the basic organization of society (Edelman, 1988).

The social psychology of child abuse. More importantly, child abuse has been able to generate considerable public support because it speaks to the personal experience of so many people. As the work of Alice Miller (1981) illustrates, many people have been abused and neglected as children, and are thus able to identify with the "abused child" as a metaphor for their own violated childhood. The "abused child" is actually a symbol for the little child within all of us who feels inadequately loved.

The metaphor of the "abused child" is a powerful expression of violated innocence. When the professional community and the public identifies with the suffering of the abused child, they share in the child's innocence and purity. In a sense, they use the abused child psychologically to establish their own innocence (Steele, 1989). This process allows a sharp distinction to be drawn between "them," who are blamed for causing harm and suffering to children, and "us," who as child advocates are benevolent and innocent. By identifying with the innocence of the abused child, the rest of society is able to protect itself from the insight that they may have something in common with "abusive parents," share to some degree the character flaws of those who abuse children, or have any degree of responsibility for creating or supporting economic and social structures that allow child abuse and neglect to occur (Nelson, 1984: Edelman, 1988).

CHILD ABUSE IN THE PROFESSIONAL MIND

Defining Child Maltreatment

How a social problem is defined, according to Best (1987), establishes the proper domain of the problem, identifies what is and is not relevant and offers a general orientation toward the problem. Critics have argued for a number of years that definitions of child abuse and neglect are unnecessarily vague and fail to clearly specify standards for reporting and case assessment. As Giovannoni and Becerra (1979) have stated, "many assume that since child abuse and neglect are against the law, somewhere there are statutes that make clear distinctions between what is and what is not child abuse or neglect. But this is not the case. Nowhere are there clear-cut definitions of what is encompassed by the terms'' (p. 2).

There is, in fact, a myth of shared meanings in the whole area of child maltreatment (Haugaard & Reppucci, 1988). Words like ''child abuse,'' ''child neglect,'' ''sexual abuse'' and so on have no commonly accepted meanings. They are evocative terms that appeal as much to the emotions as to the intellect. As Gelles (1980) has argued, the term ''child abuse'' is a political concept designed to attract attention to a phenomenon which is considered undesirable or deviant.

Vague laws. According to Besharov (1985), the major cause of the system's decision making problems is the vagueness and overbreadth of legal standards governing child protective services. While many cases of abuse and neglect are serious and clear-cut and warrant social intervention, the majority of child abuse and neglect reports are ambiguous and fall within the ''borderline'' or ''gray'' area. It is in these types of situations, that decision-makers rely on their personal interpretations and values, rather than on clearly articulated social guidelines. Because existing standards do not provide clear guidelines for decision making, Besharov says there is an increased risk of unwarranted intervention into families.

Child abuse and neglect laws are so vague and imprecise that they allow state intervention not only when a child has been clearly harmed by parental behavior but also when parents have improper habits or attitudes. For example, many state laws provide for social intervention in a family when a child is not receiving ''proper parental care,'' ''proper attention,'' or whose parents do not provide the child with the ''care necessary for his health, morals or well-being.'' (Pelton, 1989)

Ultimately, determining when parenting becomes abusive is a matter of professional judgement. The problem is that while some discretion is reasonable, the extent of ambiguity in existing definitions provides insufficient guidelines for case decision making (Melton, 1987). It also fails to give caretakers, as required by due process of law, a clear idea of expected behaviors (Duquette, 1982). If child abuse and neglect is a crime that can result in the loss of liberty or custody of a child, then current definitions need to be less ambiguous. As Melton (1987) has pointed out, predictability is the sine qua non of law. He states that ''in the absence of clear guidelines, the law cannot be expected to guide the behavior of the citizenry or as an ethical matter, to ensure justice in the conduct of affairs of state'' (p. 81).

Social workers as gatekeepers. Many believe that case finding and case assessment are best left to the discretion of social workers assigned to investigate cases. Social workers thus wield enormous power as they are in a position to define the meaning of ordinary situations involving parents and children. Consequently they are able to control what explanations are used to explain these situations and what remedial actions are brought to bear.

Social workers make decisions without the benefit of clear guidelines or precise definitions. As Johnson (1986) points out, most social workers develop an "occupational ideology" for the handling of cases which includes their perceptions, thoughts, values and feelings about the nature of child maltreatment. Whether or not a case is "substantiated" depends on the subjective assessment of a number of interacting factors. There is a great deal of variability in how clinicians define abuse and in how they use their discretion to assess cases. Factors that influence the outcome of a case include the sex, race, and social class of the participants. In addition, the personal beliefs and biases of investigators about child development, child discipline, and family development also play a key role. All of this occurs in an "organizational context" which includes formal and informal rules for how decision making is handled by those in a particular work setting (Johnson, 1986; Knudsen, 1988; Wells, 1988).

Social workers essentially function as gatekeepers for the child protective system. They are given broad discretion and decisions tend to be essentially free of supervisory review or public accountability (Knudsen, 1988). While many social workers use their discretion in a prudent manner, because of the nature of the work, all CPS workers are prone to making clinical errors. As Pecora, Adams, and McGovern point out in this volume, clinical judgment is always fallible. The ability of workers to correctly assess whether or not a child has been maltreated or whether or not maltreatment will occur in the future is always limited (Wells, 1988).

Incidence

In addition to a problem's parameters, advocates also try to estimate its incidence. Best syas that claim-makers like to use big numbers when estimating the scope of a problem. The more widespread the problem, the more attention and resources it can attract (Best, 1987, 1989).

One common estimate was that one million children a year were the victims of maltreatment (Zigler, 1983). Estimates like this, or that "one in four girls" and "one in nine boys" have been sexually abused gain credibility by being repeated so often (Peters, Wyatt & Finklehor, 1986, p. 15). The "fact" of one million victims of child maltreatment has been taken for granted as a legitimate estimate of the problem. It is not that the figures are necessarily wrong, but that they are taken for granted as a legitimate estimate, representing the great magnitude of the problem (Gusfield, 1981).

While the figures presented may or may not be a reasonable estimate of the true incidence of child maltreatment, they do dramatize and draw attention to the problem. They form what Pelton (1989) refers to as the "numbers illusion," which is the belief that the true incidence of child maltreatment can be counted, and that these cases refer largely to serious cases of physical and sexual abuse. As Cohen and Sussman (1975) said,

> estimates of the number of maltreated children in the U.S. abound in the literature. Authors are fond of presenting alarming figures in order to alert their readers to the breadth of the problem. The data advanced vary among the experts; and the suggested figures often stated in probabilistic terms, are highly unreliable. Additional confusion results from the fact that authors tend to blur distinctions between suspected and confirmed cases of abuse, as well as between cases of child battering and all other forms of maltreatment. (p. 433)

Claims about the numbers of children that are maltreated rely on reports made to public authorities. By 1986, AHA (1988) noted that over 2 million reports of child maltreatment were received that year, and that about 40% were substantiated. Less than 3% were said to involve serious physical abuse such as battering, scalding, cuts, bone fractures, etc. The majority of cases involved "deprivation of necessities," including inadequate food, clothing, shelter, medical care and supervision. The large numbers of "maltreated" children reported to public authorities actually include many cases of "mild" abuse, marginal and inappropriate care, and poverty-related neglect (Pelton, 1989). While no one really knows the true extent of the problem, even the most conservative estimate indicates that child abuse and neglect is a significant and widespread social problem.

The epidemic of child abuse. A claim that is often made about child maltreatment is that the problem is getting worse and is reaching "epidemic" proportions. The use of the word "epidemic," a medical metaphor, has the effect of suggesting that the problem is out-of-control, is outside the range of normal social and political discourse, and is so widespread and serious, that drastic actions are required.

Moreover, it is claimed that those cases that have been identified by public authorities are "only the tip of the iceberg." The use of this metaphor suggests that child abuse and neglect is greatly underreported and that any child may be vulnerable to maltreatment. Best (1987) states that the claim that the range of a social problem extends throughout a society serves an important rhetorical function. "By arguing that anyone might be affected by a problem, a claims maker can make everyone in the audience feel that they have a vested interest in the problem's solution" (p. 108).

This creates an atmosphere of suspicion towards parents and adults in general.

Thus, by the 1980s, the child protection movement had generated considerable public attention. The large numbers of children who were said to be maltreated had become alarming to public sensibilities and persuaded the public that something had to be done. These statistics helped generate a "moral panic" about child abuse (Best, 1989).

Creation of a Moral Panic

Moral panics develop during periods of rapid social change, particularly when the pace of change outstrips the public's ability to emotionally and intellectually cope with the experience. During the 1960s and 1970s, changes in sexuality, sexual identity, and family roles threatened the viability of the "traditional family." Many people were disturbed by the increase of women working outside of the home and children in daycare, as well as the ascendence of abortion rights, gay rights, and the "sexual revolution" of recent years. Child abuse became a convenient focus for public anxiety about changing social conditions related to the family (Scheper-Hughes & Stein, 1987).

Moral panics involve condemning persons who are perceived as a threat to social values and structures. As Goode (1989) has written, "A 'moral panic' is a widespread feeling on the part of the public that something is terribly wrong in their society because of the moral failure of a specific group of individuals, a subpopulation defined as the enemy. In short, a category of people has been deviantized."

Parents and others who are accused of abuse of children thus take on the role of social scapegoats onto whom we project our anxieties and anger about things gone wrong. As objects of intense, negative social transference, they generate considerable moralistic outrage. Some persons who have been accused of abuse complain that investigations are conducted in an atmosphere of hostility and implied guilt from the moment the accusation is made. The social outrage about child abuse and neglect in the mid 1980's was reflected in a Minnesota survey, where nearly half of the respondents indicated they were willing to throw people accused of child abuse off of buildings, string them up, or dispatch them in a sundry fashion (*Minneapolis Star and Tribune*, May 19, 1985). In this atmosphere, it was difficult to raise the possibility that some persons may have been falsely accused.

Sacrifice of children. As Scheper-Hughes and Stein (1987) point out, it is a paradox that "the time of greatest public outcry against child abuse is also the time of the widespread, official planning of sacrifice of children in public policy" (p. 342). The authors note that many Americans, while expressing moralistic outrage toward individuals suspected of abusing children, continue to support policies that have had serious detrimental effects on children and their families.

The early 1980's began a period of major cutbacks in programs specifically designed to meet the needs of children. Little political protest was generated by the budget cuts in children's programs, which led one author to wonder if there was "an unconscious national conspiracy against children" (Rothenberg, 1980). The programs that were cut included Aid to Families with Dependent Children, day care, food programs, child abuse programs and many other programs that affect the well-being of children (Edelman, 1987). By the end of the decade, the process of gutting programs for children had become so extreme that the cover of *Time* magazine asked, "do we care about our kids?" (October 8, 1990).

The program cuts enacted in the 1980's have had a negative impact on children resulting in needless pain, hunger and even death. Many thousands of children went hungry when they lost access to food stamps, school lunches and the WIC program (Edelman, 1987). Moreover, increasing poverty, unemployment and federal housing cutbacks have resulted in large increases of homeless children. And because of cutbacks in maternal and child health services, infant mortality rates, particularly among blacks, began to rise in the early 1980's for the first time in 30 years and in certain areas continue to rival and exceed the infant mortality rates of many third world countries (Robin, 1984). Clearly, many more children in our country suffer from poverty and social neglect than from child abuse and neglect at the hands of their parents. How is it then that we as a society cope with our guilt feelings for participating in this "official sacrifice" of children (deMause, 1984)?

Creating scapegoats. Lloyd deMause (1984) has suggested that we cope with our guilt feelings by displacing them onto selected "criminal" scapegoats. As Kenneth Burke (1945) has written, "criminals, either actual or imagined, may serve as scapegoats in a society that 'purifies' itself by 'moral indignation' in condemning them" (p. 406). When attention is focused on isolated individuals who abuse their chidren, we project our guilt for supporting abusive social policies for children onto others. Our national preoccupation with punishing those who beat or sexually molest their children, say Scheper-Hughes and Stein (1987) "conceals the extent to which we are an abusive society" (p. 341).

The moral panic about child abuse and neglect is also sustained and enhanced, says Parton, by the convergence of child abuse and neglect with other social problems such as crime, drug abuse, breakdown of the family, a decline in sexual morals, etc. Convergence is created by drawing links between these phenomenon or by simply listing a series of problems and presenting them as part of a larger, underlying problem. This creates what Parton calls a "signification spiral" where the net effect is to amplify the "threat potential" to society (Parton, 1985).

Battered child as root metaphor. The "threat potential" of child abuse to society has been sustained by the dominance of the "battered child" as the root metaphor by which child maltreatment has been understood. Kempe and Helfer (1972), in regards to the term "battered child," state:

> For some this term means only the child who has been the victim of the most severe form of physical punishment, i.e., that child who represents the far end of a child abuse spectrum. For others, the term implies the total spectrum of abuse, beginning with the parents (or future parents), who have the potential to abuse their small children and ending with the severely beaten or killed child. Our view of the battered child is one that encompasses the total spectrum of abuse . . . . (p. xi-xii)

As Giovannoni and Becerra (1979) point out, for many persons the term "child abuse" conjures up an image of a tiny child brutalized by a disturbed parent, however the terms abuse and neglect actually refer to a wide variety of situations that vary in their nature and the degree of harm inflicted on the child.

Atrocity tales. Public attention has always focused on the most extreme and sensational instances of abuse and neglect (Nelson, 1984; Johnson, 1989). The recent trial of Joel Steinberg for the beating death of his six year old daughter is a case in point. The death of Lisa Steinberg, and the trial of her father drew great attention to a large extent because they were the exception that proved the rule. The drama of this case was fed by the reports of Steinberg's wife, Hedda Nussbaum. Nussbaum claimed that she was Steinberg's psychological captive. While this family presented itself to the public as a model middle class, professional family, it was in reality, according to Nussbaum, dominated by strange and violent behavior. This case gave the impression of being a "typical" case of child abuse and neglect (Johnson, 1990).

As Scheper-Hughes and Stein (1987) point out, national attention has always tended to focus on those "criminal" or "psychopathological" parents who beat or sexually molest their children, however, recent data demonstrates that physical battering and sexual molestation are clearly not the most serious or most frequent types of child abuse. They argue that "by far the most pervasive, costly, intractable and potentially fatal risks to American children today is that of child neglect, not child abuse" (p. 353). Neglect accounts for more than 60% of child abuse reports. While a small core of neglect cases involve serious, life threatening behavior the majority of neglect cases, according to Besharov, involve forms of emotional or developmental harm to children that, although serious, pose no immediate physical danger to children. The danger of these cases are due to their damaging cumulative effects. The overwhelming majority of these cases are rooted in familial poverty and social deprivation and involve situations of marginal or inadequate care that warrant social intervention, but should be distinguished from cases of brutal battering or sexual molestation (Besharov, 1988).

Nonetheless, the publication of child abuse "horror stories" has played a significant role in the shaping of public perceptions about the nature of child abuse and neglect. The focus on "horror stories," by dramatizing the most extreme examples of child maltreatment reinforces the psychopathological orientation of child abuse programs. The "horror story" or "atrocity tale," selected for its ability to capture public attention, has become the referent for the problem in general (Best, 1987; Johnson, 1989). In fact, a leading textbook in the field, "The Battered Child" (Helfer & Kempe, 1987) has gone through four editions with this title despite the fact that its contents involve a much wider scope than its title implies. Ultimately, the focus on child abuse horror stories generates intense emotional reactions, and creates a sense of urgency to "do something."

The discovery of sexual abuse. The height of public sensitivity about child abuse peaked in 1984 (Crewsdon, 1988). By that time, media accounts of child sexual abuse cases were becoming commonplace. A cover story in *Newsweek* (May 14, 1984) described the sexual abuse of children as a "hidden epidemic" and much more common than most Americans realized or were willing to admit. What was particularly disturbing was that children were being abused, in many cases, by their own parents or by other trusted members of the community such as doctors, teachers, and even clergymen.

As Haugaard and Reppucci (1988) point out, the issue of child sexual abuse was dramatically brought to public attention by two cases that year. The first was in Manhattan Beach, California where seven employees at the McMartin Day Care Center were arrested and accused of molesting more than 125 children over a ten-year period. Later in 1984, 24 adults were accused of abusing more than 50 children in Jordan, Minnesota.

These cases, and others, helped focus public attention in the mid-1980's firmly on the problem of child abuse and neglect, and particularly that of sexual abuse. These same cases however, would later come to be associated with the problem of false allegations.

CHILD ABUSE AND NEGLECT REPORTING

With increased public exposure to the problem of the maltreatment of children, there has been a significant increase in the reporting of child abuse cases. By 1989, more than 2.5 million reports of child abuse and neglect had been made to public authorities. Since there are no reliable records of child abuse and neglect that predate current reporting laws, it is impossible to know for sure if the incidence of child abuse is actually increasing or decreasing. There are many, however, who believe that increased reporting is most likely the product of greater social awareness of the problem. There is the possibility that while the number of reports of child abuse and neglect have been rising dramatically in recent years, the actual incidence of child victimization may be decreasing.

Underreporting

The number of reports of child abuse and neglect have increased dramatically in recent years, nonetheless underreporting still remains a serious problem. A recent study, the *National Study of the Incidence and Severity of Child Abuse and Neglect* estimated that only 50% of maltreated children seen by professionals are reported to the appropriate public authorities (Sedlak, 1987). Many professionals do not report because they fear the case will be mishandled by CPS, or that their judgments and perspectives will be ignored by inexperienced and poorly trained workers (Zellner & Antler, 1990).

There is considerable evidence that a great deal of child abuse and neglect goes unreported by victims themselves. For example, retrospective studies show that many adults have been sexually abused as children, but only a small percentage of cases are reported to public authorities at the time of the abuse (Berliner, 1989). According to Berliner (1989) and Sauzier (1989), many victims do not report the abuse for fear of being disbelieved, or because they have been threatened into silence. And some fear the consequences of telling, since revealing the abuse can be as stressful as the abuse itself. At this point, no one knows the full extent of nonreporting of child abuse and neglect, but there is little doubt that it is extensive.

Overreporting

Just as the numbers of reports have risen dramatically in recent years as has the incidence of non-reporting, there has also been a steady increase in the number and percentage of unfounded reports since 1976 when approximately 35% of reports were unfounded (Besharov, 1985). Today about 60% of all child abuse cases are classified as "unfounded" or "unsubstantiated" (Besharov, 1990; Finklehor, 1990). There are some who refer to this process as a move from frequent underreporting to frequent overreporting (Schetky, 1986). However, this is an error. Both underreporting and overreporting are serious problems which compromise the efficacy of child protective services. Unfortunately, the issue tends to get polarized by advocates who claim one or the other is the "real" problem (Terr, 1989).

Besharov (1985) acknowledges that many of the reports that are labeled unfounded are not made inappropriately. Given the fact that child abuse reporting laws require the reporting of suspicions, it is inevitable that a certain portion of reports will be determined to be unfounded. However, according to Besharov, unfounded rates of the current magnitude go beyond anything reasonably needed. Besharov worries that the large number of unfounded reports are overwhelming the limited staffing resources of many agencies and might ultimately be inhibiting the ability of CPS to respond quickly and effectively when children are in genuine danger.

Unfortunately, there are some who consider unfounded reports the same as "false reports." But as Giovannoni (1989) points out, unfounded reports are a heterogenous group and should not be equated with "false" reports. While some portion of unfounded reports involve "false" reports, there are actually many reasons that account for the inability to substantiate a case. For example, a perpetrator could not be identified or was able to cover up an abuse incident, a child was too young to give a credible account, or perhaps a worker lacked experience and investigative skills and misdiagnosed the case. In some situations, cases are labelled unfounded as a means of caseload control or when services are not available to offer a family (Faller, 1985; Besharov, 1985).

There are many who claim that because a case is labelled "unfounded," does not necessarily mean that abuse did not occur. While these situations (false negatives) occur, there has been no published study that has assessed the extent of false negatives among unfounded reports. If it is indeed true that many unfounded reports involve actual abuse, then the rate of misdiagnosis is extraordinarily high. On the other hand, the claim that an unfounded report does not necessarily mean that abuse did not occur, leaves no room for the accused to clear their name when abuse did not occur. Some states have taken steps to create a new language for case identification that is intended to correct the ambiguities of the terms "substantiate" and "unfounded." In Minnesota, for example, the new categories are "maltreatment occurred" or "maltreatment did not occur."

That some portion of child abuse and neglect reports will be "unfounded" is legitimate (Besharov, 1985), however, the problem is that so little attention has been devoted to what happens to families when an accusation is unfounded. Some of the key concerns that need to be attended to by clinicians include: (1) how family relationships are affected by CPS investigations, (2) how parents cope with the stress of an accusation, (3) what type of support services, if any, are offered to parents, (4) do social workers show adequate concern for the welfare of the family following an unfounded report, and (5) finally, how children are affected by a child abuse investigation that is unfounded (Cleaver, 1989). As the papers in this volume by Carbino, and Hicks and Nixon show, unfounded reports can result in considerable stress for families, requiring the need for support services to heal from the experience.

Need for Family Based Services

Ultimately, many child abuse and neglect reports are, according to Besharov, "at base, not about child abuse or child neglect but are really requests for needed family-oriented social services" (Besharov, this volume). Many of these reports involve child and adolescent behavioral problems, school problems, drug abuse and parent-child conflicts and difficulties that do not necessarily constitute child maltreatment. Giovannoni (1985) noted that in a study of 1,000 adjudicated cases of child maltreatment, 25 percent of the reports involved complaints of children's behavior without an allegation of parental mistreatment. Many of these reports were initiated by the parents themselves in a desperate effort to obtain needed help.

Besharov's analysis on this point has been reinforced by the work of Sheila Kamerman and Alfred Kahn. In their study, *Social Services for Children, Youth and Families in the U.S.* (1989), Kamerman and Kahn noted that Child Protective Services has emerged as the dominant public child and family service, and has become the "portal of entry" for children and families in need of services. Funding for child welfare services tends to focus on either child protective service investigations or foster care placements. The majority of family service programs are for families where a child is at high risk of immediate placement, rather than for troubled children and families whose problems are not necessarily in crisis. A refurbishing of the child welfare system would help relieve the burden on the child protective system which is overextended by more cases than it can adequately handle. (Kamerman & Kahn, 1989)

EMERGENCE OF FALSE ALLEGATIONS AS A SOCIAL PROBLEM

The high level of attention and anxiety about child abuse has led in recent years to increased case reporting to child protective services. The mandatory reporting campaigns, the broadened definitions of child abuse and neglect, and the decline of voluntary, community-based family services have greatly enlarged the pool of children referred to local child welfare authorities as potentially in need of protective services. The reporting net that has been established has included large numbers of maltreated children.

But inevitably, it includes a certain portion of cases where no abuse occurred. Some of these cases involve questionable parenting practices rather than actual or potential maltreatment (Daro, 1988); the reporting of conditions such as inadequate food, clothing, housing, supervision, etc., that have more to do with the conditions of poverty than inadequate parenting (Pelton, 1989); the reporting of child behavior problems that do not involve parental abuse (Besharov, this volume); and the reporting of altogether innocent persons. Many of these persons experience the report as "false" regardless of the motivation of the reporter or disposition of the case.

While many believe that false allegations are becoming more common, no one knows for sure how extensive the problem is truly. It is unfortunate that there has been so many exaggerated claims and counter-claims about the problem. Many child protection professionals argue that "false allegations" are rare, while advocates for those who claim to be "falsely accused" say the problem is widespread and has reached "epidemic" proportions. The truth is likely to be somewhere in between.

Case Examples

By the mid-1980's, a series of cases gained national attention where the accused claimed to be "falsely accused." Some of these include the Kelly Michaels (Nathan, 1988; Rabinowitz, 1990) and Larry Spiegel (Spiegel, 1986) cases in New Jersey; the Jordan, Minnesota case (Rigert, Peterson,

& Marcotty, 1985); and the McMartin Day Care Center case in California (Crewsdon, 1988). These cases are terribly complex. Advocates and supporters have made claims and counter-claims of what is supposed to have happened, but the truth, in most of these cases, may never be known.

Take the case of Hillary Foretich as an example. Hillary's mother, Dr. Elizabeth Morgan spent 25 months in jail for contempt-of-court charges for failing to reveal the whereabouts of Hillary. Dr. Morgan accused Hillary's father, Dr. Eric Foretich of sexually abusing Hillary when she was a toddler, which he denies. Both parents have engaged the support of reputable professionals who have reached opposing conclusions of what is supposed to have taken place (Myers, 1989a).

Or consider the McMartin case. In 1983, a mother told Manhattan Beach, California police that her 2 1/2 year old son had been sexually molested by a "Mr. Ray," a teacher at a local nursery school operated by his family. Ray Buckey, his mother and sister, and four other McMartin teachers were arrested and charged with 321 counts of child sexual abuse, involving dozens of other children. Before the trial began in 1987, charges were dropped for five defendants, as were all but 65 of the counts. In January of 1990, the jury after deliberating for nine weeks, acquitted Peggy Buckey (mother of Raymond Buckey) on all charges, and acquitted Raymond Buckey on all but 13 counts. A second trial in July of 1990 acquitted Raymond Buckey on all charges. While many of the jurors believed that some of the children had been abused, they were not able to determine what the children actually said on their own volition, and what had been suggested to them by the therapists and investigators who handled the case. This trial, which was the longest criminal trial in our nation's history, has left many people frustrated and confused as to what actually happened (Crewsdon, 1988; Goldberg, 1990).

In 1984, a national organization was formed to represent the interests of those who claimed to be "falsely accused" of child abuse. Initially founded in Minnesota, Victims of Child Abuse Laws or VOCAL quickly spread to other states. By the end of the decade, VOCAL was claiming chapters in nearly every state and thousands of members. VOCAL is a controversial organization and an unbiased account of its origins and development has yet to be written. While VOCAL has hurt its credibility by making unwarranted and exaggerated claims about the issues, it has raised many legitimate questions about the manner in which child abuse investigations are conducted in our society (Myers, 1989b, 1990; Hechler, 1988).

Faulty Evaluations

Much of the controversy about false allegations tends to focus on the credibility of children. But the root of the problem, according to Schetky (1989), is not that children are frequently making false claims about abuse or that our society is unwilling to believe that children can be abused, but that faulty evaluations are leading, in some cases, to the misdiagnosis of abuse. There have been situations where inexperienced or overzealous investigators, with a strong bias that "children don't lie about abuse," have rationalized the use of suggestive or coercive investigatory techniques in an effort to "validate" their case (Coleman, 1986). An investigator who is prematurely disposed to believing a child has been abused when it is alleged, and who fails to conduct a thorough and unbiased assessment of the case, risks either eliciting or confirming a "false" report (Farr & Yuille, 1988).

Quinn (1989) and Schetky (1989) summarized some of the common errors found in child abuse investigations. These include:

1. Investigators who pursue an agenda.
2. Failure to obtain an adequate psychosocial and psychosexual history of the child and the family.
3. Failure to interview all of those involved in the allegation.
4. Failure to inquire about family attitudes and practices regarding privacy, nudity, and sexuality.
5. Misinterpretation of medical findings.
6. Inadequate time spent with the child or too many prolonged interrogations of the child.
7. The use of biased, either/or, coercive, repetitive, or age inappropriate questions.
8. Interviewing techniques that introduce leading or educational materials.
9. Differential reinforcement of child responses in an interview.
10. Selective interpretation of the child's behavior.
11. Failure to understand the nature of false allegations.

Schetky says that a faulty evaluation may lead to the conviction of innocent persons but also may result in cases against defendants being dropped or the acquittal of guilty persons.

Defining False Allegations

The several meanings of the word false make it difficult to define the concept of false allegations. False refers to that which is simply untrue or wrong, but it also includes the narrow definition of one who is intentionally deceitful. Much of the controversy over "false allegations" is based on the distinction between truth and truthfulness. As Bok wrote in her book, *Lying* (1978), "the two domains overlap, and up to a point each is indispensable to the other. But truth and truthfulness are not identical, any more than falsity and falsehood" (p. 6). Unfortunately, the current usage of the term "false allegation" usually fails to take into account its two domains: (1) the moral domain which refers to whether or not one is telling the truth, and (2) the larger domain of truth and falsity in general (Bok, 1978).

According to Sink (1988), the term "false allegation" has created considerable confusion as it fails to differentiate situations of intentional falsification, situations of misunderstanding or situations where inadequate information is available to assess an allegation. The nature and extent of the problem depends on the definition that is used. While some apply the term to any situation where abuse did not occur, others only apply the term to those situations in which a report was intentionally falsified. Depending on one's perspective, a false allegation may involve a substantiated case that was misdiagnosed, an unfounded report of legitimate concern, a report that was intentionally falsified, or any report that falls outside of the legal definition of abuse or neglect, regardless of the motivation of the reporter. The term "false allegation" has evolved from its initial consensual meaning, which took account of its two domains, into a narrow pejorative term. It is assumed by many that a "false allegation" only involves cases of malicious intent (D. Perrin, personal communication, October 6, 1990).

University of Wisconsin professor Rosemarie Carbino has undertaken the most comprehensive study of the uses of the word "false" when applied to child protective investigations. Her studies, which have primarily involved abuse reports in foster care, have relevance for investigations in other settings. She notes that the word "false" is emotionally charged and means different things to different people. Carbino (1989) has pointed out that in the "objective" language of child protection, the word false does not exist. Child protective language, according to Carbino, is designed to be legally neutral and clinically objective, but fails to take into account the experience of those who are investigated. She writes that "where agency staff speak of child abuse 'reports,' (foster) parents often speak of being accused, or where agency staff speak of the report being 'unsubstantiated' or 'services not indicated,' (foster) parents speak of accusations which were 'false' and 'untrue,' and "the legal requirement to protect the confidentiality of the reports, is often experienced by parents and others as not being allowed to know their accuser and of what they are said to have done" (pp. 38-39). These differing language systems create a gulf that makes it difficult for both sides to understand the experience of the other, and often results in considerable resentment and conflict.

Denial. The word "denial," like the word "false," has a dual meaning. A denial is a claim that an allegation is not true. When a person makes a denial, it may be a true denial or it may be a false denial. Therefore, when a person claims they have been falsely accused, their claim needs to be critically assessed and should not be taken at face value. As Ayoub and her colleagues in this volume show, many child abusers will make a false denial to protect themselves from the consequences of their actions. On the other hand, it is possible that an accused person's denial is truthful and accurate. While it may be true that many sex offenders will deny they have abused a child, it does not follow that those who deny abuse are most likely giving a false denial.

Studies of False Allegations

Despite the considerable controversy regarding the issue of false allegations of sexual abuse, there have been relatively few studies that have addressed this issue. Peters (1976) in an early report on false disclosures, found that of 64 cases of alleged sexual abuse examined at a hospital emergency room, 4 cases were considered to be false. In a similar vein, Goodwin, Sahd, and Rada (1978) reviewed 46 sexual abuse cases referred to a child abuse agency and concluded that 3 were probably false. One case was initiated by a child, and two were by parents, both of whom were mentally ill.

The study by Jones and McGraw (1987) is the only to date to use a naturally occurring sample to analyze the incidence of false reports. The authors reviewed 576 reports of child sexual abuse to the Denver Department of Social Services in 1983. Of the total sample, 53% were considered reliable and 47% were unfounded. Of the unfounded reports, 22% had insufficient information to be substantiated, 17% were made on the basis of a legitimate concern but had alternative explanations than abuse and 8% involved "fictitious" cases. Fictitious cases were defined as deliberate falsifications, misperceptions and confused interpretations of nonsexual events. Most of the "fictitious" reports were made by adults who were emotionally disturbed. Most readers of this article use the 8% figure regarding the incidence of false allegations rather than the larger 47% of cases where there was little or no evidence that abuse occurred.

The second phase of the Jones and McGraw study included 21 cases of child sexual abuse considered to be false after an evaluation. Of the 21 cases, five were made by the child, nine by an adult, and 7 were initiated by both parent and child. Four of the five children who initiated allegations had been sexually abused before the current allegations, and were suffering from untreated post-traumatic stress disorder when the current allegation arose. Of the nine fictitious accounts made by adults, all were females, most of whom were embroiled in custody/visitation disputes, had histories of abuse and neglect and were currently emotionally disturbed. In these cases little information was provided by the child. In the mixed cases all 7 mothers were psychologically disturbed and had enmeshed relationships with their children. In three of these cases, the mother's abuse occurred at around the same age of the child who was currently alleged to have been abused.

Divorce/Custody Disputes

The context of divorce and custody disputes does seem to increase the incidence of allegations of sexual abuse, although there is considerable controversy over whether false allegations of sexual abuse are disproportionately high in custody and visitation disputes (Thoennes & Tjaden, 1990). Much of the present information about abuse allegations in custody disputes derives from clinical evaluations performed by physicians. While these studies are based on non-random samples, and cannot be used to generalize about the relative incidence of the problem, they can provide useful information on the dynamics found in these cases.

Benedek and Schetky reported on 18 cases referred for custody evaluation that involved sexual abuse allegations. They were not able to substantiate 10 of the 18 reports. All of the false reports were initiated by the adults rather than children. They noted that the false reports arose out of misperceptions of reality, not out of vindictiveness or the desire for personal gain.

Paradise, Rostain and Nathanson (1988) studied 31 cases involving sexual abuse allegations, 12 (39%) of which involved a custody or visitation dispute. Allegedly abused children whose parents contested a custody or visitation arrangement were significantly younger than those for whom custody or visitation was not an issue. Sexual abuse allegations tended to be substantiated less frequently than those without co-existing parental conflict but were nevertheless substantiated more than half of the time. Paradise and colleagues concluded that the younger age of the child in the disputed cases may have contributed to the higher rate of unsubstantiation, because histories of sexual abuse are more difficult to obtain from younger children. A younger child is more likely to be the focus of contention as they are more easily influenced and less able to provide a detailed and consistent history.

Jones and Seig (1988) reviewed 20 consecutive cases that were evaluated within the Kempe Center where both sexual abuse allegations and a parental custody dispute co-existed. Of the 20 cases, 14 were reliable, 4 were fictitious, one was unsubstantiated suspicion and one remained uncertain. The authors conclude that the setting of the divorce and custody dispute does seem to raise the likelihood of finding an increased number of false allegations. The assessment of false allegations is usually based upon a constellation of factors including an inconsistent, sparse or unreliable sounding account from the child, an accusing parent prematurely convinced that her child may have been abused, and an acrimonious custody or visitation dispute.

Green (1986) analyzed four cases of "false allegations" among a sample of 11 children reported to be sexually abused by a non-custodial parent. False disclosures may occur, according to Green, when a vindictive parent, usually the mother, fabricates an allegation to punish the ex-spouse, or when a delusional parent projects their own unconscious sexual fantasies onto the spouse. These parents often have histories of sexual abuse and psychiatric disturbance. Green states that the accusing parent will reinforce the child's compliance by withholding love and approval if the child denies the abuse or has positive feelings toward the non-custodial parent. These children usually behave in a hostile manner toward their fathers in the presence of their mother, but become friendly when they are no longer in her presence.

Schuman (1986) discussed seven cases in which sexual and/or physical abuse was alleged in the context of a divorce dispute. All the reports were found to be invalid by judicial determination and psychiatric investigation. Schuman claimed the children's ambiguous statements were overinterpreted by an anxious parent and projected back onto the child in a "positive feedback loop" which increased the initial distortions. Schuman points out that the stress of a divorce situation can have a negative impact on the psychological functioning of family members. Parents under the influence of domestic stress may interpret their children's statements or behavior narrowly within the context of sexual abuse and exclude other plausible explanations.

Yates and Musty (1987) reviewed sexual abuse allegations in 19 of 80 cases where there was a custody and/or visitation dispute involving pre-school children. Sexual abuse was substantiated in four of the 19 cases. Most allegations were declarations by one parent about the other, without the direct involvement of the child. Allegations were less likely to be valid when they were initiated by an adult than when they were initiated by a child. The authors suggest the following mechanisms by which young children come to make erroneous allegations that they perceive to be true: (1) through the persuasion or suggestion of a caretaker, (2) through sexualized perceptions emanating from the Oedipal conflict, (3) through the emergence of primary process material, and (4) through the secondary involvement of the child in the projective identifications of a dominant care-giver.

Review of the few studies available regarding false sexual abuse cases indicates that the majority of false reports were initiated by parents, not children. They were usually made by parents with emotional disturbances, parents who had distorted or misperceived an ambiguous situation, or who were in the midst of a custody/visitation dispute. Most false allegations of sexual abuse, either by parents or children, do not appear to be made maliciously.

Studies of False Allegations of Physical Abuse

While most studies of false allegations involve sexual abuse, there are several studies that have examined false allegations of physical abuse. For example, Kirschner and Stein (1985) report on 10 cases where emergency room physicians misdiagnosed certain illnesses and injuries as child abuse. In all of the cases, the parents were truthful and their reports were consistent with the results of the physical exam. The authors suggest that the physicians lack of experience and their attitude of hostility and suspicion contributed to the false allegations. The authors conclude that when the stress of a serious illness or death of a child is compounded by a false allegation of child abuse, this becomes a form of medical abuse.

Likewise, Hurwitz and Castells (1987) described three children with metabolic diseases who were erroneously reported as being abused. The authors state that when children with metabolic diseases and bleeding disorders are erroneously reported as abused the families are often devastated. Some physical conditions that sometimes present symptoms that appear to be related to child abuse include osteogenesis imperfecta, hemophilia, failure-to-thrive, liver diseases causing vitamin K deficiency, vasculitis, and Ehlers-Danlos syndrome.

ASSIGNMENT OF STIGMA

There is considerable social stigma when a person is reported for child abuse is significant. To be labelled a potential abuser can result in the loss of reputation, social status, money or employment. While many investigations are handled sensitively and may even be helpful to a family (Fryer et al., 1990), investigations are by nature intrusive, involving sensitive personal or family issues, and are often resented whether or not the charges are dropped or the case is unfounded.

For parents, a child abuse report is an explicit accusation that they have failed their obligation to protect and nurture their child. As Faller (1985) states, "While the worker may be supportive and may present her/himself as someone who can help, the essential message to the parent is that they have failed as parents" (p. 65). Faller notes that for many parents, the role of father and mother is at the core of their personal identity. Thus, to be accused of child abuse can result in considerable stress, loss of confidence, fear of losing their children, or anger at those who are perceived as being responsible for the report (Faller, 1985).

An accusation of child abuse is a form of what Garfinkel (1956) calls a "degradation ceremony." A degradation ceremony involves the assignment of stigma. A person who is accused of the maltreatment of a child is stigmatized, and by definition, a person with a stigma is not quite human (Goffman, 1963). The accused, feeling shamed and isolated, takes on a new identity in the eyes of the community. According to Garfinkel (1956), "It is not that the new attributes are added to the old nucleus. He is not changed, he is reconstituted . . . the former identity stands as accidental; the new identity is the basic reality. What he is now is what 'afterall' he was all along" (p. 421). A child abuse allegation is therefore as much a statement about a person's character and moral status as it is about what a person may have done. The trauma of a child abuse accusation is that it violates a person's sense of self and redefines their status in the community. The accused person is, in effect, "de-graded." It is not just that one has abused a child, but that one is therefore fundamentally flawed as a human being. That is, the person is disturbed and immoral and has in Goffman's term, a "spoiled identity" (Goffman, 1963).

Coping with Victimization

Clinical psychology shows that people tend to live their lives on the basis of an "illusion of invulnerability." That is, they overestimate the likelihood of positive events happening to them and underestimate the likelihood of negative events (Janoff-Bulman & Lang-Gunn, 1988). A child abuse report often shatters that sense of personal invulnerability. Individuals who have lost their sense of personal invulnerability often exaggerate the degree to which they or others might be vulnerable to similar fates. This dynamic may account, in part, for the tendency of some of those who claim to be "falsely accused" to exaggerate the extent of their particular problem.

Victims of negative events tend to be blamed for their situation by those around them and often fail to receive needed social support. According to the "just world theory" (Lerner, 1980), people have a need to believe in a just world, a world where people get what they deserve. By blaming victims for their fate, the rest of society is able to believe that, because of their own good character, they are not vulnerable to a similar fate. The result is that people accused of abuse find that others tend to believe something must have happened. Even when the case is unfounded, or there is an acquital in a criminal trial, many accused persons are frustrated by their inability to remove the "shadow of doubt" that lingers over their reputation.

Thus, for many persons accused of child maltreatment, state intervention becomes a crisis from which they feel powerless to overcome. These persons may manifest a wide variety of symptoms of psychological distress. The symptoms are shock, excessive fear, angry outbursts, confusion, anxiety, obsessive thoughts about the events, difficulty resuming normal activities, sleep and eating disturbances, helplessness, and what Carbino calls a sense of unending vulnerability. Many persons also experience financial and job losses, family disbandment, and social isolation (Tyler & Brassard, 1984; Schultz, 1986; Carbino, 1989; Spiegel, 1986).

The shock and horror of being accused of abuse of one's child has been eloquently described in Larry Spiegel's book, *A Question of Innocence* (1986). Spiegel (1986) wrote,

> The story began the day I was arrested in the parking lot of my office in Morris County, New Jersey. That day, December 9, 1983, I was a successful clinical psychologist with a growing private practice. That afternoon, I was escorted to a waiting police car, charged with sexually molesting my then 2½-year-old daughter, handcuffed, and taken to police headquarters. Suddenly, my work, my dreams, my life—everything I had struggled for—were shattered. The confusion, disbelief, fear, and anguish I had experienced at that moment became an ongoing nightmare which continued for over two years. This charge was filed by my ex-wife about 2 weeks after our divorce was finalized. (p. 1)

In another case, a therapist won a defamation suit against a former employer who falsely claimed she had sexually abused two young female clients. In a letter to the editor of *Harper's Magazine*, Jane E. Johnston (1990) wrote, "It is impossible to describe the despair, loneliness, isolation, and feelings of helplessness that result from such a reprehensible allegation and the guilty-until-proven innocent mentality associated with such accusations. Seven years of my life have been spent dealing with a false accusation. It ruined my career, and I was plagued with depression and suicidal thoughts as I struggled to put my life back together" (p. 5).

Unfortunately, there has been a tendency to dismiss the potentially negative impact of child abuse investigations for children as well as for adults. For example, one prominent professional has flippantly suggested, "we never had a child die of an investigation" (Brannigan, 1989). But children do suffer when a parent is wrongly accused of abuse. They suffer when the parental relationship is strained or disrupted, when they are placed into foster care unnecessarily, or when they endure medical examinations or psychological evaluations and therapies for abuse that never occurred (Benedek & Schetky, 1987).

The stress of a child abuse investigation can have detrimental effects for all members of the family. As Faller (1984) has written, "the protective service investigation itself can increase the level of stress in the home and place a child at greater risk than before. Thus, the system we have instituted to enhance our ability to identify children and intervene to help them may have very negative consequences for parents and their children. These consequences impact not only on the guilty but the innocent as well" (p. 65). Therefore, all persons accused of child maltreatment deserve to be treated with dignity and respect and should receive compassionate and humane social support regardless of whether the case is "substantiated" or "unfounded" (Carbino, 1989).

Professional Denial

While recognition is often given to other social accusations that prove unfounded, in the child abuse field it is difficult to even raise the possibility that a complaint is false or untrue, or that some percentage of cases involve false allegations. Many professionals have difficulty accepting the possibility that some alleged offenders are innocent, that some children give inaccurate accounts of abuse, or that faulty evaluations can lead to the misdiagnosis of abuse.

The child protective service movement has created a powerful negative image of those who challenge their practices. To call into question the efficacy of child protective services is to become suspect oneself. After all, to be "for" those accused of child abuse has no standing in our political culture. Some of those who have advocated for people who they believe were falsely accused, or have testified for the defense in criminal trials, have found themselves with their own personal and professional integrity called into question, and have experienced considerable peer pressure not to testify at criminal trials or present their views in public forums. Critics of the system are often presented as being part of a "backlash" against child protection in general, rather than as people motivated, in most cases, by the desire to correct deficiencies or to create balance and moderation in the system (Hechler, 1988).

Much of the tendency of professionals to minimize the extent and impact of false allegations is based, in part, on their belief that false reports are rare and when they do occur, they have clear and decisive characteristics that can be identified by the trained professional. For example, several authors have recently claimed that the "experienced professional" is usually able to correctly differentiate true from false allegations (Myers et al., 1989). This claim is made despite the evidence that many cases are very complex and have conflicting opinions among the various professionals as to what may have occurred (Corwin et al., 1987).

There is a strong tendency among clinicians doing diagnostic work to overestimate their clinical skills and to exaggerate their ability to correctly identify true cases (Faust & Nurcombe, 1989). In the child protection field, some workers have been heard to claim that they seldom, if ever, misdiagnose a case. Much of the overestimation of clinical abilities in child protection is rooted in the status anxieties of those engaged in this type of work. While scientific studies about child abuse are much improved in recent years, this field is still in its infancy and much of its scientific foundation is not well developed. Moreover, many of those who work in the field have not received extensive professional training and have not been exposed to the major theories and supporting scientific knowledge that exists.

The denial of fallibility and error making are also related to issues of personal identity. Social critic Lionel Trilling has stated, "only the self that is certain of its existence; of its identity, can do without the armor of systematic certainties" (cited in Katz, 1984, p. 203). Assuming a facade of infallibility serves to maintain the illusion of professional competence and control over a clinical decision making process that is fraught with numerous complexities and uncertainties (Katz, 1984). When child abuse professionals claim that false allegations are "rare," they are in effect claiming that they rarely make mistakes. This is a strange assertion given the complexity of the cases and the lack of training that is so endemic to this field.

Error making and fallibility are an inherent part of any clinical work. As Pecora's review of risk assessment systems shows, workers using current assessment instruments have a limited ability to correctly identify whether maltreatment has occurred or whether it will occur in the future. The errors go both ways. There are still many cases of underdiagnosis as well as overdiagnosis.

Ultimately, clinicians assessing child abuse cases will need to acknowledge the uncertainties inherent in their work and the potential for misdiagnosing a case. Clinicians insensitive to the complexities of diagnosis run the risk of making decisions on limited information. Unfortunately, it seems that many clinicians have great difficulty maintaining in the child abuse field, an appreciation and awareness of the extent to which uncertainty affects their work (Katz, 1984).

CONCLUSION

What is significant is not that false allegations happen, but the indifference of the professional community when they do happen. The injustice of false allegations is based not only on the immediate circumstances of the problem but also on the unwillingness of the professional community to acknowledge the phenomenon and to then take the necessary steps to prevent and/or ameliorate its negative consequences. This is an example of what the philosopher Judith Shklar (1990) refers to as passive injustice.

If the professional relationship is viewed as a covenant based on the ethical tenet, "above all else do no harm," then clinicians have an obligation to apologize to clients when they cause them harm or suffering. As Robert ten Bensel has said, "compassion is the knowledge of harm to others and the ethical response to help in reducing pain" (R. ten Bensel, personal communication, April 12, 1988). Because a child abuse accusation and investigation can cause considerable pain and suffering, then professionals and others who might be responsible have an obligation to make amends. The act of apology is a form of atonement as it reestablishes relationship with others and pays homage to what is right. To contribute to healing, the apology must be honest, genuine, and acknowledge the point of view of the client (Murphy & Hampton, 1988).

Much of the trauma associated with false allegations is rooted in the unwillingness of the professional community to acknowledge its mistakes. In most cases involving the possibility of a false accusation, individuals and agencies steadfastly deny any degree of responsibility for making errors in judgement. This refusal is apparently based on the fear that an apology might be interpreted as an admission of guilt in a potential lawsuit. It is possible, however, that if professionals were more willing to apologize, and made greater efforts to correct deficient practices, then aggrieved clients would be less likely to sue.

Victims need to have their experience acknowledged by others. Persons who are "falsely accused" of child abuse often have an intense desire for vindication, that is, to have their reputation and self respect restored. Many become preoccupied with their "victimization," and are able to talk about little else. For the victim of false allegations, forgiveness involves letting go of the immediacy of the trauma, so that it no longer dominates one's life. The process of healing would be greatly enhanced if the professional community was willing to acknowledge its mistakes, apologize and listen to the accused's interpretation of their experience (Robin, 1989).

There are many who are concerned that giving attention to false allegations will undermine public trust in the child protective system. But to pose the issue of false allegations as a serious social problem is not to suggest that children should be disbelieved when they claim to be abused or that the child protection system needs to be rolled back. Child abuse and neglect still remains a serious problem that demands a social response, professional competencies and even greater public support than it now receives. Recent calls for increased public funding and support for CPS services are an effort in the right direction. But "child protection" cannot be a social value that supersedes all other values. The public wants to know that the child protection system is fair, and in conducting its mission, adequately takes into account the rights and needs of the accused. Therefore, advocacy for children must be framed and balanced within a larger structure of values. These include family rights, family preservation, due process of law, justice, fairness and truth.

REFERENCES

American Humane Association. (1988). Highlights of official child neglect and abuse reporting, 1986. Denver, CO: Author.

Benedek, E., & Schetky, D. (1987). Problems in validating allegations of sexual abuse part 2: Clinical evaluation. *Journal of the American Academy of Child and Adolescent Psychiatry, 26*, 916-921.

Berliner, L. (1989). Resolved: Child sex abuse is overdiagnosed: Negative. *Journal of the American Academy of Child and Adolescent Psychiatry, 28*, 792-793.

Besharov, D. J. (1985). Doing something about child abuse: The need to narrow the grounds for state intervention. *Harvard Journal of Law and Public Policy*, *8*, 539-589.

Besharov, D. (1988, August 4). The child-abuse numbers game. *Wall Street Journal*.

Besharov, D. (1990). Gaining control over child abuse reports. *Public Welfare*, *48*(2), 34-40.

Best, J. (1987). Rhetoric in claims-making: Constructing the missing children problem. *Social Problems, 34*, 101-121.

Best, J. (Ed.). (1989). *Images of issues: Typifying contemporary social problems*. New York: Aldine de Gruyter.

Bok, S. (1978). *Lying*. New York: Vintage Books.

Brannigan, M. (1989). Child-abuse charges ensnare some parents in baseless proceedings. *Wall Street Journal, 70*(218), 1, 12.

Burke, K. (1945). *A grammar of motives*. New York: Prentice-Hall.

Carbino, R. (1989). Child welfare issues in how social service systems respond to allegations of foster home abuse/neglect. In J. Sprouse (Ed.), *Allegations of abuse in family foster care: An examination of the impact on foster families*. King George, Virginia: American Foster Care Resources.

Cleaver, H. (1989). *Parental perspectives on suspected child abuse and its aftermath*. Unpublished manuscript. Dartington Social Research Unit, Devon, England.

Cohen, S. (1972). *Folk devils and moral panics*. London: Macgibbon and Kee.

Cohen, S. J., & Sussman, A. (1975). The incidence of child abuse in the United States. *Child Welfare, 54*, 432-443.

Coleman, L. (1986). Has a child been molested? *California Lawyer, 6*(7), 15-18.

Corwin, D., Berliner, L., Goodman, G., Goodwin, J., & White, S. (1987). Child sexual abuse and custody disputes. *Journal of Interpersonal Violence, 2*, 91-105.

Crewsdon, J. (1988). *By silence betrayed: Sexual abuse of children in America*. Boston: Little Brown.

Daro, D. (1988). *Confronting child abuse*. New York: Free Press.

deMause, L. (1984). *Reagan's America*. New York: Creative Roots.

Dubowitz, H., & Newberger, E. (1989). Pediatrics and child abuse. In D. Cicchetti & V. Carlson (Eds.), *Child maltreatment*. Cambridge: Cambridge University Press.

Duquette, D. (1982). Protecting individual liberties in the context of screening for child abuse. In R. H. Starr, Jr. (Ed.), *Child abuse prediction: Policy implications*. Cambridge, Mass.: Ballinger.

Edelman, M. (1987). *Families in peril: An agenda for social change*. Cambridge, Mass.: Harvard University Press.

Edelman, M. (1988). *Constructing the political spectacle*. Chicago: University of Chicago Press.

Faller, K. (1984). Is the child victim of sexual abuse telling the truth? *Child Abuse and Neglect, 8*, 473-481.

Faller, K. (1985). Unanticipated problems in the United States child protection system. *Child Abuse and Neglect, 9*, 63-69.

Farr, V., & Yuille, J. (1988). Assessing credibility. *Preventing Sexual Abuse, 1*(1), 8-13.

Faust, D., & Nurcombe, B. (1989). Improving the accuracy of clinical judgement. *Psychiatry, 52*, 197-208.

Finklehor, D. (1990). Is child abuse overreported? *Public Welfare, 48*(1), 22-29.

Fryer, G., Bross, D., Krugman, R., Denson, D., & Baird, D. (1990). Good news for CPS workers. *Public Welfare, 48*(1), 38-41.

Garbarino, J. (1989). The incidence and prevalence of child maltreatment. In L. Ohlin & M. Tonry (Eds.), *Family violence*. Chicago: University of Chicago Press.

Garfinkel, H. (1956). Conditions of successful degradation ceremonies. *American Journal of Sociology, 61*, 420-424.

Gelles, R. (1973). Child abuse as psychopathology: A sociological critique and reformulation. *American Journal of Orthopsychiatry, 43*, 611-621.

Gelles, R. (1980). A profile of violence toward children in the United States. In G. Gerbner, C. J. Ross, & E. Zigler (Eds.), *Child abuse: An agenda for action*. New York: Oxford University Press.

Giovannoni, J. (1985). Unanswered cries: The problem of unsubstantiated child abuse. *Social Welfare, 1*, 14-15.

Giovannoni, J. (1989). Substantiated and unsubstantiated reports of child maltreatment. *Child and Youth Services Review, 11*, 299-318.

Giovannoni, J. M., & Becerra, R. M. (1979). *Defining child abuse*. New York: Free Press.

Goffman, E. (1963). *Stigma: Notes on the management of spoiled identity*. Englewood Cliffs, New Jersey: Prentice-Hall.

Goldberg, M. Z. (1990). Child Witnesses: Lessons learned from the McMartin trials. *Trial*, October, 86-88.

Goode, E. (1989). *Drugs in American society*. Third Edition. New York: Alfred A. Knopf.

Goodwin, Sahd, D., & Rada, R. (1978). Incest hoax: False accusations, false denials. *Bulletin of the American Academy of Psychiatric Law, 6*, 269-276.

Green, A. (1986). True and false allegations of sexual abuse in child custody disputes. *Journal of the American Academy of Child Psychiatry, 25*, 449-456.

Gusfield, J. (1981). *The culture of public problems: Drunk driving and the symbolic order*. Chicago: University of Chicago Press.

Gusfield, J. (1989). Constructing the ownership of social problems: Fun and profit in the welfare state. *Social Problems, 36*, 431-441.

Haugaard, J., & Reppucci, N. D. (1988). *The sexual abuse of children*. San Francisco: Jossey-Bass.

Hechler, D. (1988). *The battle and the backlash*. Lexington, Massachusetts: Lexington Books.

Helfer, R. E., & Kempe, R. S. (1987). *The battered child*. Fourth Edition. Chicago: University of Chicago Press.

Hurwitz, A., & Castells, S. (1987). Misdiagnosed child abuse and metabolic diseases. *Pediatric Nursing, 13*, 33-36.

Janoff-Bulman, R., & Lang-Gunn, L. (1988). Coping with disease, crime, and accidents: The role of self-blame attributions. In L. Abramson (Ed.), *Social cognition and clinical psychology*. New York: Guilford Press.

Johnson, J. (1986). The changing concept of child abuse and its impact on the integrity of family life. In J. Peden & F. Glahe (Eds.), *The American family and the state*. San Francisco: Pacific Research Institute for Public Policy.

Johnson, J. (1989). Horror stories and the construction of child abuse. In J. Best (Ed.), *Images of issues*. New York: Aldine de Gruyter.

Johnson, J. (1990). *What Lisa knew: The truth and lies of the Steinberg case*. New York: G. P. Putnam's Sons.

Johnston, J. (1990). Letter to the editor. *Harper's, 281*, (1683), 5.

Jones, D., & McGraw, J. (1987). Reliable and fictitious accounts of sexual abuse to children. *Journal of Interpersonal Violence, 2*, 27-45.

Jones, D., & Seig, A. (1988). Child sexual abuse allegations in custody or visitation disputes. In E. Bruce Nicholson (Ed.), *Sexual abuse allegations in custody and visitation cases*. Washington, D.C.: American Bar Association.

Kamerman, S., & Kahn, A. (1989). *Social services for children, youth and families in the United States*. The Annie E. Casey Foundation.

Katz, J. (1984). *The silent world of doctor and patient*. New York: Free Press.

Kempe, C. H., & Helfer, R. E. (1972). *Helping the battered child and his family*. Philadelphia: J. B. Lippineott.

Kempe, C. H., Silverman, F. N., Steele, B. F., Droegemueller, W., & Silver, H. K. (1962). The battered child syndrome. *Journal of the American Medical Association, 181*, 17-24.

Kirschner, R., & Stein, R. (1985). The mistaken diagnosis of child abuse: A form of medical abuse? *American Journal of Diseases of Children, 139*, 873-875.

Knudsen, D. (1988). *Child protective services*. Springfield, Illinois: Charles C Thomas.

Lerner, M. J. (1980). *The belief in a just world*. New York: Plenum Press.

Melton, G. (1987). Law and random events: The state of child mental health policy. *International Journal of Law and Psychiatry, 10*, 81-90.

Miller, A. (1981). *Prisoners of childhood*. New York: Basic Books.

Murphy, J., & Hampton, J. (1988). *Forgiveness and mercy*. Cambridge: Cambridge University Press.

Myers, J.E.B. (1987). *Child witness and the law*. New York: John Wiley.

Myers, J.E.B. (1989a). Allegations of child sexual abuse in custody and visitation litigation: Recommendations for improved fact finding and child protection. *Journal of Family Law, 28*, 1-41.

Myers, J.E.B. (1989b). Protecting children from sexual abuse: What does the future hold? *Journal of Contemporary Law, 15*, 31-50.

Myers, J.E.B. (1990). The child sexual abuse literature: A call for greater objectivity. *Michigan Law Review, 88*, 701-725.

Myers, J.E.B., Bays, J., Becker, J., Berliner, L., Corwin, D., & Saywitz, K.

(1989). Expert testimony in child sexual abuse litigation. *Nebraska Law Review*, *68*, 1-145.

Nathan, D. (1988, August 2). Victimizer or victim? Was Kelly Michaels unjustly convicted? *Village Voice*.

Nelson, B. (1984). *Making an issue of child abuse*. Chicago: University of Chicago Press.

Paradise, J., Rostain, A., & Nathanson, M. (1988). Substantiation of sexual abuse charges when parents dispute custody or visitation. *Pediatrics*, *81*, 835-839.

Parton, N. (1981). Child abuse, social anxiety and welfare. *British Journal of Social Work*, *11*, 391-419.

Parton, N. (1985). *The politics of child abuse*. New York: St. Martin's Press.

Pelton, L. (1989). *For reasons of poverty*. New York: Praeger.

Peters, J. (1976). Children who are victims of sexual assault and the psychology of offenders. *American Journal of Psychotherapy*, *30*, 398-421.

Peters, S. D., Wyatt, G. E., & Finklehor, D. (1986). Prevalence. In D. Finklehor (Ed.), *A sourcebook on child sexual abuse*. Beverly Hills, California: Sage.

Quinn, K. (1989). Resolved: Child sex abuse is overdiagnosed: Affirmative. *Journal of the American Academy of Child and Adolescent Psychiatry*, *28*, 789-790.

Rabinowitz, D. (1990). From the mouths of babes to a jail cell. *Harper's*, *280*(1680), 52-63.

Rigert, J., Peterson, D., & Marcotty, J. (1985, May 26). The Scott County case/ How it grew, why it died. *Minneapolis Star and Tribune*.

Robin, M. (1982). Sheltering arms: The roots of child protection. In E. Newberger (Ed.), *Child Abuse*. Boston: Little, Brown.

Robin, M. (1984). Black babies: The right to the tree of life. *The Nation*, *238*(22), 698-700.

Robin, M. (1989). The trauma of allegations of abuse and neglect for foster parents. In J. Sprouse (Ed.), *Allegations of abuse in family foster care: An examination of the impact on foster families*. King George, VA: American Foster Care Resources.

Rothenberg, M. (1980). Is there an unconscious national conspiracy against children in the United States? *Clinical Pediatrics*, *19*(1), 10-24.

Sauzier, M. (1989). Resolved: Child sex abuse is overdiagnosed: Negative. *Journal of the American Academy of Child and Adolescent Psychiatry*, *28*, 793-795.

Scheper-Hughes, N., & Stein, H. (1987). Child abuse and the unconscious in American popular culture. In N. Scheper-Hughes (Ed.), *Child survival*. Dordrecht: D. Reidel Publishing Co.

Schetky, D. (1986). Emerging issues in child sexual abuse, editorial. *Journal of the American Academy of Child Psychiatry*, *25*, 490-492.

Schetky, D. (1989). Resolved: Child sex abuse is overdiagnosed: Affirmative. *Journal of the American Academy of Child and Adolescent Psychiatry*, *28*, 790-792.

Schultz, L. (1986). *One hundred cases of wrongfully charged child sexual abuse: A survey and recommendations.* Unpublished manuscript. School of Social Work, West Virginia University.

Schuman, D. C. (1986). False allegations of physical and sexual abuse. *Bulletin of the American Academy of Psychiatry and the Law, 14,* 5-21.

Sedlak, A. (1987). *Study of national incidence and prevalence of child abuse and neglect.* Bethesda, Md.: Westat.

Shklar, J. (1990). *The faces of injustice.* New Haven: Yale University Press.

Sink, F. (1988). Studies of true and false allegations: A critical review. In E. Bruce Nicholson (Ed.), *Sexual abuse allegations in custody and visitation cases.* Washington, D.C.: American Bar Association, Washington, D.C.

Spector, M., & Kitsuse, J. (1977). *Constructing social problems.* Menlo Park, CA: Cummings.

Spiegel, L. (1986). *A question of innocence.* New Jersey: The Unicorn Publishing House.

Steele, S. (1989). I'm black, you're white, who's innocent? *Harper's Magazine, 279,* 45-53.

Terr, L. (Ed.). (1989). Debate forum: Resolved: Child sex abuse is over-diagnosed. *Journal of the American Academy of Child and Adolescent Psychiatry, 28,* 789-797.

Thoennes, N., & Tjaden, P. (1990). The extent, nature, and validity of sexual abuse allegations in custody/visitation disputes. *Child Abuse and Neglect, 14,* 151-160.

Tyler, A., & Brassard, M. (1984). Abuse in the investigation and treatment of intrafamilial child sexual abuse. *Child Abuse and Neglect, 8,* 47-53.

Wells, S. (1988). Factors influencing the response of child protective service workers to reports of abuse and neglect. In G. Hotaling, D. Finklehor, J. Kirkpatrick, & M. Straus (Eds.), *Coping with family violence.* Newbury Park: Sage Publications.

Yates, A., & Musty, T. (1987). *Young children's false allegations of molestation.* Paper presented at the 140th Annual Meeting of the American Psychiatric Association, Chicago, IL.

Zellner, G., & Antler, S. (1990). Mandated reporters and CPS: A study in frustration. *Public Welfare, 48*(1), 30-37.

Zigler, E. (1983). Understanding child abuse. In E. F. Zigler, S. L. Kagan, & E. Klugman (Eds.), *Children, families and government.* Cambridge: Cambridge University Press.

POLICY ISSUES

Child Abuse and Neglect Reporting and Investigation: Policy Guidelines for Decision Making

Douglas Besharov

ABSTRACT. This report seeks to provide guidance to state and local officials, professionals, and advocates seeking to improve the reporting and investigation of suspected child abuse and neglect. The need for clearer guidelines for reporting and case disposition is emphasized.

Over the past twenty years, much progress has been made in protecting abused and neglected children. Every state has passed a mandatory reporting law. The result has been an enormous increase in reported cases.[1]

Douglas Besharov is affiliated with the American Enterprise Institute for Public Policy Research, 1150 Seventeenth St. N.W., Washington, DC 20036. This report embodies the consensus of a national group of child protective professionals. The consensus-building process was conducted under the auspices of the American Bar Association's National Legal Resource Center for Child Advocacy and Protection in association with the American Public Welfare Association and the American Enterprise Institute. Financial support was provided by the National Center on Child Abuse and Neglect, Administration on Child, Youth, and Families, Department of Health and Human Services.

In 1985, more than 1.9 million children were reported to the authorities as suspected victims of child abuse and neglect. This is more than twelve times the estimated 150,000 children reported in 1963.

Increased reporting and specialized child protective agencies have saved many thousands of children from death and serious injury.

Despite this progress, major gaps in protection remain:

Professionals — physicians, nurses, teachers, social workers, child care workers, and police — still fail to report many of the maltreated children whom they see, including those with observable injuries severe enough to require hospitalization.

Many thousands of other children suffer serious injuries after their plight becomes known to the authorities. Studies in a number of communities indicate that 25 to 45 percent of the children who die under circumstances suggestive of child maltreatment have previously been reported to child protective agencies.

There is some reason to believe that, after many years of decline, child fatalities attributable to child maltreatment rose in 1986.

At the same time, the nation's child protective agencies must investigate a large number of reports that are not substantiated:

Nationwide, only about 40 percent of all reports are "substantiated" (or a similar term) after investigation. This is in sharp contrast to 1975, when about 65 percent of all reports were "substantiated."

Each year, over 500,000 families are investigated for reports that are not substantiated.

These simultaneous problems are unfair to the children and parents involved, and they threaten to undo much of the progress that has been made in building child protective programs. There is widespread confusion about what should be reported and investigated — and what should not be. This report recommends policy changes designed to reduce such confusion.

Almost all the recommendations made in this report can be implemented through changes in child protective agency administrative procedures and training manuals. In most states, no new laws need be passed. Moreover, the recommendations are consistent with the Federal Child Abuse Prevention and Treatment Act, so that their adoption will not threaten a state's eligibility for grants under that Act.

THE "CHILD PROTECTIVE MISSION"

Child abuse and child neglect are serious national problems. Only firm and effective government intervention protects many children from serious injury and even death.

The Role of Child Protective Services

The responsibility to receive and investigate reports of suspected child abuse and neglect is primarily assigned to a single, statutorily created public agency, usually called the "Child Protective Service Agency" (or CPS). To protect children from abuse or neglect, Child Protective Service Agencies perform the following functions: report taking, screening, investigation, initial risk assessment, crisis intervention, report disposition, case planning and implementation, and case closure.

The objective of Child Protective Service Agencies is to protect children from abuse and neglect. They do so by strengthening families so that children can remain within or be returned to their families; by temporarily removing children from situations of immediate danger; and by pursuing the termination of parental rights and assuring the child permanency in a substitute family if the custodial family cannot be preserved without serious risk to the child.

The Wider Role of Community-Based Services

Nevertheless, the protection of children from abuse and neglect is a community-wide concern. Child protective services must be provided as an integral component of a larger array of child welfare services designed to enhance the well-being of children, and of an even broader continuum of human services designed to help meet the needs of children and families. Special responsibility is placed on child welfare, law enforcement, medical and public health, mental health, and educational agencies and professionals.

Across the nation, however, Child Protective Service Agencies are being pushed to respond to the absence of other, more appropriate services. *Child abuse* hotlines, for example, are receiving thousands of "reports" that, at base, are not about child abuse or child neglect, but are really requests for needed family-oriented social services. Many of these reports involve adolescent behavioral problems (such as truancy, delinquency, school problems, substance abuse, and sexual acting out); child who need specialized education or treatment; and chronic parent-child conflicts with no indication of abuse or neglect. Some of these reports result in the family receiving much needed services, but most do not. In any event, these additional, inappropriate calls to CPS hotlines significantly increase the number of unsubstantiated cases.

In effect, callers are trying to use Child Protective Service Agencies to fill gaps in what should be a comprehensive child welfare system. To prevent this misdirection of scarce resources, and to reduce the number of unsubstantiated cases, Child Protective Service Agencies must develop policies and procedures that specify the kinds of calls that are appropriate and that should be accepted for investigation.

Law Enforcement

Child abuse is a crime and, therefore, a legitimate concern — and responsibility — of police and other law enforcement agencies. A number of calls made to CPS agencies may involve matters that are the sole or joint responsibility of law enforcement to evaluate and investigate. Recognizing this, there is a need to eliminate unnecessary multiple interviews of children and other unnecessary duplications of effort, to promote proper and expeditious collection and preservation of physical and other evidence, and to carry out the statutory mandate in the majority of states for law enforcement and CPS agencies to cross-report such cases. Joint efforts with law enforcement — police and prosecutors — should be made to develop a coordinated system for identifying and investigating appropriate calls.

A recent tendency has been to broaden the definition of those who may be reported for "child abuse and neglect," particularly in cases of sexual abuse, to include all adults, whether or not in the child's home and whether or not responsible for the child's care.[2] Cases of maltreatment by babysitters, adults not in the child's home, and strangers are more appropriately assigned to law enforcement agencies. They should not be investigated by Child Protective Service Agencies unless the parents appear unwilling or unable to protect the child.

Institutional Abuse

Child Protective Service Agencies are family-oriented. Therefore, although the abuse and neglect of children in public and private institutions is intolerable, its investigation is beyond the scope of functions best performed by child protective service workers. Child Protective Service Agencies should be assigned investigatory responsibility only over intrafamilial or quasifamilial child maltreatment, broadly defined to include parents, guardians, foster parents, and other persons (such as boyfriends or girlfriends) continuously or regularly in the child's home.

The investigation of child maltreatment in out-of-home care, on the other hand, requires specialized units of professionals (often law enforcement or licensing) with the necessary expertise and authority. Furthermore, such units must be independent of the agency or facility being investigated, so that there is no conflict of interest.[3]

Parental Rights

If the parent declines help from the Child Protective Service Agency — or refuses to cooperate altogether — the agency and the courts must decide whether the danger to the child is so great that specific treatment services must be imposed or the child removed from the home.

Laws against child abuse and child neglect are an implicit recognition that parental rights are not absolute, and that society, through its courts and social service agencies, should intervene into private family matters to protect endangered children. But in seeking to protect helpless children, it must be remembered that, in large part, only suspicions are being reported. The parents' innocence should be presumed — unless evidence establishing the suspected maltreatment is obtained. CPS Agencies cannot impose treatment services on unwilling parents without a court order.

Poverty Issues

Many of the families reported to Child Protective Service Agencies are poor and on welfare. If the child is actually neglected, that is, if parental failure poses a danger to the child, protective action is required. Even some serious situations, however, reflect not parental failure but, rather, social factors beyond the control of individual families.

Poor children and their families have a right to the assurance of their basic needs, including food, clothing and shelter. These needs must be ensured, however, through reform of income support programs (such as public assistance, child support, and food stamps) or through the use of family-centered or family preservation services. Child Protective Service Agencies have not been established as society's response to poverty, and for them to assume, or be assigned, this role misdirects those services and resources from their proper mission.

Meeting Unmet Needs

Children and families have many unmet social service needs for which the label "child abuse and neglect" and a child protective response are inappropriate. Institutionally, Child Protective Service Agencies should advocate and broker for the remedies these families need. Individually, Child Protective Services workers, like all other human service professional, have a responsibility to help provide necessary crisis services for all children and their families.

DEFINITIONAL CLARIFICATION

Statutory and agency definitions of "child abuse and neglect" establish reporting responsibilities; they also determine what reports will be investigated, and their disposition. Most existing definitions, however, are broad and imprecise. Potential reporters and child protective workers need clearer and more specific guidelines to help their decision making.

While statutory reform would be helpful, existing laws can be clarified through a combination of more specific administrative rules and better training materials (consistent with relevant state judicial precedents). Such materials should reflect the following policy and definitional considerations.

Sufficient Severity

The Federal Child Abuse Act requires the reporting of instances of physical and mental "injury . . . under circumstances which indicate that the child's health or welfare is harmed or threatened thereby." No one, therefore, would suggest that minor scratches, which are indeed "injuries," should, by themselves, be a reason to require a report.[4]

Involuntary Child Protective Service Agency intervention (action taken *after* a report has been investigated) should be limited to situations of serious harm or threatened harm to the child. This limitation is meant to protect the rights of parents to exercise their best judgement about how to raise children and to protect regional, religious, cultural, and ethnic differences in such beliefs.

There has been much confusion about the concept of sufficient "seriousness," however. It is not restricted to life-threatening situations. Reflecting the need to specify the level of severity, the National Center on Child Abuse and Neglect (1983) provides the following definitions:

"Physical injury" means death, or permanent or temporary disfigurement or impairment of any bodily organ or function.

"Mental injury" mean an injury to the intellectual or psychological capacity of a child as evidenced by an observable and substantial impairment in his ability to function within his normal range of performance and behavior, with due regard to his culture.

Any narrower definition of "serious" would threaten the state's eligibility under the Federal Child Abuse Act.

Threatened Harm

Deciding to intervene is relatively easy when the child has already suffered *serious* physical or mental injury. If the parents cannot satisfactorily explain what happened—and there is reason to believe that the parents are responsible—protective action must be taken.

Society, however, does not wait until a child is seriously injured before taking protective action. The purpose of child protective intervention is also to protect children from *future* injury. Hence, the laws of all states authorize Child Protective Service Agencies and courts to intervene before children have suffered an injury, even a minor one.

This authority (requirement, in fact) to protect children from "threatened harm"—that is, to predict future danger to the child—adds immeasurably to the subjectivity of reporting and investigatory decisions. Despite years of research, there is no psychological profile that accurately identifies parents who will abuse or neglect their children in the future.

Children who have already been abused or neglected are in clear danger of further maltreatment. So are their siblings. But—and this is the key to understanding when a prediction of future danger is justified—the parents' conduct need not already have seriously injured the child for it to be considered "abusive" or "neglectful," and for it to be the ground for Child Protective Service intervention. If the parent did something that was *capable of harming the child*, the parent has demonstrated that he is a continuing threat to the child. It is reasonable to assume that—unless there is a change in circumstances—a parent who has already engaged in harmful conduct toward the child will do so again. Of course, such behavior must be relatively recent; ordinarily, involuntary intervention should not be based on behavior from the distant past.

Therefore, involuntary Child Protective Service intervention should be authorized only if:

1. the parent has seriously harmed the child or engaged in behavior capable of seriously harming the child, whether or not actual harm resulted; or
2. the parent is suffering from a severe mental disability[5] that *demonstrably* prevents the parent from adequately caring for the child.

The latter condition requires a specific assessment of parental functioning and the risk to the child.

The Forms of Child Maltreatment

Early child protective laws focused only on physically abused and battered children. But sexual abuse can leave lasting psychological scars on its young victims, and child neglect can be just as damaging, and just as deadly, as physical abuse. Therefore, Child Protective Service Agencies should respond to all forms of physical, sexual, and psychological maltreatment, in accordance with the following definitions.

Physical Abuse — physical acts (such as striking, punching, kicking, biting, throwing, burning, or violent shaking) that caused, or could have caused, physical injury to the child.

Reasonable corporal punishment is not child abuse, and it is therefore not reportable. The laws of all states recognize the right of parents to physically discipline their children — as long as the punishment is "reasonable" or not "excessive."

Sexual Abuse — vaginal, anal, or oral intercourse; vaginal or anal penetrations; or other forms of contacts for sexual purposes.

Sexual Exploitation — using of a child in prostitution, pornography, or other sexually exploitative activities.

Physical Neglect — failing to provide needed care (such as food, clothing, shelter, protection from hazardous environments, care or supervision appropriate to the child's age or development, hygiene, and medical care) that caused, or over time would cause serious harm.

Abandonment — leaving a child alone or in the care of another under circumstances that demonstrate an intentional abdication of parental responsibility.

Psychological Maltreatment[6] — acts or omissions that caused, or could cause, serious conduct, cognitive, affective, or other mental disorders (American Psychiatric Association, 1980).

Psychological maltreatment is a serious problem requiring Child Protective Service intervention. Its subjectivity and potential overbreadth, however, require that Child Protective Service Agencies exercise special care in this area. There is insufficient professional knowledge about the harmfulness of certain parent/child interactions. In many cases, there is no way of predicting, with any degree of certainty, whether a particular parent's behavior will result in severe harm to the child.

Therefore, a two level approach to the definition of psychological maltreatment is recommended. For such extreme acts of torture and close confinement, no demonstrable harm to the child is required. For less severe acts, such as habitual scapegoating, belittling, and rejecting behavior, demonstrable harm is required. Similarly, some extreme forms of developmental neglect have unambiguous signs, for example, non-organic failure-to-thrive. In less severe cases, assessment by a mental health professional is necessary before proceeding. In these cases, consideration must be given to the severity, chronicity, and context of the parent's acts or omissions. Another important factor can be the parent's failure to seek (or accept) help for such emotional problems in the child.

The meeting participants could not reach agreement on the role of Child Protective Service Agencies in cases of educational neglect. All agreed that parental failure to send a child to school is a serious problem. There was broad feeling, however, that this is not an appropriate area for Child Protective Service intervention. A substantial number of participants would have limited Child Protective Service responsibility to cases of *active* parental interference with the child's school attendance. An even larger number would have Child Protective Service Agencies play no role in such cases, leaving intervention entirely to school authorities unless other forms of abuse or neglect are present.

DECISION MAKING GUIDELINES

Child protection is a multi-stage process of intervention, ascending in accordance with the child's need for protection. The level of intervention rises at a number of discrete points. At each stage of decision making, the Child Protective Service Agency must consider two interrelated factors: (1) the degree of harm or threatened harm to the child, and (2) the certainty of evidence.

Thus, most reports are based on a *suspicion*, usually described as "reasonable cause to suspect,"[7] that the child has been abused or neglected. To determine that a report is substantiated, states require either "some credible evidence" or sufficient reason to conclude that the child has been abused or neglected. For the imposition of involuntary court ordered services, state laws require either a "preponderance of the evidence" or "clear and convincing evidence." Similarly, most court opinions on the subject require serious harm or the threat of serious harm for the imposition of involuntary court ordered services.

Decision-makers do not have specific and widely accepted guidelines that would help ensure uniform and more appropriate reporting and case disposition. More specific operational definitions and decision making criteria must be developed for each stage of the child protective process.

Public and Professional Education

Potential reporters are not required to be sure that a child is being abused or neglected, or to have absolute proof of maltreatment. Instead, reports are required if there is "reasonable cause to suspect" or "reasonable cause to believe" that a child is abused or neglected. This is not, however, an open-ended invitation to report whenever one has a vague, amorphous, or unspecified concern over a child's welfare. Better public and professional materials are needed to obtain more appropriate reporting.

For the general public, educational materials and programs should: (1) clarify the legal definitions of child abuse and neglect, (2) give general descriptions of reportable situations (including specific examples), and (3) explain what to expect when a report is made. Brochures and other materials for laypersons, including public service announcements, should give specific information about what to report—and what not to report.

Professional education should include more specific information about the basis for a report. Keyed to the specific professions most likely to report, it should explain the importance of obtaining—and of providing to the Child Protective Agency—information about the nature of the child's injuries or maltreatment; the history of prior injuries or maltreatment of a child; the condition of a child, including his personal hygiene and clothing; the statements and demeanor of a child or parent—especially if the injuries to the child are at variance with the parental explanation of them; the condition of the home; and the statements of others. The need for the professional who made the report to continue to be involved in efforts to protect the child should also be stressed.

"Behavioral indicators" of child abuse, especially of sexual abuse, have a valid place in decision making. Particularly when there is an otherwise unexplained change in behavior, they provide important clues for potential reporters to pursue, and they provide crucial corroborative evidence of maltreatment. However, the lists of "behavioral indicators" now being circulated, standing on their own and without an accompanying full history of past and present behaviors, should not be the basis of a report. Such behaviors have many other possible explanations. Nevertheless, some alarming and unusual child behaviors may, in and of themselves, warrant a report by qualified professionals. More work needs to be done in developing descriptions of such behaviors and educating professionals about them.

Education for both public and professional audiences should describe the range of community resources — beyond Child Protective Services — available for children and families with problems other than child abuse or neglect.

Receiving Reports

Not all calls to Child Protective Service Agencies are reports of suspected child abuse and neglect. Because of the volume of calls they receive, the danger of harassment, and the need to limit unnecessary investigations, Child Protective Service Agencies have an obligation to determine whether a call is appropriate for investigation. Agencies that carefully screen calls have lower rates of unsubstantiated reports and expend fewer resources investigating inappropriate calls.

Child Protective Service Agencies should develop more specific policies and procedures for determining whether to accept a call for investigation. Such policies should require a determination that the call falls within the state's statutory definition of reportable suspected child maltreatment. Factors to be considered include: (1) the age of the child, (2) the identity of the responsible caretaker and relationship to the child, (3) the suspected existence of an incident or circumstance falling within the state's definition of child maltreatment, and (4) the existence of demonstrable harm or risk of harm to the child. When appropriate, calls may be referred to other agencies that can provide services needed by the family.

This kind of intake decision making cannot be done by clerks, nor by untrained caseworkers. A sophisticated judgement about the child's need for protection must be made. In addition, the intake staff must be able to provide advice and consultation to the person on the telephone. Experienced and qualified CPS workers should be assigned to intake — where they can do the most to improve agency decision making.

Case/Dispositional Decision Making

Definitions of child abuse and neglect must distinguish between those child rearing situations that society thinks are less than optimal — and for which voluntary services should be offered — from those of such severity that society is prepared to impose, through court action, treatment services and, if necessary, removal of the child. This is meant to protect the rights of parents to exercise their best judgement about how to raise children and to protect regional, religious, cultural, and ethnic differences in such beliefs.

In effect, Child Protective Service Agencies need specific guidelines for deciding what kind of intervention is needed, and for determining whether to pursue involuntary intervention. The National Association of Public Child Welfare Administrators (NAPCWA, 1987), has identified the relevant factors to be considered in assessing the severity of danger to the child and the certainty of evidence:

1. Action or failure to act of the parent or caretaker
2. Impact of parental/caretaker behavior on child/severity of the alleged abuse
3. Age of child
4. Frequency/recency of the alleged abuse
5. Credibility of reporter
6. Type and amount of evidence and corroboration
7. Relationship of alleged perpetrator to the child
8. Location of child
9. Parental willingness to protect the child
10. Parental ability to protect child.

These guidelines need to be reviewed and operationalized.

Interdisciplinary Consultation

Reporting, investigatory, and dispositional decision making often entail a complex weighing of medical, social work, child development, and legal considerations. Decision making becomes easier—and more accurate—when it is made in consultation with other professionals whose skills and experience can help assess the situation. Consultation can be accomplished informally or through the more formal mechanism of a "Multidisciplinary Team" (sometimes called a "Suspected Child Abuse and Neglect" or "SCAN" Team) comprised of professionals from many disciplines.

INVESTIGATORY DETERMINATIONS

Child Protective Service Agencies must determine the validity of reports so that basic case-handling decisions can be made. This is especially true because the laws under which Child Protective Service Agencies operate give them the right to intervene against parental wishes. In addition, procedures for the sealing or expunging of records often depend on such determinations.

Some Unsubstantiated Reports Are Necessary

Nationwide, only about 40 percent of all reports are "substantiated." The rest are dismissed after investigation (American Association for Protecting Children, 1987). Although rules, procedures, and even terminology vary (some states use the phrase "unsubstantiated," others "unfounded" or "not indicated"), in essence, an "unsubstantiated" report is one that is dismissed after an investigation finds insufficient evidence to warrant further Child Protective Service involvement.

Many unsubstantiated cases involve situations of poor child care that, though of legitimate concern, simply do not amount to child abuse or neglect. In fact, a substantial proportion of unsubstantiated cases are referred to other social agencies that can provide needed services to the family. Others involve situations in which the person reporting, in a well-intentioned effort to protect a child, overreacts to a vague and often misleading possibility that the child may be maltreated.

Moreover, an unsubstantiated report does not necessarily mean that the child was not actually abused or neglected. Evidence of child maltreatment is hard to obtain, and may not be uncovered when agencies lack the time and resources to complete a thorough investigation or when inaccurate information is given to the investigator. Other cases are labelled unsubstantiated when there are no services available to help the family. Some cases must be closed because the child or family cannot be located.

A small percentage of unsubstantiated reports are deliberate misstatements. Studies of sexual abuse reports, for example, suggest that, at most, from 4 to 10 percent of these reports are knowingly false (Berliner, 1988). Malicious reports are illegal. In appropriate cases, a referral for civil or criminal prosecution should be considered.

A certain amount of unsubstantiated reporting is an inherent—and legitimate—aspect of reporting *suspected* child maltreatment and is necessary to ensure adequate child protection. We ask hundreds of thousands of strangers to report their suspicions; we cannot ask that they be certain.

These realities make it important, for both programmatic effectiveness and agency image, that the meaning of statistics about unsubstantiated cases be clarified. *First*, the categories of reasons for closing a case after an initial investigation should be standardized across the states. *Second*, to document the role of Child Protective Service Agencies in providing services to families, the category of "unsubstantiated" reports should be divided into two parts:

1. Unsubstantiated—no further action taken, and
2. Unsubstantiated—services provided or arranged.

CONCLUSION

This report has sought to provide policy guidelines for improved reporting and investigatory decision making. Its recommendations can be summarized as follows:

1. Child Protective Services should be defined as a program limited to abused or neglected children and their families within a broader child welfare service system, not as *the* child welfare program.
2. The community, not the Child Protective Service Agency alone, has the primary and ultimate responsibility for preventing and treating child abuse and neglect. The community and professionals do not satisfy this obligation merely by reporting cases.
3. Child Protective Service Agencies should be assigned investigatory responsibility only over intrafamilial or quasifamilial child maltreatment, broadly defined to include parents, guardians, foster parents, and other persons (such as boyfriends or girlfriends) continuously or regularly in the child's home.
4. Investigating nonfamilial abuse and neglect should be the responsibility of law enforcement, licensing, or other agencies with the expertise and authority to investigate such cases, not of the Child Protective Service Agency. Furthermore, such units must be independent of the agency or facility being investigated, so that there is no conflict of interest.
5. Consistent with the need to safeguard the welfare of endangered children, every effort must be made to protect parental rights.
6. Definitions of child abuse and neglect and implementing rules should be redrafted to be more specific and to clarify the types of cases that should be reported—and not reported—to the Child Protective Service Agency.
7. Involuntary Child Protective Service intervention should be authorized only if: (1) the parent has engaged in seriously harmful behavior toward the child, whether or not actual harm resulted; or (2) the parent is suffering from a severe mental disability that *demonstrably* prevents the parent from adequately caring for the child.
8. Decision-makers do not have specific and widely accepted guidelines that would help ensure uniform and more appropriate reporting and case disposition. More specific operational definitions and

decision making criteria must be developed for each stage of the child protective process.

9. Public and professional education should provide clear information about what to report (and not to report), give descriptions and examples of reportable conditions, explain what to expect when a report is made, and give information on appropriate alternative resources for other child and family problems. Professionals should be asked to give more specific information than the general public when making a report.

10. "Behavioral indicators" of child abuse, especially of sexual abuse, have a valid place in decision making. However, the lists of "behavioral indicators" now being circulated, standing on their own and without an accompanying full history of past and present behaviors, should not be the basis of a report.

11. State law should allow for, and guidelines should support, the screening of reports by qualified staff — in order to limit the Child Protective Agency's involvement in inappropriate cases.

12. The extent of Child Protective Service Agency intervention should vary with the degree of harm or threatened harm to the child and the certainty of the evidence. Guidelines to assess both should be developed.

13. Reporters should not be expected to decide if abuse or neglect has occurred before making a report. Thus, a certain number of unsubstantiated investigations is necessary to ensure adequate child protection.

14. Uniform categories and definitions of investigative findings should be developed. They should accurately reflect the disposition and the services provided in cases that are not substantiated.

ENDNOTES

1. The following statistics concerning reported cases are derived from various reports of the American Humane Association.

2. This expanding of the definition goes beyond child maltreatment in out-of-home care, which is discussed in the next section.

3. See 45 Code of Federal Regulations sec. 1340.14 (e) (January 26, 1983).

4. For the definitive exposition of how severity of injury effects — and should effect — child protective decision making, see Giovannoni and Becerra (1979).

5. Including severe mental illness, severe mental retardation, severe drug abuse, and severe alcohol abuse, as defined in American Psychiatric Association (1980).

6. This category is often labelled "emotional maltreatment." The broader

phrase was adopted to reflect the fact that it encompasses the full range of serious psychological disorders.

7. Some states adopt a probable cause standard, that is, "reasonable cause to *believe.*"

REFERENCES

American Association for Protecting Children. (1987). *Highlights of official child neglect and abuse reporting (1985).* Denver, Co: American Humane Association.

American Psychiatric Association. (1980). *Diagnostic and statistical manual of mental disorder (DSM III).* Washington, D.C.: American Psychiatric Association.

Berliner, L. (1988). Deciding whether a child has been sexually abused. In B. Nicholson (Ed.), *Sexual abuse allegations in custody and visitation cases.* Washington, D.C.: American Bar Association.

Giovannoni, J., & Becerra, R. (1979). *Defining child abuse.* New York: Free Press.

National Association of Public Child Welfare Administrators. (1987). *Guidelines for the development of protective services for abused and neglected children and their families.* Washington, D.C.: National Association of Public Child Welfare Administrators.

National Center on Child Abuse and Neglect. (1983). *Child protection: A guide for state legislation.* Washington, D.C.: National Center on Child Abuse and Neglect. (Draft).

Unsubstantiated Reports:
Perspectives of Child Protection Workers

Jeanne M. Giovannoni

ABSTRACT. The "unsubstantiated" child abuse report has become a matter of great concern and controversy. Despite their role as gatekeepers of the Child Protection System, there has been little study of CPS workers' views on this problem. This study of CPS workers from three states will assess their attitudes about issues of reporting, screening, and substantiation of cases as they relate to the "unsubstantiated" report.

Although increasing attention has been focused on unsubstantiated reports of maltreatment and critics have demanded that they somehow be reduced (Besharov, 1985), there has been no examination of CPS workers' opinions and attitudes about the problem, although they are the ones closest to the situations and in fact are the gatekeepers of the Child Protective System. This article is based on a survey of 117 workers in 6 rural and 3 urban county agencies located in California, Idaho, and Virginia. The opinion survey was part of a larger project. The other component was a study of the outcomes of 1150 actual reports of maltreatment made to these agencies including 125 that were screened out before investigation. That data has been presented elsewhere but where findings complement the results of the opinion survey they are noted (Giovannoni, 1987 and 1989).

The interviews were semi-structured and content analysis was used to categorize the open-ended responses. The questions centered on three major areas: (1) screening of cases before investigation in the three urban counties that used screening; (2) issues in substantiation; and (3) within each, reporter differences between private individuals and mandated professionals. Two caveats are in order. Given the limitations of sampling no

---

Jeanne M. Giovannoni is affiliated with the School of Social Work, University of California, Los Angeles, CA.

51

inferences of generalizability can be drawn, and since the intent of the research was to gather ideas, responses made by even a small fraction of the workers are noted without any implication that these were typical of a majority.

SCREENING ISSUES

One potential avenue for reducing investigative activity is the screening out of reports before investigation. In the interviews the 81 workers in the three urban counties that used screening were asked to identify: (1) the three most important factors that prompted rejection of initial reports; (2) factors that should be considered in the decision not to investigate and (3) issues that gave them "second thoughts" about rejecting cases for investigation. Data on 125 reports that had been screened out had been collected as part of the report survey and where there is an overlap between the workers' responses and these data on actual reports it is noted (Giovannoni, 1987).

The most commonly cited reasons for screening out cases involved factors in the report that fell outside the legislative mandates of the agency or agency policy. Included here are reports of family or child problems that do not constitute abuse or neglect such as marital conflicts and adolescent behavior problems, the older age of the child and third party perpetrators. These were the kinds of problems most commonly screened out in the survey of reports. Beyond these jurisdictional matters were judgments about the reliability of the information given by reporters, the nebulousness of evidence that anything had occurred and the absence of concrete information such as addresses which would preclude investigation.

The other set of responses referred to the questioning of the motivations of reporters, a matter germane to the issue of "false reporting." The two main ones pertain to custody disputes and those referred to as "malicious." The idea that the resolution of custody disputes is being sought through child protective services is one commonly identified in the survey of screened reports, with "Absent Spouses and In-Laws" being among the groups of reporters most likely to have been screened out. Workers in the interview survey at times graphically noted that such reports were even being made by the secretaries of the attorneys of the conflicted parties. We know from the report survey that by no means are all reports reflective of custody disputes automatically screened out, but clearly these are a source of reports that are of widespread concern, even though they constitute a very small percentage of all reports. Other kinds of "malicious" complaints were also cited, particularly ones suspected to be motivated by family or neighborhood feuds.

The next two sets of questions dealt with the workers' opinions about the screening process and their subjective experiences with it. The responses to both indicate that for a majority the practice of screening is problematic. When asked if they thought other factors should be included in screening decisions, the respondents were almost evenly divided between those who mentioned factors that would screen out more cases and those that would, in effect, screen in more. Among the former were a variety of factors, the most common being reports of problems not appropriate to CPS intervention, especially those involving acting-out adolescents. Workers thought that CPS had little or nothing to offer these youth because they are difficult to hold in foster care.

Other responses referred to the reporters' past pattern of reporting, when the case had last been investigated, and stricter adherence to non-intervention if the child was not at substantial risk or if another agency was already involved. A few urged more frequent use of "information only" dispositions, i.e., simply recording the call but not reporting it or investigating, while others called for greater discretion in using their own judgement, including their own intuitive assessment of the veracity of the caller and the risk to the child.

Slightly less than half the respondents offered no further criteria that would screen out cases but rather ones that would have the effect of screening in more cases. In direct contrast to other workers, they would investigate all reports of emotional maladjustment, children out of control without any help, third party perpetrator situations to see that the child victim is getting services, situations where there is a history of abuse of another child, and those involving drug addicted or mentally ill caretakers or violent homes where there is no known current abuse or neglect. The division of opinion among these workers indicates screening is problematic. Responses to the next set of questions bear this out.

The initial question was, "Do you ever have second thoughts about any of the reports that are rejected at the point of initial contact?" Depending on the response they were then asked, "If not, why not?" or "If yes, what are the issues in a case that bother you the most?" We deal first with the negative responses and then with those that did reveal "second thoughts."

Slightly less than half the workers who responded to this question said they had no second thoughts. However, when we looked at the reasons given why they did not, it appears that their lack of concern is not necessarily a validation of their comfort with the process. In roughly half of these responses the workers indicated that they had no second thoughts because the supervisor makes the final decision and in the other half the reason given was that if they did have any doubt they sent the case on to investigation. Only five indicated that the reasons they had no second thoughts was because of the clarity of the criteria for rejecting a report. These responses indicate that rejecting reports is problematic for these workers.

Not surprisingly the reasons given by workers as to what prompted them to have second thoughts are similar to the situations noted above as to what they would like to see considered in screening in more reports: high risk or potentially abusive situations and the problems of teenagers, children described by one worker as the "ones who fall through the cracks."

SUBSTANTIATION ISSUES

We turn now to examination of the responses of workers to questions in the interview which focused on issues of substantiation. But first a word about "substantiation." None of the agencies used the term. In the report survey the agreed upon definition of "substantiated" was "opened for services." Among the reports designated as "unsubstantiated," in over half, some maltreatment had been noted or validated in the investigation. The major difference between these cases and those substantiated was that the maltreatment was less serious or there was an absence of multiple kinds of maltreatment. Hence the claim "unsubstantiated" does not equal "false report." The workers were asked their views about agency priorities, reasons why maltreatment was not validated, how they experienced the situation of unsubstantiation, how they viewed the use of their time in such cases, what might be done to facilitate more cases being substantiated, and finally questions concerning service needs.

Agency Priorities

Workers were asked to rate on a four point scale ranging from (1) "Not important at all" to (4) "Very important," how important it was to the agency to investigate reports from professionals, and then from private individuals. And then questions were put to them regarding the importance of "opening" cases, which was the operational definition of substantiation used in the study.

To these workers the importance of investigation of reports to the agencies was clear: over 85% responded that investigating reports from either agencies/professionals or private individuals was "very important." When asked why, the overwhelming majority simply stated: "That's my job." A few mentioned maintaining good public relations with agencies, or CPS agencies' potential liability if they did not investigate.

With respect to opening cases, over 90% stated that opening cases was of little or no importance in relation to the source of the report. When asked, the majority responded that reporter differences had no bearing on the matter, rather the protection of children was the central issue in the decision to open cases. Apart from this very common type of response there were a few who noted liability risks in not opening cases, public relations issues as a reason for priority in opening cases reported by professionals, and the capacity of Protective Services to provide appropriate resources.

In sum, the workers generally thought that the agency in which they worked set a high priority on investigating cases, but no such priority on opening cases or substantiating them.

Workers' Subjective Experiences

The respondents were asked, "How do you feel when you investigate a report that is not validated?" The majority of the workers gave responses that indicated varying levels of discomfort. The most common of these expressed a mixed reaction such as "sometimes you worry if you did all you could, but sometimes you feel relieved that there was nothing there." Others expressed stronger feelings of uneasiness and a sense of frustration, such as "it can be really frustrating when you feel in your gut that something is going on but you can't pin the evidence down to validate it." About a third of these negative reactions referred to feelings of embarrassment and even guilt at having intruded into families' lives. Only a few reported indifference to the situation, while the remaining responses were generally positive expressions of relief that the investigative activity itself was an opportunity to assist families in other areas, regardless of whether a case was opened or not.

A related question was, "How would you describe the use of your time in these instances?" The greatest proportion of respondents felt that time spent investigating reports that were not validated was used to offer other services. Others simply described the use of time in these instances as appropriate. Only a fourth said it was a waste of time, with half of these referring specifically to situations associated with custody disputes and malicious reporting.

Next they were asked, "What do you think needs to happen to maximize the use of your time in responding to reports?" Almost one-fifth said that they were doing the best they could with respect to the use of their time. The remaining responses focused primarily on intra-agency changes that might be helpful. These included: better telephone interviewing techniques that would improve the specificity and comprehensiveness of the information received at the time of the initial report; adjustments in staffing patterns such as specialization according to function and/or extent of training and, assignments according to geography, and less frequently mentioned, increased staff. Other internal changes cited referred to office procedures (e.g., allocation of cars, greater privacy, assigned clerks) and increased latitude and time to ask more questions over the telephone as well as more time to develop and establish collateral information. Only a handful suggested more information and training for the community.

Why Reports Are Not Validated

Workers were asked, "What, in your opinion, are some of the commonest reasons why reports are not found to be valid?" Following this they were then asked, "How do these reasons differ when the report is from a private individual or from an agency/professional?"

There were 296 responses given by the 117 workers as to why reports were not found to be valid. The most common (39% of the responses) was "lack of proof," including such factors as the absence of concrete information, failure of child to corroborate report, denial by perpetrator and the untimely (i.e., long after the fact) report of abusive incidents.

The "malicious report" was given as the next most frequent reason for non-validation (16%). Neighbors particularly were described as using the Protective Services system as a retaliatory weapon against one another. Closely coupled with this reason for not validating complaints were those referring to family disputes (12%), where most related to custody disputes. Of note, was the observation of some workers that reports of abuse were initiated by attorneys of the opposing spouse as part of "building a case." Both malicious and family dispute reports were attributed to private individuals rather than professionals. These responses should not be interpreted as workers saying either maliciousness or family disputes are characteristic of private individuals' reports only that agencies are unlikely to have such motivations.

Another 15% of the reasons cited concerned a genuine misinterpretation of the event or situation by the reporter, for example, a continuously crying baby who upon investigation was observed as colic. Private individuals were seen as more likely to make such misinterpretations but some said this was a problem with professionals as well. Situations that did not meet the states' legal criteria of severity of maltreatment constituted 10%

of the reasons given for non-validation, where the event or behavior was not judged severe enough to be covered by the reporting legislation and in the opinion of some constituted the imposition of reporters' own values on the situations, such as reports of neglect where the parenting standards of the reporter far exceeded the requirements of the law.

Finally, 8% of the reasons given for non-validation related to a lack of understanding about the functions of child protection agencies, like the hope that families would be policed or children placed in foster homes. Similarly, agency professionals were said sometimes to make reports because they didn't want to provide services for a family, or they reported indiscriminantly just to ensure they have met their obligation under the mandatory reporting requirements.

Information Given in Reports

The second question was: "What kinds of information are more likely to lead to validated reports?" Thirty-six percent of these responses referred to documentable facts: a specific allegation by the child, availability of an eye witness, medical reports, first hand knowledge of the incident by the reporter, an allegation by the non-offending parent, admission by the perpetrator, and physical evidence of injuries or neglect. Specific identifying information was cited in 21% of the responses, including exact location, names and ages of the victims and other family members. The remaining 16% of the responses fell evenly among the following categories: information suggesting reporter reliability, availability of collateral informants; timeliness and history of abuse in family. Neither agencies nor private individuals were particularly perceived as better informants.

Improving Reporting from Agencies
and Private Individuals

Asked first with reference to agency/professionals and then for private individuals the question was: "What do you think needs to happen to facilitate more reports that can be validated?" There were notable differences between the responses to this question with respect to agency/professionals and report source.

With reference to agencies/professionals, a third of the respondents said that "Nothing should be done." A few thought agencies were already reporting satisfactorily, but, the majority cited concern about reducing any impetus to report. Examples of this type of response were: "All they have to do is suspect. If reporting is more stringent then they become the investigators," and "Nothing needs to happen because it is better to be cautious. We do not want the professionals to do their own investigations." Other responses were focused not on making changes in the reporters but on improving CPS workers' skills in obtaining information, such as in-service training in interviewing and in obtaining information both in the taking of reports and in conducting investigations.

Contrary responses all focused on changes that would facilitate agencies and professionals making reports that could more easily be validated. These included suggestions for agencies "to check it out" or "talk to the child," making timely reports on current situations, and training reporters in how to screen reports. Some focused on addressing training to particular categories of reporters including law enforcement, physicians, teachers, and therapists, particularly educating them to the proper functions of CPS. These three responses were typical:

> Take the health department, some report, some don't. Education is needed; need to know exactly what we do; we stop abuse if we know about it and investigate. We treat families.

> There is a need to reduce reports. Professionals report to protect themselves. But they are hostile because they have unreal expectations. Need more public awareness of what can and can't be done, what should and shouldn't be reported.

> More education—we are advocates, not child snatchers.

When asked what could be done to facilitate reporting by private individuals over half indicated concerns about discouraging reports from these people or cited the difficulty of reaching this amorphous audience compared to a professional one. The most common response cited a need for improved CPS skills rather than any intervention directed at reporters. Examples were:

> Hard to reach private individuals. I'd rather have them report than not, even if it is unfounded. Some is really "junk"; neighbors are mad at each other and make malicious reports just to give trouble. Some know we'll go out no matter what—even though we might already know there's nothing there.

> A lot has to do with the way we question. They should call; we should know how to get useful information.

Responses related to positive change efforts were similar to those for professionals, but there were also distinctive suggestions particular to these individuals: general community education about child abuse and neglect, including what information to give, the necessity for timely reporting, the need to give specific details, and a better understanding of CPS functions.

Interestingly, some of these were seen as ways that a better understanding of CPS limitations might influence not so much reporter behavior but the responses made by alleged perpetrators. An example of such a response is:

> People don't know what to expect when they are investigated; they might not be so defensive if they were better informed.

An interesting approach mentioned by several workers concerned the utility of broad based community education in normal child development as a way of distinguishing different values about appropriate parental behavior from abuse and neglect. One such response was:

> People need to realize the kinds of things that we do. People now see just about everything as "abuse or neglect." e.g., "child riding bike in road," "child playing in the creek." They need to consider what's normal. I had to learn to put my own personal feelings aside and had to learn to deal with no plumbing and inadequate housing.

A final, though small minority of responses referred to educating people to the seriousness of making malicious reports and to enforcing legal sanctions against those who do. A majority of workers would like to see some educational efforts aimed at private individuals, but a significant portion of workers were fearful of any efforts that might have the effect of reducing serious and valid reports.

Services Rendered During Investigation

Overall a referral to at least one agency outside CPS was made in 35% of the substantiated and 20% of the unsubstantiated cases. When the responsible caretaker was the alleged perpetrator, referrals were made in 27% of the cases, and where the perpetrator was someone else, in 37% of the cases, a referral was made for the responsible caretaker. Interestingly, in cases where the alleged perpetrator "denied" the allegation, referrals were made in 45% of these cases and in 55% where the response was other than denial indicating denial is not to be equated with uncooperativeness in all instances.

Where some maltreatment had been noted in the investigation, 39% of such cases had referrals, but even where no maltreatment had been noted,

17% of the cases did. Thus, whether maltreatment is validated or cases substantiated or not, service rendering is a part of CPS investigatory activity and indicates investigation is not necessarily a hostile or adversarial process.

We turn now to the workers' perceptions of service needs. They were asked first about service needs among cases where maltreatment was not validated and then about those situations where it was validated but was not deemed to warrant CPS intervention and thus the report was unsubstantiated.

Overall, a little less than half the workers responding to the question about situations where maltreatment was not validated said that at least 60% or more of the families where reports could not be validated needed some other kind of service ranging from counseling to health care, child care, legal assistance and job training.

When the question shifted to cases where maltreatment was verified but CPS intervention was not warranted, almost three-quarters of the workers felt that over 60% of these cases not taken into the system had need of other services especially counseling but also frequently mentioned were food, housing, money, self-help groups for parenting skills along with health care and legal assistance. The most frequently cited barriers to the provision of perceived service needs were: Internal agency policies mainly eligibility requirements followed by client resistance, lack of community services, and lack of agency resources.

CONCLUSIONS

Child Protection workers stand as gatekeepers between the community and the Child Protection system. As such they are the object of diverse, conflicting interests within the community and they must struggle constantly to maintain a delicate balance between the adequate protection of children, and the unjustified intrusion into family privacy. The strains this situation places on them are revealed in many of the responses given in this study.

These workers were virtually unanimous in their perception that their most important and, indeed unique, function is investigation, regardless of the outcome of the investigation. This was suggested not only by the responses to the direct questions about the importance of investigation to them and to their agencies but also in the rather general reluctance to either expand the kinds of reports that might be screened out before investigation or steps to reduce reporting especially from private individuals. In a sense, they see their role in investigation as that of an arbitrator between conflicting community claims and fulfillment of that role is achieved when a judgment is made about the existence of maltreatment, regardless of which way that judgment goes.

Nonetheless, it was also clear that a majority do experience uneasiness when in their role as gatekeepers they do not bring cases into the system. There is an awareness that some individuals do attempt to manipulate the protective service system for their own ends, including custody battle pursuits and just plain maliciousness. Yet, there was no strong support for categorically excluding such potentially manipulative reports from investigation, but rather that such a judgment about a report should be made only after a sufficient investigation.

On balance both the responses of these workers as well as the data from the survey of actual reports to their agencies go against the notion that a high proportion of "unsubstantiated" reports is a valid indicator of the level of "false reports." "Unsubstantiated" reports are a heterogeneous lot and in no way synonymous with "false reports." Still it must be acknowledged that some proportion of families are put through investigations when in fact the children involved have not been endangered. Can this be avoided when the complaint is one of a situation, that if valid, falls within the legal mandates of child protective intervention? Another way of looking at this question is as a choice between "false positives" and "false negatives" with the "false positive" being the invalid complaint and the "false negative" being the uninvestigated complaint that was in fact valid. Taken in concert, the responses of the workers interviewed would indicate the majority would opt for taking the risk of the false positive over the risk of the false negative. While concerned with the rights of families when there is a conflict, the protection of children comes first even if on occasion it must be at the cost of unnecessary intrusion.

The situation does not warrant complacency, and such was not the response of most of these workers. We note here their many suggestions for improvements in the investigative process centered less on changing reporters than on making changes within the system, including the upgrading of their own skills in interviewing and gathering evidence. There should be a continuing concern in child protective services to keep unnecessary investigative activity to a minimum, but realistically some measure will persist. Reporters, including professionals, not acting out of maliciousness but in good faith, will consider some parental behavior to warrant protective intervention Child Protective Services does not. Perhaps one avenue to be pursued in mitigating the negative effects of unnecessary investigative intrusion is the development of positive mechanisms to officially recognize those cases that, following investigation, were demonstrated not to involve maltreatment. Since the term "unsubstantiated" has such diverse meanings, additional recorded statements of exoneration in these kinds of situations are a means of addressing what may be a relatively rare occurrence, but nonetheless an unfortunate one.

There was a divergence of opinions among these workers with respect to both the screening out of more cases and the advisability of efforts to reduce reporting. Such divergence does not indicate indifference to the level of unsubstantiated reports. On the contrary, the very divergence indicates the salience of the issues and controversy over the solutions.

The divergence of opinions among these workers as to solutions to the "unsubstantiated report" are no more pronounced than they are in the field in general. Efficiency in resource utilization and protection of family integrity must be continuing concerns. In opting for solutions that would maximize these interests, however, the protection of children must always remain paramount. Solutions that might protect the interests of a few but endanger the interests of others, such as the wholesale screening out of custody issues, cannot be countenanced. The concern shown by the workers augurs well for the potential for collaboration and cooperation between Child Protective Services and parties interested in combating "false reports." Such cooperation is necessary for any success. Advocacy efforts devoid of a cooperative element are likely to end only in stalemate.

REFERENCES

Besharov, D. J. (1985). Doing something about child abuse: The need to narrow the grounds for state intervention. *Harvard Journal of Law and Public Policy*, *8*(3), 539-589.

Giovannoni, J. (1987). *Private Individuals' Reports of Child Abuse and Neglect*. Final Report. OHSDS Grant #90-CA-1007.

Giovannoni, J. (1989). Substantiated and unsubstantiated reports of child abuse and neglect. *Children and Youth Services Review*. *11*, 299-318.

Responding to Reports
of Child Abuse and Neglect

Susan J. Wells
Jane Downing
John Fluke

ABSTRACT. This paper examines screening and substantiation practices in CPS intake and investigation. The authors note a large degree of variation in screening practices. In the context of false allegations, they note that most reports of maltreatment are specific, and those that are not specific or do not allege maltreatment are generally not investigated.

Screening in Child Protective Services has recently received a great deal of attention due to the increasing numbers of CPS reports and the resulting inability to investigate thoroughly every complaint that is received. In addition to prioritizing cases for investigation, many states are adopting policies and laws which permit some degree of freedom in determining whether to conduct a full scale investigation. A few recent examples include the California law permitting workers to make inquiries about a contact without performing in-person investigations; the Louisiana law which has two different definitions of abuse and neglect—one for the purpose of reporting and the other for conducting investigations; and policies in numerous states (written and unwritten) which specify which types of complaints will not be investigated, e.g., Texas, Arizona, and Maine. These policies generally focus on interpreting the legal definitions of

Susan J. Wells and Jane Downing are affiliated with the National Legal Resource Center for Child Advocacy and Protection, American Bar Association, Washington, DC 20036. John Fluke is affiliated with the American Association for Protecting Children. The work on which this article is based was made possible by the National Center on Child Abuse and Neglect, Administration for Children, Youth and Families, Office of Human Development Services, Department of Health and Human Services through Grant Number 90-CA-1265.

abuse and neglect and do not usually encourage screening out actual complaints of child maltreatment. In addition, some localities and states such as the State of Washington are screening out what they believe to be "low risk" reports, often reports of chronic neglect without injury.

SCREENING PRACTICES

It is clear that screening should not be thought of as one uniform act and that it does not usually begin with the process of exclusion. It is a set of practices and policies which: (1) set definitions of child maltreatment through laws and policy; (2) guide preliminary assessment of a contact to determine congruency with the intent of law and policy, for example, identifying complaints in which a caller is known to be subverting the CPS system by continually making harassing complaints, or where there is not enough information to proceed; and which may (3) eliminate actual reports of maltreatment before investigation. While there may be a lot of controversy about what should be "in" or "out" in accordance with laws, policies and preliminary assessments, these are basically policy decisions regarding what constitutes a potentially valid (and investigatable) report. In the last alternative, everyone agrees that there is a report of some degree of maltreatment by a caretaker but that there are not enough agency resources to investigate every report that is made to the agency. This final level of screening appears to take place locally and may be done systematically according to written or unwritten procedures or it may occur as a de facto result of prioritization of investigations.

Screening of contacts made to child protective services may be conducted at several levels. At the time of first contact the receiving worker may determine that the complaint is not within the scope of the reporting law and refer the caller to a more appropriate agency. After a complaint is accepted by the "front line" worker, the supervisor for the unit of workers receiving the calls reviews the allegation and may decide at that time that the contact is not within the scope of the law. For example, the perpetrator may not be the child's caretaker, making the contact a police matter.

The next level of review is the supervisor who assigns the investigations. In large offices this will be another person. In small offices it will probably be the same person who supervises incoming complaints. If the supervisor assigning investigations is another person, he or she will review the allegation a third time before assigning it to a worker. At any level of review, preliminary inquiries may be made to determine whether the allegation is supported by other evidence or whether it is a bogus or frivolous complaint. Records are checked for previous reports and any workers in the agency with knowledge of the family may be contacted for additional information.

While the system of review varies according to size and administration of the agency, the basic task of the supervisors is to determine whether the contact is credible, specific, within the scope of the state's laws and agency's policies and an indication of actual harm or threatened harm to a child.

Uses of Risk Assessment

Work currently being done in evaluation of risk assessment instruments suggests that accurate distinctions between serious and non-serious cases can be made to some degree from the information gained at the time of the report. Johnson (personal communication, 1988) found that in Alameda County, worker judgments predicted substantiation of sexual abuse 54% of the time, physical abuse 68% of the time, and neglect 68% of the time. Using a list of risk factors known at the time of the contact to predict disposition the researchers were able to create models to predict substantiation of abuse reports 73% of the time and sexual abuse reports 68% of the time. The model for neglect had some predictive value but did not exceed the workers' clinical judgments.

English (personal communication, 1988) also reports hopeful findings regarding ability to correctly classify less serious reports at the time of the complaint, citing a success rate of 90% in predicting that a report was low risk. Yet she also found that 80% of those believed to be at moderate or high risk initially, became low risk at a later date. These are recent findings and will be available in more detail shortly.

The point here is that research regarding predictive validity of information known at the time of the contact is underway and generating some preliminary information regarding judgments made at the time the contact is received. The study on which this paper is based concerns the screening of contacts at intake and the workers' reasons for investigating or not investigating a report.

A STUDY OF SCREENING IN CHILD PROTECTIVE SERVICES

This study was funded by the National Center on Child Abuse and Neglect to examine screening and substantiation practices in CPS intake and investigation. The remainder of the paper will report on findings of that research with specific attention to types of allegations of abuse and neglect and reasons why workers and supervisors chose to investigate them or screen them out. Data will be presented regarding case decisions and practices in 12 sites (referred to as Sites A-L). A site may be a county, city, or district (which is composed of a conglomerate of cities or counties). Workers were given checklists to record source of contact, type of maltreatment and problem alleged, as well as disposition and reason for disposition. They were asked to record every call, letter or complaint where the reporter had some concern about the welfare of a child. All inquiries regarding other services such as food stamps and day care were referred out and are not represented in our sample. Any calls making vague allegations or expressing concerns about children were recorded. Types of problems alleged could range from maltreatment (e.g., hitting, locking out, lack of supervision) to parental or child problems only (e.g., parental drug abuse, child mental health problems). In addition, a reporter may have alleged injuries without maltreatment or vice versa.

Site Description

The child population of the study sites ranged from 9,663 to 424,044 according to the 1980 census. A few examples may give the reader an idea of the range of communities studied: Site A is an urban, relatively poor area with a population fairly evenly divided between white and non-white. Site C, in the same state, has roughly the same child population, is suburban and 90% white. Site I is very poor, rural and virtually all white. Three sites have a Hispanic population of 10-20%. There are two to three sites in each state studied. The number of contacts for the twelve sites is 2,556. The number of contacts for individual sites ranges from 63 to 401. This figure includes multiple referrals on the same child and family.

Types of Injuries and Maltreatment Alleged

Of the 2,556 complaints received, 86% alleged some form of maltreatment. The remainder (363 contacts) concerned allegations of parental, child, or familial problems, e.g., problems in caring for children, parental alcoholism, or the lack of housing. No maltreatment was alleged four percent of the time in Site F and 30% of the time in Site H. Most contacts had one type of maltreatment alleged (57 to 83%) with 8 to 24% having two or more.

Neglect. In terms of neglect, lack of supervision was alleged for 23% of the sample. Failure to provide food, clothing, shelter and/or health care was alleged for 15% of the contacts. Other types of neglect were alleged in 13% of the population with relatively little variation. In addition, unspecified neglect was alleged in 4% of the contacts and abandonment in 3%.

Physical abuse. Unspecified physical abuse was alleged in 6% of the contacts made and hitting in 14%. Reports of more severe types of physical abuse (repeated hitting, beatings, suffocation, the use of a weapon, throwing, burning or shaking the child) were, as expected, much more rare occurrences, with a range of 5 to 18% and an average of 9%. Other physical abuse (biting, unacceptable confinement, etc.) was alleged in 7% of the contacts.

Sexual abuse. Unspecified sexual abuse complaints were made in 5% of the contacts. Exposure, suggestive talk, use of pornography or fondling were alleged in 7% of the contacts. Intercourse was alleged for 2% and exploitation or other types of sexual abuse was alleged for 4% of the contacts.

Other complaints. Emotional maltreatment was alleged for 138 contacts (5%) and fostering delinquency for 78 contacts (3%), and for 363 contacts, no maltreatment was alleged. Parental and familial problems alleged for these complaints included: (1) health and mental health problems (28% of those alleging no maltreatment, N = 363); (2) marital problems including family violence (13%); (3) problems in caring for the children, e.g., discipline too harsh, too many child care responsibilities, don't know how to care for children (9%); (4) other family problems, e.g., no housing, inadequate housing, insufficient income (17%); (5) custody dispute (8%); (6) parental alcoholism (7%); and (7) parental drug dependency (7%). Child problems described when no maltreatment was alleged were: health and mental health problems (30%); behavioral problems (21%); and unspecified (4%).

Injuries. Two hundred and ninety-four contacts (12%, N = 2,556) alleged minor injuries. In this variable, as in some others, there are several within-state similarities and between-state differences. One hundred and thirty-five contacts (5%) alleged severe injuries. Other injuries or physical conditions were alleged in 6% of the contacts. In 63% of the contacts no injuries were alleged.

Screening Practices by Type of Maltreatment and Type of Injury

Forty-two percent of the 2,556 contacts received were not investigated. Screening percentages vary widely, with Site K investigating 29% of the contacts received and Site B investigating 97% of their contacts. One other site (J) investigated almost all contacts. Five sites (C, D, F, K and L) investigated 60% or less of the contacts received. (All referrals to CPS agencies in other jurisdictions are excluded from this analysis.)

Maltreatment. Recalling the earlier discussion of maltreatment, for the entire sample, 86% of the contacts made involved some type of maltreatment. The remainder involved other complaints such as child behavior problems or family/parental problems, as noted earlier. Categories of maltreatment alleged in the following analyses are recoded so that they are mutually exclusive. That is, neglect includes only neglect, abuse is only abuse and so on.

For neglect, the following categories were used: abandonment, failure to provide, lack of supervision, other, not specified and multiple types of neglect. There are 904 contacts in this category. Fifty-nine percent of these contacts were screened in. Unspecified neglect was investigated in 37% of the contacts. The remaining types of maltreatment in this category were investigated between 55 and 71% of the time. On the whole, contacts alleging abandonment were very rare (25 contacts for the entire sample). Lack of supervision, the most common category for many sites was screened in 100% of the time in Site B, and 11% of the time in Site K. Multiple types of neglect, often the next most frequent types of neglect alleged, was screened in 97% of the time in Site B and 32% of the time in Site K. Failure to provide was the most frequent problem reported in Site H and was screened in 70% of the time in that site and 5% of the time in Site K.

Two additional categories of maltreatment include fostering delinquency and emotional maltreatment. Forty percent of contacts alleging fostering delinquency were screened in. Forty-one percent of contacts of emotional maltreatment were screened in. Contacts alleging emotional maltreatment and fostering delinquency were also rare (38 and 43 contacts for the entire sample, respectively).

For physical abuse, the mutually exclusive categories are: hitting; repeated hitting, beating and other "severe" forms of abuse; other physical abuse (e.g., locking up, biting, etc.); unspecified abuse and multiple forms of physical abuse. There are 527 contacts in this category. The most common categories are hitting only and repeated hitting only (298 contacts - 57% of physical abuse contacts) with 60% of all physical abuse screened in. Unspecified abuse was screened in 42% of the time, followed by other physical abuse which was screened in 49% of the contacts. Multiple types of physical abuse and more severe abuse were screened in the most: 74 and 72% respectively.

The last category, sexual abuse, was alleged in 302 complaints. The most common category was exposure/fondling (38% of sex abuse contacts) followed by unspecified (25%). Fifty-seven percent of all sexual abuse contacts were screened in. Multiple types of sexual abuse were screened in 72% of the time. All others were screened in from 46 to 70% of the time.

Injuries. Types of injury were also recoded so that they would represent mutually exclusive categories. That is, minor injury would mean that the contact alleged minor injury only, and involved no other type of injury. There were 2,399 contacts for which type of injury was recorded. Where the information was unknown or there were no injuries alleged, 52% of the contacts were screened in.

Reasons Given for Screening Out Reports Alleging Maltreatment

Of the 2,556 contacts made to CPS, 32% alleged some type of maltreatment and were not investigated. Of those contacts alleging maltreatment (N = 2,193), 62% were investigated.

To get some beginning notion of why contacts which had actually alleged some form of maltreatment were not investigated, reasons given by workers and supervisors in response to a closed ended question on the screening form were examined. Three percent were screened out because the incident was not intentional. Four percent of the screened-out contacts were rejected due to impressions of the worker that the caller was harassing the family and 5% were screened out because the alleged incident happened "too long ago." In 6% of these contacts there was no apparent way to locate the parent or child. Eight percent were not investigated because the perpetrator was not a caretaker. Custody dispute was given as a reason for not investigating in 8% of the contacts alleging maltreatment but screened out. Insufficient information was given as the reason for 16% of these contacts. Problem should be handled by another agency was given as a reason 17% of the time and child not currently at risk was given in 22% of the responses. Twenty-two percent were not investigated because no specific act was alleged. Thirty-six percent were not investigated because no injury was alleged.

Response to Unspecified Allegations

As noted earlier, unspecified allegations were very few. These were complaints where the reporter alleged some type of maltreatment but was unclear or not specific about what was alleged. One example might be that a reporter called to say that the Jones children were being neglected but had no further information. Contacts containing only unspecified allegations comprise nine percent of all contacts recorded. Including contacts alleging fostering delinquency and emotional maltreatment which were not accompanied by more specific allegations of maltreatment, 60% of these contacts were not investigated.

Reasons for Investigating When No Maltreatment or Injury Was Alleged

Fourteen percent of all contacts had no allegation of maltreatment or injury alleged. Approximately 29% of these contacts involved parental health or mental health problems and nine percent alleged that the parents were unable or unwilling to properly care for their children. Thirty percent described child problems including health or mental health problems.

Most of these contacts were not investigated. Eighty-four of them were referred for investigation (24%). The reasons given for investigating contacts where no maltreatment or injury was alleged were that: (1) act of maltreatment was not specified but the child may be at risk (24%); (2) specific act alleged [in this case, this item refers to parental and child problems that were not included with allegations of maltreatment, e.g., parents unable to care for children] (17%); (3) reporter is believable (13%); (4) all reports must be investigated (11%); (5) parent worried about harming child (9%); (6) previous reports suggest a need for investigation (7%); (7) other (34%). (Reasons for investigation are not mutually exclusive.)

CONCLUSION

There is a large degree of variation between sites in types of contacts received and in screening practices. In at least two of the sites studied, large numbers of allegations of maltreatment are regularly screened out. As expected, these sites also screen out most contacts which do not specifically allege some form of maltreatment. Five sites screened out over 40% of the allegations of maltreatment received (this includes unspecified allegations of physical abuse, neglect or sexual abuse). In addition, workers in these sites did not generally investigate contacts in which no maltreatment was alleged: seven to 17% were investigated as compared to 25 to 92% in other sites.

One site referred almost every contact for investigation while others screened out the large majority of contacts, both those alleging maltreatment and those which were less specific. False complaints containing specific allegations are much harder to detect at the time of the complaint.

While workers do make an effort to identify and screen out those complaints that are obvious attempts at harassment, these are difficult judgments to make from the information included in a report. Reasons for not investigating are more often based on absence of injury, lack of a specific allegation, insufficient information or absence of apparent risk to the child.

The issues for CPS agencies which are highlighted by this report are many. The first is that it is virtually impossible to think of child protective services in this country as having one consistent approach to protecting children. Many factors impinge on the decision to intervene in family life. Not the least of these is the number of workers available to do the job. The sites with the highest numbers of reports received were also the sites that screened out contacts to a considerable degree. Other factors, ranging from state policies to types of contacts received also impact on worker decision making. For example, compared to other study sites, Site H received a considerable number of complaints which did not allege maltreatment. They, in turn, screened out large numbers of these complaints.

In the context of concern regarding excessive numbers of false or ambiguous reports, one of the most valuable pieces of information is that most complaints to CPS agencies are specific in regard to the type of allegations made. In addition, those that are not specific or which do not allege maltreatment or injury are generally not investigated. This suggests that, contrary to what has often been expressed in the popular literature, the major problem for CPS is not in investigating too many "bogus" reports but, rather, in not having enough resources to investigate the large number of reports which are specific allegations of maltreatment. These results do not suggest a need for more screening. Rather, it appears that, in some sites, the practice of screening out reports far exceeds the limits circumscribed by current laws and policies.

The inevitable question, concerning the necessity of changes in specific laws and policies hinges on two very different views of the role of CPS agencies in U.S. society. Is it the role of the CPS to protect children from all forms of abuse or neglect or should the energies of CPS agencies be restricted to cases of physical injury and sexual abuse? At those sites where screening is used a great deal, the choice seems to have been made. Cases of physical injury and sexual abuse already appear to take priority. This approach is a remedial one, waiting until the worst abuse or neglect has occurred. In addition, it excludes children for whom the results of maltreatment are some of the most devastating, those who experience chronic neglect (Wells, 1989). Obviously, the role of the CPS in addressing child abuse and neglect is not a question for policy-makers alone, but for society as a whole.

In addressing those few complaints which do not allege maltreatment but focus on other concerns regarding the welfare of the children, general child welfare services (without the need to go through child protective services) would be the treatment of choice. Finding such services, however, is less than easy in this time of fiscal constraint in service delivery. As noted in this volume, current policy initiatives have recognized this problem and have begun to search for better ways to serve this population.

Meanwhile, to assist workers in distinguishing between valid and invalid reports, research on factors predicting later abuse or case substantiation should be vigorously pursued. With more valid and reliable indicators, further accuracy in decision making at intake may be increased.

REFERENCE

Wells, S. J. (1989). *Current NCCAN funded research*. Paper presented at the Eighth National Conference on Child Abuse and Neglect, Salt Lake City.

Investigating Allegations of Child Maltreatment: The Strengths and Limitations of Current Risk Assessment Systems

Peter J. Pecora

ABSTRACT. This article discusses the common strengths and limitations of the major types of risk assessment systems currently implemented in the United States with respect to their effectiveness in assisting child protective services workers in investigating allegations of child maltreatment, documenting current child and family conditions, and predicting the occurrence or re-occurrence of child maltreatment.

Risk assessment has received increased attention as one of the main challenges facing workers and administrators in child protective services and in child welfare generally. The term "risk assessment" is used to define a number of different assessment and decision making processes, but essentially is concerned with predicting whether or not a child will be maltreated at some future point in time. This process involves examining the child and family situation to identify and analyze various "risk factors," family strengths, family resources, and available agency services. This assessment information can then be used to determine if a child is safe, what agency resources are necessary to keep a child safe, and under what circumstances a child should be removed from their family. In some

Peter J. Pecora is affiliated with the Casey Family Program and the School of Social Work, University of Washington, Seattle, WA. The research for this project was partially supported by a grant from the Administration for Children, Youth, and Families, Office of Human Development Services, U.S. Children's Bureau (Grant No. 08CT0058/01). Special thanks to Diane DePanfilis and Michael Wald for their review of an earlier version of this paper.

cases, risk assessment instruments can be used to help judge whether a child who has been in foster care can return home safely. After briefly describing the major approaches to risk assessment being used in America, this article will discuss some of their common strengths and limitations.

DEFINING RISK IN CHILD WELFARE

Risk assessment information is important for making a number of critical decisions in child protective services (CPS) during the investigation phase by helping workers determine such things as:

1. If the child is in immediate risk of maltreatment;
2. What services or worker action are necessary to protect the child during the investigation;
3. Whether the child should be removed from the home to protect him or her; and
4. What initial case plan will address the field of forces that are placing the child at risk (Holder & Corey, 1986).

The term "risk assessment" refers both to a structured form of decision making as well as to the specific instruments that are used in this process. A number of child welfare agencies and organizations have developed models and instruments for assessing risk. The various systems being developed may be used to address one or all of the above decisions. Because there is no standard definition or set of purposes ascribed to risk assessment, there exists some confusion in the practice community regarding this area.

Yet risk assessment systems are being rapidly developed, aided in part, by the increasing amount of research and "practice wisdom" regarding what factors are associated with various forms of child maltreatment.[1] Some of these risk factors are used to predict the likelihood of maltreatment, while other "indicators of maltreatment" are important for identifying children or adolescents who are currently being maltreated. Both types of information are useful to child welfare workers as they assess risk to children.

Part of the impetus for developing these systems stems from the need for agencies to screen out spurious CPS reports or allegations that constitute such a low risk that they do not meet the criteria of the reporting statute. Some states such as Washington are experimenting with diverting "low risk" cases to community agencies for assistance rather than investigating them. Another motivating factor is the need to improve the ability of workers to detect high risk cases before children are injured.

Risk assessment systems *per se* cannot be used as the method for determining if the allegation(s) of child maltreatment can be supported by the facts of the case (i.e., case substantiation). These systems, instead, are more appropriate for structuring the assessment process, predicting the likelihood of future maltreatment, and documenting case facts and worker observations. Most of the assessment instruments currently being implemented, however, are unable to achieve a high degree of predictive accuracy because of limitations in the current knowledge base and methodology. But implementation of the better systems is beginning to strengthen assessment and case decision making in many child welfare agencies.

Current Risk Assessment Systems

Given the developments in research and the need for agencies to implement better procedures for screening and prioritizing reports, four basic types of risk assessment systems have emerged.[2]

The matrix approach. This is one of the first systems to be developed. The matrix approach uses a table comprised of 16-35 factors which are rated in terms of their severity or risk to the child (e.g., parenting skills, severity and/or frequency of maltreatment, child age, accessibility of perpetrator to child, substance abuse of caretaker or perpetrator). Each of the risk factors is rated using a 3-5 point scale that describes a level of child, parent or family functioning or some other factor in terms of its contribution to low, moderate and high levels of risk to a child.

One of the earliest systems was developed in Illinois by the Department of Children and Family Services in 1982. Early versions of the Illinois matrix have been adapted for implementation in a number of states, while Washington, Florida and other states have devised their own types of matrices. The Illinois matrix and some others, however, have undergone major revisions in the last year to allow for recording risk factors not on the matrix and family strengths (Martinez, 1989).

The factors chosen for inclusion in the matrix represent some of the more commonly cited factors associated with one or more forms of child maltreatment. Workers use the matrix to assess the family in relation to these and other factors to make casework decisions and formulate initial casework plans. In certain states, the factor scores are displayed by area (e.g., parent, household), or averaged across all of the scales. In other states, workers are instructed to use professional judgement in analyzing the high scoring or serious factors for case decision making.

Empirical predictors method. A second and (probably the most concise approach to risk assessment) is modeled after the risk studies conducted in public health and juvenile corrections (Baird, 1988; Johnson & L'Esperance, 1984). These systems generally focus on identifying a small set of risk factors most predictive of child maltreatment (e.g., caretaker abused as a child, mother figure's parenting skill, presence of more than one child in the home, reasonableness of the mother figure's expectations for the child). Thus parent, family, or child characteristics associated with child maltreatment are considered but not included in the final set of risk factors unless they actually predict the recurrence of one or more types of child maltreatment. In other words, these risk assessment systems try to include only those factors actually predictive of child maltreatment, as compared to including factors "associated" with child maltreatment through prospective or other types of studies (Leventhal, 1982; Miller, Williams, English, & Olmstead, 1987). With this approach, risk factors that are identified are provided to CPS intake personnel, and in some cases, CPS investigators to assist them in assessing the risk of future maltreatment.

Ideally, the risk factors incorporated into these instruments would be the same factors that predict first-time occurrences of maltreatment as well as the recurrence of child abuse, because often the CPS worker is investigating cases where child maltreatment has already occurred and the primary concern is whether or not the child may be maltreated again. Much more research, however, must be undertaken to confirm whether the same set of factors for various forms of child abuse and neglect can be used for both types of situations.

Family assessment scales. The third approach uses behaviorally anchored scales to assess the levels of parent, child, family and household functioning to identify areas of concern. These assessment scales typically use the "Child Well-Being" or "Family Risk" scales developed by the Child Welfare League of America (Magura & Moses, 1986; Magura, Moses & Jones, 1987) or the Family Assessment Form developed by the Children's Bureau of Los Angeles (McCroskey & Nelson, 1989). These various packages contain some of the most clearly anchored assessment scales available in the field. For example, the Child Well-Being scales measure concepts related to one or more physical, psychological or social needs that all children possess. The degree to which these needs are not being met is intended to help define a child's state of overall "well-being." Each scale has between four and six levels of descriptors for child, parent, family, or other capability ranging from an adequate level to increasing degrees of inadequacy (Magura & Moses, 1986).

Generally, this approach to assessing risk is more of a structured assessment system than a risk assessment system *per se;* assessment of child and family functioning is the primary focus of the instrument, not identification of risk factors. The family is rated at multiple points during the casework process and workers are requested to identify a range of risk factors present in the case, as well as family strengths and resources (Utah Child Welfare Training Project, 1987).

Child at risk field. The fourth major approach to risk assessment is the Child at Risk Field (CARF), which was developed by ACTION for Child Protection. This risk assessment system uses an ecological approach and is organized around five "force fields": Child, Parent, Family, Maltreatment and Intervention. A series of 14 open-ended questions and anchored rating scales are used to help workers identify "risk influences" that may be operating in the family situation (Holder & Corey, 1986). The Child at Risk Field is probably one of the most comprehensive approaches to risk assessment available in that it promotes the consideration of a variety of risk influences, helps workers make decisions about initial safety, and promotes the use of risk assessment throughout the entire casework process.

The strengths and limitations of any of these systems must be viewed in relation to the objectives of that particular system. Most system developers, however, state that prediction of future child maltreatment is a major objective. While certain risk assessment approaches seem more promising than others in this area, a lack of validation and implementation data preclude definitive answers at this time regarding how much faith to place in the ability of these systems to predict the likelihood of future child maltreatment.[3] Many of the systems available need to be refined to be more culturally sensitive to particular ethnic groups, tested for gender bias, and adjusted for specific types of child maltreatment (especially if risk scores are calculated and used in case decision making).

However, the focus on risk factors and structured decision making is having a number of positive effects on worker practice which relate to other important objectives, including focusing worker attention on critical areas for assessment, structuring documentation, improving decision making procedures, reducing worker bias in decision making, and reminding workers to examine family strengths as well as limitations. Consequently, this review will point out some common strengths and limitations, rather than focus on any one risk assessment system in particular.

How Risk Assessment Systems Can Strengthen CPS Practice

The use of certain types of risk assessment systems in state and local child welfare agencies is helping to improve CPS practice in a number of ways. The following sections will highlight some of the more important benefits of using a high quality risk assessment system.

Focus worker attention on the most critical risk factors. One of the benefits of many risk assessment systems is that they help workers focus on the most critical aspects of child, parent, family, environment and other areas of functioning rather than diffusing their attention upon interesting but non-relevant aspects of the case situation (see Note 1). For example, part of the rationale for the empirical predictors approach is that (1) agencies want to use an empirically derived set of factors; and (2) workers can realistically only assess a small number of factors over the phone or as part of the initial investigation. The body of research and practice wisdom guiding worker assessment has many limitations, including the fact that small sample sizes of previous research studies have prevented the identification of a larger number of empirically derived factors (for critiques of risk factor research studies or scales, see Howing, Wodarski, Kurtz, & Gaudin, 1989; Leventhal, 1982; Plotkin, Azar, Twentyman, & Perri, 1981; Starr, 1982). However, these new approaches are nonetheless helpful to workers because in the past, most CPS staff conducted their investigations with only vague state policies to guide them.

Structure worker documentation and decision making. No risk assessment system will be able to replace professional worker judgement, but the better systems do help workers consider the nature, surrounding circumstances, duration, and pervasiveness of the contributing factors, as well as other issues in their decision making process (e.g., Holder & Corey, 1986). These systems help workers analyze and synthesize the information that they gather about child, parent and family functioning. In other words, the more refined systems help caseworkers go beyond merely adding up the scores on a risk matrix or scoring sheet, but require critical thinking regarding what the assessment information means in terms of child safety and necessary services. Thus the role of worker judgement is emphasized and supported within a structured decision making approach.

Reduce bias in decision making. Any risk assessment system should also help reduce the effects of various personal/professional biases and errors that are inevitably part of worker decision making (Stein & Rzepnicki, 1984). There are a number of approaches being used by some agencies to address these problems. Some of the problems in worker bias or variation can be evaluated through studies of interrater reliability (Nasuti, 1990; Weedon, Torti, & Zunder, 1988). More behaviorally specific assessment scales and rating criteria can then be employed. Some systems also emphasize that workers use more behaviorally specific language when they describe clients in order to avoid vague, negative, label-filled descriptions of child or parental functioning (Kinney, Haapala, & Gast, 1981). Supervisors in some agencies are fulfilling an important role by carefully reviewing worker initial assessments and case plans. Finally, many child welfare agencies are finding it necessary to conduct periodic state-wide training, using case examples, to identify common areas of worker bias and improve decision making consistency across caseworkers.

Encourage careful documentation. Fair and thorough investigation of an allegation of child maltreatment requires the careful documentation of client behaviors, home conditions, and other areas to provide the necessary justification for casework decisions. For example, as part of encouraging careful documentation, states such as Montana or Utah, and those states using the Child at Risk Field system, require workers to record the source of their assessment information (e.g., direct observation, medical records, medical exam, child report) as part of the identification of risk factors or ratings of parental functioning. This provides a means for double-checking the authenticity of the information, and assists the worker and district attorney in gathering the documentation necessary for court hearings.

Help eliminate the overemphasis upon severity of maltreatment. The central focus of risk assessment should not be on the severity of the child's injuries, but on the likelihood of future maltreatment. Some CPS caseworkers place too much emphasis upon the nature or severity of the maltreatment when there are other factors that must be considered in assessing the likelihood of future maltreatment (Holder & Corey, 1986). While cases in many states require prosecution of caretakers who maltreat their children or adolescents in certain ways, some CPS referrals involving serious injuries requiring medical treatment may indeed be low risk. In contrast, other cases involving mild injury may be high risk.

A example illustrating this was developed by Eric Oleson of ACTION for Child Protection: Consider the case where Mark, an 11-year-old boy, receives a concussion and head lacerations because he fell accidentally into a coffee table when his father pushed him during a heated argument over his first curfew violation. The family usually functions in a healthy fashion, and the father is aware that his concern for his son was translated inappropriately into an angry incident that had tragic results. This case would be considered low or moderate risk by most child welfare staff.

Contrast Mark's case with the situation of a 19-year-old parent who lives with her one-year-old infant in a one-bedroom mobile home 10 miles outside of a small town. The child, Susan, has been spanked over eight times a day but there are no bruises on her buttocks. However, Susan has colic, and her mother feels trapped in the house while her husband is traveling for business for weeks at a time. She expresses a great deal of frustration and anger with her situation and Susan's fussy behavior, but does not recognize any solutions. Which child's injuries are more severe? Which child is more at risk of future maltreatment? As this example indicates, in assessing risk to children or adolescents, a variety of child and family factors should be examined, not just the type or severity of maltreatment.

But precise methods for weighing severity in relation to other factors are not yet available. For example, the amount of emphasis depends upon the nature of the case. For many cases, severity of past maltreatment is a critical variable to consider because "the best predictor of future behavior is past behavior." Furthermore, it depends on the rates of serious injury. If the rate of serious injury to children is higher for physical abuse, then even though no physical abuse has been committed, if the risk of physical abuse is high, workers may be more likely to intervene. So, decision making guidelines will have to assist staff members to consider the consequences of child maltreatment in relation to the risk or likelihood that maltreatment may occur without intervention (M. S. Wald, personal communication, January 17, 1990). Some risk assessment systems try to balance maltreatment severity and actual risk, but attention must also be paid to avoiding unnecessary state intervention into the lives of families by handling very conservatively those cases where child maltreatment has not occurred, but the risk of maltreatment may be high (see Wald, 1976, 1980).

Help workers assess risk not only at intake but throughout the whole life of the case. As the risk assessment systems are refined, many of the analytical frameworks should assist caseworkers to assess risk at critical points throughout the entire casework process (intake to case closure) and service continuum (e.g., child protective services, home-based services, foster care). With some systems, workers are required to conduct a formal risk assessment not only for determining whether a child should be placed, but also for every formal case review and when a child is about to be returned home from substitute care.

Focusing on family strengths as well as limitations. Because of the nature of their work and the tragic family situations that they encounter daily, CPS workers understandably will often focus on the negative aspects of the family situation. The better systems encourage CPS and other child welfare workers to actively assess the family strengths that may be present or the resources that may be readily available. Some agencies are also trying to develop assessment guidelines and resource materials to help caseworkers recognize and assess family strengths in culturally appropriate ways (e.g., Horejsi, 1987; Three Feathers Associates, 1989).

Practice-Related Limitations of Risk Assessment Systems

As with any recent set of practice innovations, risk assessment systems are not perfect. Major differences do exist among the various systems and a number of national projects are undertaking reviews or comparative research studies of the major systems in use.[4] Thus the strengths or benefits described in the first part of this article may not be included in some risk assessment systems, representing serious barriers to effective assessment and un-biased decision making. In this section, three major practice-related limitations will be described. Subsequent sections will discuss limitations related to psychometric properties of the scales and system implementation.

Systems are incorrectly used. Risk assessment systems are designed to facilitate different aspects of decision making at various points in the casework process. This makes some systems less effective or inappropriate for particular purposes. For example, some of the lists of risk factors derived through predictive studies of criterion validity are most useful for screening cases at intake because they contain parent-related risk factors that will not change over time or with casework services (e.g., number of prior reports of abuse, history of previous maltreatment).

Criterion validity is one of the most important forms of validity that must be established for any risk assessment instrument that purports to be a formal prediction device through the use of one or more summary scores or scale ratings. The type of criterion validity typically examined, predictive validity, involves assessing the extent to which scores on a particular inventory or rating scale can be used to predict the occurrence of future maltreatment (Brown, 1983, pp. 98-113).

In addition, risk assessment systems should not be used in a way that obscures the larger child welfare objective concerned with promoting child and family development. Unfortunately, too many child welfare agencies are taking an overly legalistic approach to child protective services instead of promoting some of the traditional social work practice values and methods that result in a more family-centered approach to practice (Corey & Holder, 1986; Thomas, 1990).

Child neglect may be minimized. Depending upon the design of the risk matrix and the scoring system, cases involving neglect (e.g., lack of supervision, malnutrition) may be scored "low risk" and screened out of the CPS system in some states. Yet neglectful conditions cause some of the most harm to children, and represent the primary cause of death in almost half of the child fatalities reported (Daro & Mitchel, 1989; Polansky, Chalmers, Buttenweiser, & Williams, 1982). Systems need to be tested and revised in relation to this scoring bias.

Complex cases are not assessed adequately. Risk assessment systems that rely exclusively on matrices with 15-20 specific factors are not effective for assessing complex CPS cases or for developing risk-oriented case plans without supplemental case analysis procedures and recording guidelines. With these models, workers are less likely to assess risk factors not listed on the matrix, as well as consider family strengths. For example, one risk matrix being used by a western state does not include scales for caretaker employment status or history of assaultive behavior.

More specifically, any system not limited to screening intake calls should promote an assessment process that takes into account the complexity and individual nature of CPS cases. The system therefore should require that workers consider other risk factors present in the case in addition to those contained in a matrix or set of behaviorally anchored scales. Some risk assessment systems fail to do this because they use decision making tools that do not encourage workers to consider risk factors beyond those printed on the risk scales or matrix recording sheet.

Furthermore, the decision making forms (and worker training) should emphasize how various risk factors can interact to increase or lower risk in case situations. In other words, the assessment model should use an ecological approach that takes into account not only a variety of risk factors, but how they interact to produce "volatile combinations" (Holder & Corey, 1986). Most risk factor scoring systems are currently unable to adjust for how factors interact, threshold effects, and non-linear relationships, in part because of a lack of empirical data regarding which interactions are most important (Howing, Wodarski, Kurtz, & Gaudin, 1989).

Psychometric-Related Limitations of Risk Assessment Systems

As risk assessment systems become more widely used, issues related to their psychometric properties will become more important, especially as the assessment information is used in court hearings and malpractice litigation. The next sections will summarize some of the challenges in this field with respect to establishing adequate levels of validity and reliability for the risk assessment instruments.

General methodological limitations of risk assessment research. Despite the growing body of literature regarding risk factors and risk assessment, CPS case decision making procedures in many states are largely unstandardized processes structured more by practice wisdom that by empirical research. Specifying what child, parent and family information is most important is a difficult process, and few explicit decision making protocols have been developed. Unfortunately, much of the research that has been conducted to identify risk factors is descriptive, consisting largely of surveys, summaries of management information system data, case record reviews, and case studies.

Therefore, many of the risk factors used in most of the assessment systems developed thus far were found to be "associated" with child maltreatment, rather than linked in a causal manner. (The "empirical predictor" systems remain the exception as they include only predictive factors.) More specifically, few of the studies are "prospective" in design, where a cohort of families (subdivided into high and low risk according to one or more suspected risk factors, but similar in other characteristics) is followed over time to monitor rates of child maltreatment.

Many studies instead use retrospective "case control" or "incidence" approaches. Retrospective case control studies compare cases of child maltreatment with cases with similar characteristics where the type of child maltreatment under study has not occurred. Incidence studies are usually based on surveys of households, statistics compiled by child welfare agencies through registry reports and other data-gathering means (Miller, Williams, English, & Olmstead, 1987).

While retrospective or incidence studies are useful for narrowing the assessment areas and for selecting the initial sets of variables to measure in predictive research studies, these types of studies are not sufficient for establishing whether risk assessment instruments have adequate predictive criterion validity. Sets of factors predictive of various types of maltreatment need to be identified, and then adjusted for specific ethnic groups and geographic areas.

Classification and prediction rates need to be improved. The degree of success achieved thus far with respect to predicting child maltreatment with the existing sets of risk factors is promising but not extremely high; and is somewhat similar to that of predicting other forms of violent adult behavior or juvenile delinquency (Loeber & Stouthamer-Loeber, 1986; Monahan, 1981; Starr, 1982). One of the common ways of examining the accuracy of various risk assessment devices lies in calculating their rates of "sensitivity" and "specificity," particularly if the instruments are to be used as statistical predictors of future child maltreatment.

Sensitivity is concerned with the instrument's ability to correctly identify families where child maltreatment is occurring or will occur. The correct classification rates for various studies conducted recently have ranged between 15-83% (see Dalgleish & Drew, 1989; Pecora 1989). One way of examining problems in sensitivity is to calculate the percentage of "false positives" — cases where the instrument predicted that the case was high risk, but no maltreatment was found. For example, a recent meta-analytic review of predictive instruments of abuse and neglect found a 50.7 percent average "false positive" prediction rate (Rodwell & Chambers, 1989). This means that one-half of the cases that were predicted to be cases of maltreatment were actually not found to involve child abuse or neglect.

In contrast, specificity is concerned with the percentage of cases that are correctly assessed as non-maltreating (Brown & Hollander, 1977). For example, in one of the most careful studies of child welfare cases, 16 (69.6%) of the 23 cases in the validation sample were correctly predicted as cases where re-abuse would not occur. However, this set of predictive factors had a "false negative" rate of 30.4 percent. This means that 7 of the 23 cases classified as non-maltreating by the risk factors were actually substantiated as physically abusive by the CPS workers (Johnson & L'Esperance, 1984). If a risk assessment system is designed to be used as a formal screening device, than it must have both high specificity and extremely high sensitivity given the costs and civil rights issues associated with mislabeling parents and their children (Light, 1973; Starr, 1982).

Based on reviews of the problems in classification and prediction from previous studies, a number of authors have cautioned the field against unbridled optimism regarding prediction of child maltreatment using a particular set of factors or screening inventory (Daniel, Newberger, Reed, & Kotlechuck, 1978; Rodwell & Chambers, 1989). In fact, no risk assessment system or instrument has yet been documented to have a sufficiently high level of sensitivity and specificity to allow its use as the sole means for assessing CPS referrals.[5]

Adjusting for particular forms of child maltreatment. Maltreatment-specific models have not been widely developed because of a lack of research in this area. In other words, most risk assessment systems currently implemented by child welfare agencies do not explicitly help workers to distinguish risk factors that may be unique to assessing the risk of future physical abuse, neglect, sexual abuse, and psychological maltreatment. Yet retrospective studies (see Note 1) and a series of predictive validation studies (e.g., Baird, 1988; Johnson & Clancy, 1988) indicate that risk factors will vary somewhat, depending upon the type of maltreatment. Complicating this process is the fact that most risk factor studies have not addressed the additive and interactive effects of multiple types of maltreatment occurring in the same case (Howing, Wodarski, Kurtz, & Gaudin, 1989).

Instrument reliability may be low. A risk assessment system may be valid according to the criteria listed above and still be unreliable in terms of its application in the field. Various forms of reliability may be pertinent to consider, including Internal Consistency, Test-Retest, and Interrater.[6] Along with internal consistency, interrater or inter-observer reliability is one of the most important forms of reliability; it is concerned with the issue of consistency across users of the system. For example, if two or more workers were to assess the same family, is there a high level of agreement among them regarding various risk factors or ratings?[7]

Interrater reliability is very important, considering the implications of implementing a risk assessment system statewide in both urban and rural areas. Many state administrators are concerned about a lack of consistent decision making across their CPS units and district offices. While instrument reliability can be greatly affected by the quality of worker training and supervisory support, the risk assessment instrument itself should promote worker consistency through the nature of its construction.

Implementation-Related Limitations and Problems

Assuming that the actual system is valid and reliable, a number of implementation problems have been identified related to program context, worker caseloads, supervision, and ongoing training.

The linkages between program context and the system are not addressed. The risk assessment system that is implemented should be integrated with CPS law and policy. Risk assessment operates within a legal, cultural, philosophical, political and agency context. To be successful, the risk assessment system must be supported by clear and consistent state laws and policy. This is why the more effective systems in operation today began their development process with an analysis of agency CPS policies in the context of practice realities (Pecora, Carlson, Reese, & Bartholomew, 1986/87).

The extent to which the system is integrated with and supports the agency management information system should also be carefully considered and evaluated. For example, a number of states have revised the recording forms for the CPS information system as part of the implementation of the new risk assessment system. Ideally, the management information system should reduce the amount of duplicate information caseworkers must record, providing workers instead with easy access to critical case data such as number and type of prior substantiated referrals. In addition, administrative personnel should be provided with information useful for monitoring worker, unit and agency performance in a timely manner. Unfortunately, some state and local agencies have failed to modify agency policy and information systems at the same time that they are designing the new risk assessment system. What has resulted is worker and system overload, or agency paralysis due to a conflict between the new decision making system and agency policy.

The need for specialized worker competency is overlooked. Any risk assessment system is only as effective as the person implementing it. Even the best systems will not be effective if the caseworkers lack skills in interviewing, assessment, decision making, time management, and other important competency areas. Poor working conditions and the downgrading of minimal qualifications required of CPS and other child welfare staff members have contributed to this problem of under-skilled personnel (Pecora, Briar, & Zlotnik, 1989).

In addition, some agencies have implemented their system with insufficient worker training and ongoing case consultation. The adage "a little knowledge is a dangerous thing" describes the nature of this situation as these assessment systems can result in poor decision making and tragic results if applied in an incomplete manner. The CPS workers in these agencies understandably feel frustrated and insecure in their use of what could be helpful decision making and prediction tools.

Workload and supervision requirements are ignored. Realistic caseload standards are also essential for effective implementation (e.g., assignment of no more than 15-20 new cases for investigation per month per worker). Even the best systems will fail if CPS workers continue to carry an unreasonably high number of cases (Wilson, 1989). Supervisory involvement and oversight can also determine the ultimate success of any assessment system or treatment model. An effective risk system will promote a careful supervisory review of worker action at every key decision making point in the casework process such as the determination of response times for investigation, formation of initial safety plans, and case closure (Holder & Corey, 1986). To accomplish this requires that supervisors have sufficient time and training to fulfill the core functions of administrative, educational and clinical supervision. In other words, workers need assistance in more areas than just completing the necessary paperwork. Too often supervisors lack the time and/or training necessary to review cases with workers and to teach new assessment skills.

The danger is that workers will apply the system in an erroneous or superficial manner if they lack the skills, time or supervisory support to conduct a thorough assessment. It is precisely these poor working conditions and lack of agency supports that is contributing to a new form of agency vulnerability to legal action. The existence of an explicit agency policy requiring the use of a detailed risk assessment system makes an agency more liable if the requisite worker training, caseload limits, and supervisory support have not been implemented as well.

CONCLUSION

Risk assessment systems can be important tools for assisting workers in determining the risk of child maltreatment and making case decisions. There is a growing consensus, at least at the practice level, concerning the types of risk factors that may be most important to consider in assessing children and families. Some of the risk assessment systems currently in place help workers focus their assessment efforts, structure their decision making, and document their casework efforts.

These instruments, however, are not able to be used to substantiate allegations of child maltreatment or as the sole means of predicting future maltreatment. Additional research is necessary to specify the risk factors most predictive of various types of child maltreatment, and to develop more explicit decision making protocols that require careful analysis of the risk assessment data. Finally, risk assessment systems will not replace the need for adequately trained workers, reasonable caseloads, and high quality supervision. Child welfare administrators are finding it necessary to place as much emphasis upon careful ongoing training and supervision, as is placed on the design of the system itself.

ENDNOTES

1. For reviews of the risk factors associated with various forms of child maltreatment see Dalgleish and Drew (1989); Miller, Williams, English, and Olmstead (1987); and Pecora and Martin, (1989). For studies that examined child, parent or family characteristics actually predictive of various forms of child maltreatment see Baird (1988); Johnson and Clancy (1988); and Weedon, Torti, and Zunder (1988).

2. For a review of the various risk assessment systems and examples of some of the risk assessment instruments, see the conference proceedings for the 1987, 1988 and 1989 National Roundtables on CPS Risk Assessment edited by Toshio Tatara and available through the American Public Welfare Association 1125 Fifteenth Street N.W., Washington, D.C. 20005. Also see Schene and Bond (1989), Starr (1982), Stein and Rzepnicki (1983), and Wells (1985) for additional information about risk assessment in child welfare.

3. Some risk assessment systems have been evaluated more extensively than others. For example, see Allen (1988a, 1988b, 1988c) and DePanfilis (1988) for data regarding the interrater reliability and practice improvements associated with

implementing the ACTION for Child Protection risk system. See Weedon, Torti, and Zunder (1988) for research on the Vermont Risk Matrix.

4. See for example Keller, Cicchinelli, and Gardner (1988); and Marks, McDonald, Bessey, and Palmer (1989) for examples of reports from two national projects in this area.

5. There have been, however, studies with lower false positive rates in England; one group of researchers defined child abuse in a very specific way to achieve a predictive success rate of 83%, and one of the lowest false positive rates found in the literature (3%) (Hanson, McCulloch & Hartley, 1977 as cited in Rodwell & Chambers, 1989, p. 763). An Australian study correctly classified 86.8% of the cases in terms of whether or not the risk of maltreatment was serious enough to place the child (Dalgleish & Drew, 1989, p. 497). In addition, three recent studies conducted in public child welfare agencies have identified a slightly overlapping set of factors which are predictive of the recurrence of various forms of child maltreatment (Baird, 1988; Baird & Neuenfeldt, 1988; Johnson & Clancy, 1988; and Johnson & L'Esperance, 1984). Studies of the Child Abuse Potential Inventory (CAP) have also been reasonably positive (Milner & Robertson, 1989). These studies hold promise for achieving lower rates of false positives and false negatives.

6. Internal consistency is a form of internal reliability and is concerned with the extent to which items in a particular instrument measure the same concept or behavior. For example, there should be a high correlation among the items of an inventory that measures family cohesion. Alternatively, discrete factors composed of non-overlapping scale items should be able to be identified (see Milner & Wimberley, 1980 for a description of this process with the Child Abuse Potential Inventory). Test-retest reliability is generally viewed as measuring instrument stability. In other words, how consistent will the scores be over time if conditions remain unchanged? For example, the test-retest stability of the Child Abuse Potential Inventory over a one-week period was relatively high, with a Pearson correlation coefficient of .896 between the two test administrations (Milner & Wimberley, 1980, p. 877).

7. See Allen (1988b, p. 1), Downs and Hirayama (1988, p. 63), and Weedon, Torti, and Zunder (1988, p. 17) for research data regarding the interrater reliability of three different risk assessment systems.

REFERENCES

Allen, T. C. (1988a). *Evaluation results: South Carolina Child At Risk Field implementation.* Denver, CO: ACTION for Child Protection.

Allen, T. C. (1988b). *Field testing of the Child at Risk Field system.* (Presentation for the American Public Welfare Association, Second National Roundtable on CPS Risk Assessment, July 20-21, 1988, San Francisco.) Denver, CO: ACTION for Child Protection.

Allen, T. C. (1988c). *Findings: Pilot test of safety determination and response instrument, Anne Arundel County, Maryland.* Denver, CO: ACTION for Child Protection.

Baird, C. (1988). Development of risk assessment indices for the Alaska Department of Health and Social Services. In T. Tatara (Ed.), *Validation research in CPS risk assessment: Three recent studies.* (Occasional monograph series of APWA Social R&D Department, No. 2). Washington, D.C.: American Public Welfare Association.

Baird, C., & Neuenfeldt, D. (1988). Assessing potential for abuse and neglect. *NCCD Focus,* (Newsletter of the National Council on Crime and Delinquency), July, 1-7.

Brown, B. W., & Hollander, M. (1977). *Statistics: A biomedical introduction.* New York: John Wiley and Sons.

Brown, F. G. (1983). *Principles of educational and psychological testing.* New York: Holt, Rinehart, and Winston.

Corey, M. K., & Holder, W. (1986). "Letters to the Editor." *Frontline, 2*(3), p. 3 (A newsletter of the National Child Protective Services Workers Association).

Dalgleish, L. I., & Drew, E. (1989). The relationship of child abuse indicators to the assessment of perceived risk and to the court's decision to separate. *Child Abuse and Neglect, 13*(4), 491-506.

Daniel, J. H., Newberger, E. H., Reed, R. B., & Kotlechuck, M. (1978). Child abuse screening: Implications of the limited predictive power of abuse discriminants from a controlled family study of pediatric social illness. *Child Abuse and Neglect, 2*(2), 247-259.

Daro, D., & Mitchel, L. B. (1989). *Child abuse fatalities continue to increase: The results of the 1988 annual fifty state survey.* Chicago: National Committee for Prevention of Child Abuse.

DePanfilis, D. (1988). *Final report: Determining safety in child protective services and child placement decisions.* Charlotte, NC: ACTION for Child Protection.

Downs, S. W., & Hirayama, K. (1988). *The Wayne County Child and Youth Services field test of the Family Assessment Scales – 1988.* Detroit, MI: Wayne State University School of Social Work. (mimeograph).

Finkelhor, D., & Baron, L. (1986). Risk factors for child sexual abuse. *Journal of Interpersonal Violence, 1*(2), 43-71.

Hanson, R., McCulloch, T., & Hartley, S. (1977). Key characteristics of child abuse. In A. Franklin (Ed.), *Child abuse prediction, prevention and follow-up.* Lexington, MA: Lexington Books.

Holder, W., & Corey, M. (1986). *Child protective services risk management: A decisionmaking handbook.* Charlotte, NC: ACTION for Child Protection.

Horejsi, C. (1987). *Child welfare practice and the Native American family in Montana: A handbook for social workers.* Missoula, MT: University of Montana, School of Social Work.

Howing, P. T., Wodarski, J. S., Kurtz, P. D., & Gaudin, J. M., Jr. (1989).

Methodological issues in child maltreatment research. *Social Work Research and Abstracts, 25*(3), 3-7.

Johnson, W., & Clancy, T. (1988). A study to find improved methods of screening and disposing of reports of child maltreatment in the emergency response program in Alameda County California. In T. Tatara (Ed.), *Validation research in CPS risk assessment: Three recent studies.* (Occasional monograph series of APWA Social R&D Department, No. 2). Washington, D.C.: American Public Welfare Association.

Johnson, W., & L'Esperance, J. (1984). Predicting the recurrence of child abuse. *Social Work Research and Abstracts, 20*(2), 21-26.

Keller, R. A., Cicchinelli, L. F., & Gardner, D. M. (1988). *A comparative analysis of risk assessment models: Phase I report.* Denver, CO: Applied Research Associates, Social System Division.

Kinney, J.K., Haapala, D.A., & Gast, J.E. (1981). Assessment of families in crisis. In M. Bryce & J.C. Lloyd (Eds.), *Treating families in the home: An alternative to placement.* Springfield, IL: Charles C Thomas.

Leventhal, J. M. (1982). Research strategies and methodologic standards in studies of risk factors for child abuse. *Child Abuse and Neglect, 6*(2), 113-123.

Light, R. (1973). Child abuse and neglect in America: A study of alternative policies. *Harvard Educational Review, 43*(4), 556-598.

Loeber, R., & Stouthamer-Loeber, M. (1986). Family factors as correlates and predictors of juvenile conduct problems and delinquency. In M. Tonry & N. Morris (Eds.) *Crime and Justice* (Vol. 7). Chicago, IL: University of Chicago Press.

Magura, S., & Moses, B. S. (1986). *Outcome measures for child welfare services: Theory and applications.* Washington, D.C.: Child Welfare League of America.

Magura, S., Moses, B. S., & Jones, M. A. (1987). *Assessing risk and measuring change in families: The Family Risk Scales.* Washington, D.C.: Child Welfare League of America.

Marks, J., McDonald, T., Bessey, W., & Palmer, M. (1989). *Risk assessment in Child Protective Services: A review of risk factors assessed by existing instrument-based models.* Portland, ME: National Child Welfare Resource Center for Management and Administration, University of Southern Maine.

Martinez, L. (1989). *The Family Assessment Worksheet for the Illinois Department of Children and Family Services.* Presentation for the Third National Roundtable on CPS Risk Assessment, San Francisco.

McCroskey, J., & Nelson, J. (1989). Practice-based research in a family support program: The family connection project example. *Child Welfare, 68*(6), 573-587.

Miller, J. S., Williams, K. M., English, D. J., & Olmstead, J. (1987). *Risk assessment in child protection: A review of the literature.* (Occasional monograph series of APWA Social R&D Department, No. 1). Washington, D.C.: American Public Welfare Association.

Milner, J. S., & Robertson, K. R. (1989). Inconsistent response patterns and the prediction of child maltreatment. *Child Abuse and Neglect*, *13*(1), 59-64.

Milner, J. S., & Wimberley, R. C. (1980). Prediction and explanation of child abuse. *Journal of Clinical Psychology*, *36*(4), 875-884.

Monahan, J. (1981). *Predicting violent behavior: An assessment of clinical techniques*. Newbury Park, CA: Sage Press.

Nasuti, J. P. (1990). *A test of the internal consistency and interrater reliability of the Utah Risk Assessment Scales*. (Doctoral Dissertation) Salt Lake City, UT: Graduate School of Social Work, University of Utah.

Pecora, P.J. (1989). Evaluating risk assessment systems: Methodological issues and selected research findings. In P. Schene & K. Bond (Eds.), *Research issues in risk assessment for child protection*. Denver, CO: American Humane Association.

Pecora, P.J., Briar, K.H., & Zlotnik, J.L. (1989). *Addressing the program and personnel crisis in child welfare: A social work response*. Washington, D.C.: National Association of Social Workers.

Pecora, P. J., Carlson, F., Reese, S., & Bartholomew, G. (1986-87). Developing and implementing risk assessment systems in child protective services. *Protecting Children*, *3*(4), 8-10, 15. Denver, CO: American Humane Association.

Pecora, P. J., & Martin, M. (1989). Risk factors associated with child sexual abuse: A selected summary of empirical research. In P. Schene & K. Bond (Eds.), *Research issues in risk assessment for child protection*. Denver, CO: American Humane Association.

Plotkin, R. C., Azar, S., Twentyman, C. T., & Perri, M. G. (1981). A critical evaluation of the research methodology employed in the investigation of causative factors of child abuse and neglect. *Child Abuse and Neglect*, *5*, 449-455.

Polansky, N. A., Chalmers, M. A., Buttenweiser, E., & Williams, D. P. (1982). *Damaged parents: An anatomy of neglect*. Chicago: University of Chicago Press.

Rodwell, M. K., & Chambers, D. E. (1989). *Promises, promises: Child abuse prevention in the 1980's. Policy Studies Review*, *8*(4), 749-773.

Schene, P., & Bond, K. *Research issues in risk assessment for child protection*. Denver, CO: American Humane Association.

Starr, R.H. (Ed.). (1982). *Child abuse prediction: Policy implications*. Cambridge, MA: Ballinger Publishing Co.

Stein, T.S., & Rzepnicki, T. L. (1983). *Decision making at child welfare intake: A handbook for practitioners*. Washington, D.C.: Child Welfare League of America.

Stein, T.J., & Rzepnicki, T.L. (1984). *Decision making in child welfare services: Intake and planning*. Boston: Kluwer-Nijhoff Publishing.

Three Feathers Associates (1989). Risk level assessment in rural, remote Native Indian communities. *Indian Child Welfare Digest*, (August-September), 20-23.

Thomas, G. (1990). *"Bottomed out" in a "bottom up" society: Social work education and the default and recapture of professional leadership in child welfare*. Paper presented at the 36th Annual Program Meeting of the Council on Social Work Education, Reno (March 3-6). (Available from George Thomas Associates, P. O. Box 152, Athens, GA 30603).

Utah Child Welfare Training Project. (1987). *Utah Child Protective Services risk assessment project - Dissemination manual*. Salt Lake City, UT: Graduate School of Social Work, University of Utah.

Wald, M. S. (1976). State intervention on behalf of "neglected" children: Standards for removal of children from their homes, monitoring the status of children in foster care, and termination of parental rights. *Stanford Law Review, 28*, 623-706.

Wald, M. S. (1980). Thinking about public policy toward abuse and neglect of children: A review of "Before the best interests of the child." *Michigan Law Review, 78*(5), 645-693.

Weedon, J., Torti, T. W., & Zunder, P. (1988). Vermont Division of Social Services family risk assessment matrix research and evaluation. In T. Tatara (Ed.), *Validation research in CPS risk assessment: Three recent studies*. (Occasional monograph series of APWA Social R&D Department, No. 2). Washington, D.C.: American Public Welfare Association.

Wells, S. J. (1985). *How we make decisions in child protective services intake and investigation*. Washington, D. C.: American Bar Association, National Legal Resource Center for Child Advocacy and Protection.

Wilson, D. (1989). *Child protective services: A working agenda*. In P. Schene & K. Bond (Eds.), *Research issues in risk assessment for child protection*. Denver, CO: American Humane Association.

CLINICAL EVALUATIONS OF SEXUAL ABUSE

Beyond Validation Interviews: An Assessment Approach to Evaluating Sexual Abuse Allegations

Michael Robin

ABSTRACT. This essay will examine the training and orientation of child sexual abuse investigators. Particular attention will be devoted to the manner in which investigations are conducted, and how statements and behaviors of children are interpreted.

Many child sexual abuse cases involve young children, lack witnesses, and physical evidence, thus the outcome of the investigation relies heavily on the credibility of the child and the quality of the investigatory process (Quinn, 1989). Given the serious consequences and potential harm of inadequate child sexual abuse investigations, it is vital that cases are assessed accurately. As Berliner (1988) stated,

> Determining whether a child has been sexually abused is a matter of great importance. If this judgement is wrong, a child's physical and mental health may be permanently jeopardized, additional children

Michael Robin is affiliated with the School of Social Work, University of Minnesota, 400 Ford Hall, 224 Church Street SE, Minneapolis, MN 55454.

needlessly abused and their families and communities traumatized. Just as important, an individual's reputation, access to and custody of children, and even liberty, may be lost over a false accusation. Children's recovery from the effects of abuse, the protection of the community and the protection of innocent persons depends on accurate decision-making. (p. 48)

This essay offers a perspective on assessing whether or not sexual abuse occurred when it is alleged. Particular attention will be devoted to the manner in which investigations are conducted, and how statements and behaviors of children are interpreted.

CHILD SEXUAL ABUSE INVESTIGATIONS

Training

In the United States today, training for those responsible for conducting child sexual abuse investigations is seriously deficient. Ideally, according to Farr and Yuille (1988), investigators should be well-trained in gathering reliable information to determine if the abuse occurred. Unfortunately, many of those who interview alleged child victims of sexual abuse have received little, if any, formal training in child development, child abuse, and forensic interviewing techniques appropraite for children (Farr & Yuille, 1988; Goodman & Helgeson, 1985).

In fact, only a small percentage (estimated to be about 25%) of child protection workers nationally have social work training as most states do not even require that public child welfare workers or child protective service workers have social work training (Russell, 1987). But even for those who have had social work training, most have not had comprehensive training in identifying and treating child abuse and neglect, for such training in social work education is rare, if non-existent. According to Richard Krugman of the Kempe Center, there are very few individuals in any aspect of child protection work who have had academic training relevant to their respective fields. (cited in Select Committee on Children, Youth, and Families, 1990, p. 60)

For example, physicians are coming to play a larger role in recent years in the evaluation of child abuse and neglect allegations, but they, like social workers, have had little formal training in this area. Most of the training for physicians in the area of child maltreatment consists of supervision of patient care, grand rounds and continuing education opportunities. According to Dubowitz (1988), the average amount of training for pediatricians in child maltreatment is about 8 hours a year. He noted that several studies have documented deficiencies in medical training for physicians in regards to child maltreatment. Dubowitz concluded that "there appears to be a limited commitment by residency programs to enhance the competency of pediatricians in the area of child maltreatment" (p. 477).

Many communities are relying on local "experts" to assess child sexual abuse reports. These experts are part of what Benedek and Schetky (1987a) call a "new cottage industry." Many of these experts seem to be "self-proclaimed and biased, always finding sexual abuse where alleged," and some "seem to be unaware of the long-term effects the false allegation might have on a child, parent, or a child/parent relationship" (p. 912). Many of these professionals have great difficulty accepting the possibility that some alleged offenders are innocent (Gardner, 1991).

Overall, the quality of child protective investigations suffer from too many "inexperienced and overworked" professionals who are doing only "marginally competent" work (Hechler, 1988, p. 150). In testimony to the U.S. Congress on Child Protective Services, Richard Krugman of the Kempe Center in Denver, stated that retention of quality workers has become a major issue. "Not only are we working with primitive tools, but the people whom we know to be the best qualified to serve these kids and their families are often walking away from the practice of CPS because the working conditions are too difficult" (cited in Select Committee on Children, Youth, and Families, 1990, p. 60). The problem is, according to Hechler (1988), that our society has been unwilling to commit sufficient resources so that child protective workers have the necessary training and support to adequately do their job.

Impact of Bias

According to Haugaard and Repucci (1988), there are two basic processes that a clinician can follow when assessing a child sexual abuse allegation. These are: (1) assessing whether the alleged abuse occurred or (2) getting the child to confirm the clinician's belief that abuse occurred. Many investigators unfortunately tend to assume that something must have happened or else the report would not have been made. Schuman (1984) has written, "in some quarters there is such a degree of sensitivity or outrage about possible child abuse that a presumption exists that such abuse has occurred whenever it is alleged" (p. 1). Likewise, in their study of child protective services, Jones and McGraw (1987) observed that many practitioners appeared to have had their minds made up well before sufficient information had been obtained.

Dent (1982) found that the initial beliefs about the abuse incident greatly influenced the outcome of the investigation. When interviewers have preconceptions, they tend to ask questions in a way that reinforces their own beliefs. Psychological research has clearly shown that clinicians tend to: (1) form judgments extremely quickly, (2) attend to information that supports their beliefs and ignore or discount information that is ambiguous or contradictory, (3) interpret information to confirm their pre-existing theories, and (4) when confronted with contradictory information, clinicians with strongly held beliefs tend to discount the source and content of the information. Given the inherent difficulty of having no biases about something as emotionally charged as child sexual abuse, clinicians should be trained to search for disconfirming information and how to formulate and test competing hypotheses. The problem is that when clinicians ignore disconfirming data and leave alternative theories are left unexamined, there is an increased risk of a false conclusion (Jordan, Harvey, & Weary, 1988; Turk, Salovey, & Prentice, 1988; Wakefield & Underwager, 1988).

Validation Interviews

Many interviewers take for granted that abuse occurred when it is alleged (Raskin & Yuille, 1989; Faller, 1988), thus the purpose of the investigation is to collect information to confirm or validate their prior hypothesis, hence, the term "validation" interview. In articles by Burgess and Holstrom (1978), Faller (1984), Jones and McQuistron (1985), Mrazek (1980), Sgroi, Porter and Blick (1982), and MacFarlane and Krebs (1986) on interviewing *alleged* victims of sexual abuse, no mention was made that the allegation might not have been true. Several recent discussions (Faller, 1988; Meiselman, 1990) on interviewing *alleged* victims have at least mentioned the possibility an allegation may not be true. However, the focus of this approach, according to Ruskin and Yuille (1989), is on how to create a supportive atmosphere so the child will be comfortable disclosing the abuse. Consequently, many interviews are conducted in a "therapeutic and suggestive manner instead of with an investigative and questioning approach" (p. 189). Investigators who take for granted the abuse occurred when it is alleged, tend to interpret evidence in a manner that reinforces their bias. They are less likely to explore alternative theories, search for disconfirming data, or correctly identify false allegations.

Of equal concern, according to Everson and Boat (1989), are investigators who are biased against believing children or adolescents who make claims about being sexually abused. The authors state, "neither excessive skepticism nor unexamined acceptance of every allegation is a defensible position" (p. 235). Clinicians should always keep an open mind and be willing to consider any possibile explanation. According to White and Quinn (1987), the most counterproductive interview style occurs when the interviewer has strongly-held beliefs about what is supposed to have occurred and attempts to get the child to confirm those beliefs. They say the pursuit of a prior agenda is a major reason for investigations to result in false conclusions.

Assessments

An assessment approach to investigating child sexual abuse complaints requires an altogether different orientation from that of those who conduct validation interviews (Haugaard & Repucci, 1988). White, Santilli and Quinn (1988) suggest that an objective evaluation requires the evaluator to establish independence from all sides of the dispute. They recommend that the evaluator not ally themselves with any particular individual in the investigation, and interview every person who is involved in the situation. Clinicians should also maintain "internal independence" and avoid a premature belief about what is supposed to have occurred. The role of investigator requires a neutral, fact-finding orientation, rather than a therapeutic orientation focused on the needs of the child (Raskin & Yuille, 1989).

Interviews must be conducted in a professional manner. If the interviewer's methods are called into question, as happened recently in the McMartin case, it might also lead to the unnecessary questioning of the child's credibility (Quinn, White, & Santilli, 1987). White and Quinn (1988) have offered caution about the use of coercive techniques which include: (1) demands for the truth, (2) providing rewards for correct answers, (3) repetitive questions, (4) threats, and (5) refusal to accept a child's answers. The examiner should also avoid behavioral influences that may subtly express approval or disapproval with a child's answers, such as being overly solicitous, being too harsh or too abrupt, or physical caressing (Quinn, White, & Santilli, 1987). When interviewing children, the most reliable information comes from free recall. Therefore, interviewers should allow children, whenever possible, to tell their story in their own manner and at their own pace. When leading questions are absolutely necessary, great care should be taken so the child is not unduly influenced by the interviewer. It is a paradox that the situations where leading questions may be most necessary (with young children), are also those where the child is most vulnerable to their negative effects (Myers et al., 1989).

ASSESSING CHILDREN'S STATEMENTS

It is a common belief among child abuse professionals that most children lack the motivation and experience necessary to fabricate detailed accounts of sexual abuse. This notion is based on the difficulty young children experience in revealing sexual abuse and the usual lack of knowledge very young children have of explicit sexual activity (Summit, 1983; Myers, 1987). As Faller (1984) has written, "children do not make up stories asserting they have been sexually molested. It is not in their interests to do so. Young children do not have the sexual knowledge necessary to fabricate an allegation" (p. 475).

Many clinicians then take an additional step and conclude that children "don't lie about sexual abuse" making the credibility of a child's statements a matter of faith. As Sgroi, Porter and Blick (1982) state, "determining the validity of an allegation of child sexual abuse is first and foremost a matter of belief. You either believe the child's story or you do not" (p. 69). Myers (1989) has argued that child abuse professionals have gone too far when they claim that "children don't lie about sexual abuse." Prior to the 1970's, children's reports of sexual abuse tended to be discounted. It was widely believed that children made unreliable witnesses because of their difficulty distinguishing real events from what they may have imagined to have occurred (King & Yuille, 1987). But statements that children don't lie about sexual abuse, according to Myers, are too simplistic and invite unnecessary criticism of the professional community and call its knowledge and integrity into question. The point is that children's statements need to be critically assessed rather than taken on faith.

When sexual abuse is alleged the following possibilities must be considered and evaluated:

1. The child is truthful, credible, and accurate.
2. The child is truthful but has misperceived an ambiguous or innocent situation, or has misidentified an alleged perpetrator.
3. The child does not have the mental capacity because of age or disability to give a reliable account of the alleged event.
4. The child has been inappropriately influenced by a third party or parties to make a false allegation.
5. The child is intentionally fabricating an account as an act of anger or revenge or for some type of secondary gain (Nurcombe, 1986).

Research on Children's Statements

Much of what is said about how children discuss sexual abuse is based on clinical anecdote and personal belief. There actually has been very little scientific research on children's accounts of abuse. As Raskin and Yuille (1989) point out, most research studies on the abilities of children as witnesses have none of the profound effects that are associated with a child's disclosure of sexual abuse such as placement of the child in care, breakup of the family, or imprisonment of the offender. Moreover, these studies do not carry with them the "web of inducements" or the panoply of emotions that are experienced by children in sexual abuse cases like fear, shame, trauma, anxiety, etc. They write, "in research studies, the children are usually unaffected by the events they are reporting, and their testimony has no consequences. These differences between the laboratory research context, and those of actual crime situations place severe limitations on the conclusions that may be drawn from the published literature" (p. 189).

True Allegations by Children

There is no typical victim of sexual abuse. How a child responds to sexual abuse is highly variable and depends on their (1) sex and age, (2) emotional and cognitive development, (3) the nature of the abuse, including its frequency and duration, (4) the child's relationship to the offender, (5) the possible use of threats or force, and (6) the quality of support available to the child. Many clinicians recognize that disclosing an abuse incident is often as stressful for the child as the abuse itself. Fearing the consequences of revealing the abuse, it is not unusual for a child to give a delayed, confused and inconsistent account of their experience or to deny the abuse altogether (deYoung, 1987).

Despite its importance to case identification, there has been little research devoted to the manner in which children disclose abuse and the consequences of that disclosure. Sauzier (1989) reports on a study of 156 sexually abused children, and how the abuse was revealed. In this group, 55% of the children initiated the report themselves, however in 17% of these cases the report did not lead to any intervention because the child was disbelieved or the adult took no action. While most children delayed reporting, those who did report usually experienced "minor" forms of abuse such as exhibitionism or attempted contact. Most of the children subjected to more serious forms of abuse such as intercourse never reported their victimization. In general, disclosing an abuse experience can present a heavy burden for a child. Therefore, greater awareness of the factors that contribute to a child's fear of disclosing abuse is needed.

In another study of children's accounts of being sexually abused, Faller (1988) examined 103 cases of child sexual abuse where the perpetrators acknowledged the abuse. She analyzed three aspects of victims' statements and behavior during the diagnostic interview: (1) information about the context of the sexual abuse, (2) the description or demonstration of the sexual victimization, and (3) the victim's emotional state. Faller's goal was to assess factors that are associated with true allegations. Faller noted,

> Both a description of the sexual behavior of the sort found in a true allegation, and an emotional reaction to the sexual abuse or describing it, which is characteristic of a true allegation, were found in over four-fifths of the accounts. Details of the context of the sexual abuse were found slightly less frequently, but nevertheless in over three-fourths of the cases. Seventy of the victims' descriptions (68%) contained all three of these characteristics; 16 (15.5%) contained two; 11 (10.7%) contained one; and six (5.8%) contained none (p. 395).

Faller concluded that,

> Most children who have been sexually abused will be able to provide details about the context of the abuse situation; will describe sexual behavior, which is explicit, from a child's viewpoint and/or will display sexual knowledge beyond that expected for the victim's age; and will have an emotional reaction to the maltreatment and/or having to recount it (p. 397).

In addition, Faller claimed that these factors were "valid predictors of whether children have been abused." The problem with this notion is that it does not account for the fact that many abused children's statements lack consistency and clarity, and sometimes contain information that is improbable, if not impossible to have occurred (deYoung, 1986). There is a danger that a child who does not demonstrate these "predictors" will be wrongly disbelieved.

False Allegations by Children

The trouble with the idea that children don't lie about sexual abuse is that it confuses the distinction between truth and truthfulness. Children's reports will frequently contain inconsistencies, omissions and distortions. And children, like adults, will have selective recall, forget pertinent information, or misperceive ambiguous situations. Moreover, a child may be influenced by their own dreams and fantasies or by the suggestive questioning of others (Eth, 1988; Yates, 1987).

According to Terr (1986), children under stress from an abuse experience exhibit perceptual and cognitive mistakes and fantasy elaborations. These errors depend on the child's emotional development, the nature and severity of the stress, and the child's relationship to the perpetrator. Terr concludes that a child's inconsistent account of events does not necessarily indicate that the child is lying. A child may hold on to false memories or fantasies as the truth, making it difficult to establish the truth of what actually happened (Yates, 1987; Eth, 1988).

Intentional false reports. Faller (1988) argues that false denials are the most frequent untrue statements made regarding sexual abuse, but false disclosures initiated by children do occur and most often involve an older child, who may have been previously abused, is emotionally disturbed, and seeks some type of secondary gain by making a new allegation. Goodwin, Sahd, and Rada (1978) presented the cases of two adolescents who admitted lying about sexual abuse to leave a troubled family setting. Jones and McGraw (1987) also discussed the cases of four children who made false reports. They had been sexually abused prior to the current allegation, and were suffering from untreated post traumatic stress disorder when the current allegation arose.

In their study, "False Allegations of Sexual Abuse by Children and Adolescents," Everson and Boat (1989) assessed the rate of false allegations of sexual abuse in a large sample of Child Protective Service (CPS) cases. They asked CPS workers in North Carolina to identify those cases in which a child or adolescent made an allegation of child sexual abuse that the worker concluded was false. The estimated rate of false allegations in the current sample fell between 4.7 to 7.6% of all reports of child sexual abuse. The most common reasons for concluding a report was false were the following: the report lacked credibility or was considered improbable, the report was inconsistent, or a child recanted.

The authors concluded that in 59% of the cases considered false, the abuse was deliberately fabricated by the child or, most often the adolescent for secondary gain. These included adolescents seeking changes in placement or living arrangements, adolescents retaliating against parental figures for perceived mistreatment, and children and adolescents desiring more attention or responsiveness from significant adults in their lives. In a minority of cases, the child was believed to have been manipulated by another into making a false report, and a small number of cases involved situations where no clear motivation on the part of the child was apparent (Everson & Boat, 1989).

Coaching. In some cases, false allegations involving children are initiated by adults during custody/visitation disputes. It has been noted that children have been influenced and, sometimes "coached" by a parent on statements about being abused. For example, Yates and Musty (1988) present the case of a four year old girl who described how her father rubbed her "tushy." On the witness stand, the child was unable to give details of the events herself but stated her mother told her of them. Apparently, the mother of this child gave her frequent reminders of what was supposed to have happened. The mother stated she believed the abuse did occur.

According to MacFarlane (1986), when children who have been "coached" make statements about sexual abuse, "their words are originally those of an adult and do not represent descriptions of actual situations or the real feelings associated with them. As a consequence, they seem to have several common characteristics: a lack of authenticity, a lack of variation, a lack of convincing detail, and sometimes the use of adult language and adult rationale" (p. 124).

While a lack of emotion is frequently associated with "false allegations," it can also be found in genuine abuse cases. Some children will have little overt emotional response to abuse because they have been traumatized or because they are fearful or depressed. On the other hand, a child who has been pressured to make a false accusation may show signs of psychological distress (Haugaard & Repucci, 1988).

Likewise, when a child gives an account using age-appropriate language, their credibility is enhanced. However, it certainly is possible that a child can be "coached" to use age-appropriate language (Haugaard & Repucci, 1988). Therefore, the presence or absence of emotion or the use of adult or child language when making a disclosure is not reliable in differentiating true from false allegations. As Berliner (1989) states, ". . . the professional literature does not identify a set of characteristics that discriminate abused from nonabused children or qualities of a statement that distinguish true from false claims" (p. 793).

When a Child Retracts an Allegation

It is not unusual for sexually abused children to retract their initial statements about being abused. The pressure to recant has been described by Dr. Roland Summit in his article, The Child Sexual Abuse Accommodation Syndrome (1983). According to Summit, sexually abused children go through five distinct phases: (1) secrecy, (2) helplessness, (3) entrapment, (4) disclosure, and (5) retraction. He writes that "whatever a child says about sexual abuse, she is likely to reverse it" and then goes on to describe the intense pressure a victim may experience to recant and concludes "unless there is special support for the child and immediate intervention to force responsibility on the father, the girl will follow the 'normal' course and retract the complaint" (p. 188).

Summit's theory assumes the child was abused and explains why a child may retract their initial allegation. Although not intended as a diagnostic device, many child abuse professionals use the "child sexual abuse accommodation syndrome" in this manner. (Myers et al., 1989) While Summit's theory may have a limited role in legal cases to rehabilitate the testimony of a child who has recanted an allegation, it's greatest weakness is that it gives no account for the possibility of a legitimate retraction. As one commentator said, "there is something fundamentally strange about saying that since the child denies that the event occurred, it must have occurred" (cited in Myers, 1987, p. 158).

INTERVIEWING CHILDREN ABOUT SEXUAL ABUSE

Given that many abuse reports are initiated by adults, the question becomes not whether children lie, but whether a child can be manipulated to give an honest but inaccurate account of an alleged abuse experience. While children are capable of giving an accurate account of an abuse experience, the younger the child, the more prone they are to suggestions and influence from interested adults. In general, the preschool child is particularly vulnerable to leading questions (King & Yuille, 1987).

According to Raskin and Yuille (1989), children, particularly young ones, are generally oriented to please adults in an interview situation. It is conceivable that a child questioned by an interviewer with a preconceived idea of what is supposed to have occurred, will change or alter their story simply to please the interviewer. Raskin and Yuille state the clinician should be aware of the possibility that the form of the questions or the manner of the questioning may influence a child's answers inappropriately. For example, a child who is repeatedly interviewed over an extended period of time is prone to distortions of memory. In this type of situation, a child may have difficulty distinguishing what is actually remembered from what may have been suggested. There is a possibility, according to Christiansen (1987), that if an interviewer unwittingly encourages a child to imagine some details of an event, the child may accept the fantasy as memory.

Leading Questions

The justification for the use of leading and suggestive questioning is based on the assumption that the child has in fact been abused and is too frightened to reveal the abuse. MacFarlane and Krebs (1986), for example, suggest that the fact a child is reluctant to discuss an alleged abuse incident does not mean that it did not happen. In some cases the child will be reticent to admit to abuse initially and will later give a more accurate account of his/her experience with the abuser. For this reason, they argue, the continued questioning of a child may be appropriate. The authors state that "leading questions may sometimes be necessary in order to enable frightened young children to respond to and talk about particular subjects" (p. 87). What is not mentioned, however, is that sometimes a child's denial of abuse is truthful and accurate. This raises an important question regarding the appropriate protocol for interviewing a child who initially denies being a victim (Haugaard & Reppucci, 1988). While it is indeed true that many genuine victims are reluctant to acknowledge an abuse incident and will continue to deny their experience, not all children who deny being abused are giving a false denial.

If the child has not been abused, the interview can become a lesson in learning, not recall (Christiansen, 1987). The child notices that the interviewer is unwilling to accept his/her statements that abuse did not occur, and senses he or she is expected to say certain things. So the child listens and observes, trying to anticipate what the interviewer wants the child to say. As Christiansen (1987) wrote, "it would be a strong-willed child indeed who could hold out against persistent, suggestive questioning aimed at eliciting statements that certain events took place, especially when the child knows that he will get a hug and good words, if he says that he did" (p. 713).

Coercion. Some interviewers, who become frustrated by the child's supposed unwillingness to acknowledge the abuse, will resort to coercion to get the child to confirm certain information. In their study of videotaped child sexual abuse interviewers in Texas, DeLipsey and James (1988) noted "numerous examples of bribery and coercion during our review of videotaped interviews. Uncooperative children were frequently offered candy and food or denied access to the lavatory until they completed the interview" (p. 238). Benedek and Schetky (1987a) also have noted cases where interviewers have withheld food and bathroom privileges to get the child to tell "what really happened." Some children have even been threatened with not seeing their parents or returning home until they admitted the abuse. According to Benedek and Schetky (1987a) "such coercive techniques are never appropriate" (p. 914).

When a Child Denies Being Abused

The Doe case. In a widely publicized case in Minnesota, an anonymous caller contacted the local child protective services and alleged that Mr. Doe had been sexually abusing his two and four year old daughters. The substance of the allegation was based on the fact that the two year old, while playing on the neighbor's lap, tried to unbutton his shirt. As it turned out, the two year old had been going through a period when she was infatuated with navels and was trying to determine if the neighbor had one. The two young girls were removed from the home without county investigators ever meeting with the parents to discuss the allegations. The parents attributed the agency's response to its "policy of treating as true all allegations of abuse, regardless of source and (the fact) that the county child protection's procedure manual had no reference to the possibility that the maker of a report may have improper motives. This results in a failure to investigate, contrary to statutory duty . . ." (Besharov, 1985, p. 559). The assessment that the children had been abused was supported by a psychologist who concluded that the older child's adamant denial that she had been abused by her father was unusual. He stated, "such an explicit and emphatic denial is atypical in a four year old, even a precocious one." This is an example of how even a child's denial of being abused may be used to support an allegation (Benedek & Schetky, 1987b).

Jordan, Minnesota. In Jordan, Minnesota in 1984, 25 children were removed from the custody of their parents and were placed in foster homes outside of Jordan for over one year. Most of the children were not allowed to see or have contact with their parents during this time. After a lengthy jury trail, two parents were acquited, the charges were dropped against the others, and the state attorney general's office eventually took over the investigation. The attorney general concluded that "the manner in which the Scott County cases were handled resulted in it being impossible to determine, in some cases, whether sexual abuse actually occurred, and if it did, who may have done these acts . . . The tragedy of Scott County goes beyond the inability to successfully prosecute individuals who may have committed child sexual abuse. Equally tragic is the possibility that some are unjustly accused and forced to endure long separations from their families" (Humphrey, 1985).

Most of the children were separated from their parents and placed into foster care prior to being interviewed. A number of them initially denied being abused. Disbelieved by county officials, they were told "the sooner you tell the truth, the sooner your parents will be able to get help, and the sooner you can go home." Eventually stories of sexual abuse began to proliferate. As stories were told, little effort was made to find corroborating evidence. The broad range of children's responses were interpreted narrowly and only in the context of confirming the sexual abuse allegations. Promises of families being reunited if the children accused their parents of sexual abuse, were ignored as factors in shaping the children's responses. One 12 year old reported feeling pressured by the county prosecutor: "she said she'd make a plea bargain with my mom and dad and have treatment for 24 months and then she'd return us all home and everything. That's when I started saying just a little bit . . ." (*Minneapolis Star and Tribune*, January 19, 1985). Another 11 year old denied being abused by his parents for three months, but after being questioned repeatedly, he said he was abused by 19 different adults. The boy was reported to have been questioned by social workers, therapists and detectives 74 times during the investigation (*Minneapolis Star and Tribune*, November 15, 1987).

ASSESSING CHILDREN'S BEHAVIORS

As a group, sexually abused children are quite diverse. While some children show no symptoms from being sexually abused, others manifest a wide range of emotional and behavioral problems. It is said, for example, that sexually abused children may demonstrate some of the following symptoms: helplessness, nightmares, sleep disturbances, enuresis, thumb sucking, eating disorders, social withdrawal, acting-out, fear of men, depression, anxiety, school problems, substance abuse, poor self esteem, poor peer relationships, and so on (Myers et al., 1989).

The Use of Indicators

These symptoms are often presented as "indicators" of abuse. Usually presented in the form of lists without reference to children's age, level of development or family culture, they frequently form the basis of a report. The problem with the so-called indicator lists is that they include many emotional and behavioral symptoms that are widely found in other clinical populations. They also include many symptoms that are part of normal child development. According to Melton and Limber (1989), "therefore, the probability is that children showing behaviors said to be indicative of abuse have *not* been abused" (p. 1229).

The most common behavioral indicators that are said to be suggestive of sexual abuse are precocious sexual behavior, seductiveness and knowledge of sexuality beyond what is reasonable given the child's age (Faller, 1988; Berliner, 1988). The problem with this notion is that there is little normative data on sexual interest and behavior for children of particular ages. As Wakefield and Underwager (1988) point out, a subjective impression that a child's sexual knowledge or behavior is precocious without adequate knowledge of the sexual development of children and the variety of sexual expression and behavior is unreliable. While it is indeed true that many sexually abused children are preoccupied with sexual matters, it certainly is possible that a child may have a precocious knowledge of sexuality without being abused. Some children may show symptoms or behaviors that are sometimes associated with sexual abuse, but are actually the result of an environment that is sexually overstimulating, although not necessarily abusive (Haynes-Seman & Krugman, 1989).

Unfortunately, clinicians are using these indicators as diagnostic tools. In a recent law review article, Myers and colleagues (1989) wrote that, "recent research lends empirical support to the clinical conclusion that properly qualified professionals can determine whether a child's symptoms and behaviors are consistent with sexual abuse" (p. 75). It is unclear, however, what constitutes a "properly qualified professional" or on what basis this claim is made. deYoung (1986) has questioned whether using certain behaviors and emotions are useful in diagnosing sexual abuse. She notes that the indicators are so non-specific that "the net effect is a kind of melange — a veritable grab bag of indicators that potentially bids itself to much abuse and most certainly to false positive identifications" (p. 555).

Drawings

Drawings are widely used by therapists to help children express their feelings. It has been noted that it is very rare for young children to include genitals in their drawings. From this prespective, it has been suggested says Wong, that the presence of genitalia in children's drawing may be indicative of abuse. (Wong, 1987)

Hibbard and colleagues (1987) studied the drawings of 52 children who allegedly had been sexually abused, and who were matched with 52 non-abused children. Overall, genitalia were only present in six of the children's drawings. Ten percent (5/52) of the alleged sexual victims drew genitalia compared with 2% (1/52) of the comparison group. The differences between the groups were not statistically significant at the .05 level.

The authors suggest that while there might be an association between genital drawings and sexual abuse, it is important that drawings not be overinterpreted or that sexual abuse be inferred exclusively from them. Hibbard and colleagues (1987) state emphatically that drawings cannot be used as a screening test for sexual abuse. "Without a larger and broader population study to determine sensitivity, specificity, and the positive predictive value of this tool, the potential adverse effects of any screening test, specifically false positive results, could be considerable" (p. 136).

Anatomically Correct Dolls

The use of "anatomically correct dolls" has become widespread among clinicians investigating sexual abuse complaints. The dolls are particularly useful as an aid to help young children describe their experience. According to Melton and Limber (1989), while the dolls are useful as a means to help children clarify their verbalization through demonstration, they should not be used as a "test" to prove sexual abuse.

Although doll use in sexual abuse evaluation is quite common, little is known about how they are actually used in clinical assessment. Boat and Everson (1988) surveyed 295 child protection workers, law enforcement workers, mental health practitioners and physicians to ascertain their uses of anatomically correct dolls in child sexual abuse evaluations and their interpretations of young children's interactions with the dolls. The results indicated that anatomical doll usage was widespread among all four disciplines, but the users were, for the most part, inexperienced and untrained. What training that does exist is usually little more than an occasional lecture or workshop.

A common concern about the usage of these dolls in clinical assessment is that they are suggestive and encourage the child to "play sex" (Yates & Terr, 1988). Gabriel (1985), for example, states that "many persons working in the child protection field are untrained in play therapy and do not know about the projection-evoking properties of toys. The result has been that the material produced by children in this manner can appear to confirm suspicions of sexual abuse and may actually be no more than normal reaction to the dolls and the interview situation" (p. 42). King and Yuille (1987) point out that "the dolls serve the function of a suggestive question with young children. The genitals and orifices of the doll suggest a play pattern to children, and that play may be misinterpreted as evidence for abuse. Interviewers of young children must be alert to this problem" (p. 31). Whether or not the dolls are actually suggestive has yet to be established by clinical research.

Despite the widespread use of the dolls in interviewing alleged abuse victims, there has been little research addressing the question of how abused children interact with dolls and if they do so differently than do non-abused children (Yates & Terr, 1988). In one study, White and colleagues (1986) studied 25 two to 5.6 year old children who were believed to be sexually abused and compared them to 25 young children who were not suspected abuse victims. Referred children demonstrated significantly more sexually-related behaviors when presented with the dolls than did non-referred children.

A second study was done by Jampole and Weber (1987) who examined the incidence of sexual behavior with dolls with 10 children sexually abused and 10 non-sexually abused children. Results of their experiment showed that of the children who had been sexually abused, 9 or 90% demonstrated sexual behaviors with the dolls and one or 10% did not. Of the non-abused population, two or 20% demonstrated sexual behaviors with the dolls and 8 or 80% did not. Despite their small sample size, Jampole and Weber concluded without any qualification that "the research findings show that significantly more children who had been sexually abused demonstrated sexual behavior with the anatomically correct dolls than did the non-sexually abused group. These findings suggest that anatomically correct dolls are useful instruments in sexual abuse investigations" (p. 187).

In the only study of the interaction of a large sample of non-abused children with anatomically correct dolls, Sivan, Schor, Koeppl, and Noble (1988), observed that the doll play of the children was, for the most part, free sexual concerns. They noted that the dolls themselves occupied little of the children's interest. Although the sexual body parts of these dolls were inspected by many children, role playing of explicit sexual behaviors was not observed. Since the study only included middle-class subjects, the degree to which its findings apply to other socio-economic groups needs to be determined.

Overall, these studies suggest that sexually abused children may possibly have more "sexualized play" with the dolls than non-abused children. But the presence or absence of sexual play with dolls is not useful in concluding whether or not a particular child has been abused. As in other types of investigative tools used in this field, there is a risk of both false positives and false negatives (Yates & Terr, 1988).

The problem is that there is no consensus among professionals on what constitutes "sexualized play" when children play with anatomically correct dolls. Boat and Everson (1988) found that how a child's demonstration of sexual activity with the dolls is interpreted depends on the child's age, the child's statements, and the particular discipline of the professional. For example, 50% of protective service workers, but only 6% of law enforcement officers considered placing dolls on top of each other as normal. The groups also disagreed about 50% of the time over whether avoiding the dolls or anxious behavior in response to the unclothed dolls was a normal response from a young child. Significantly, there was no single behavior, not even undressing the dolls, that all groups agreed would be normal play behavior for young children.

A California appeals court ruled in 1987 that the clinical use of anatomically correct dolls in forming an opinion about sexual abuse constitutes a novel scientific test and is inadmissable in court (In re Amber B, 1987, cited in Myers, 1988). It is clear from the preceding discussion, that the scientific foundation for knowledge about how children interact with the dolls and its meaning is still quite limited. While there are many who agree that the dolls should not be used for diagnostic or interpretive purposes, there is considerable support for the continued use of the dolls as an adjunct to the interview process (Myers & White, 1989).

CONCLUSION

The accurate assessment of child sexual abuse complaints is a matter of great importance. There are serious consequences for children, their families, the professional community, and the public when investigations are poorly handled. Therefore, greater attention must be devoted to the manner in which child sexual abuse investigations are conducted in our society. In particular, there needs to be greater awareness of the impact of the investigatory process on the quality of children's statements about abuse. Those who conduct child sexual abuse investigations must be aware of the potential effects of bias on the outcome of the investigation. Ultimately, it is important to remember, as Farr and Yuille (1988) point out, that children are victimized when they have been sexually abused or when they have been the victim of a false allegation.

REFERENCES

Benedek, E., & Schetky, D. (1987a). Problems in validating allegations of sexual abuse part 1: Factors affecting perception and recall of events. *Journal of the American Academy of Child and Adolescent Psychiatry, 26*, 912-915.

Benedek, E., & Schetky, D. (1987b). Problems in validating allegations of sexual abuse part 2: Clinical evaluation. *Journal of the American Academy of Child and Adolescent Psychiatry, 26*, 916-921.

Berliner, L. (1988). Deciding whether a child has been sexually abused. In E. B.

Nicholson (Ed.), *Sexual abuse allegations in custody and visitation cases*. Washington, D.C.: American Bar Association.

Berliner, L. (1989). Debate forum: Resolved: Child sex abuse is overdiagnosed: Negative. *Journal of the American Academy of Child and Adolescent Psychiatry*, *28*, 792-793.

Besharov, D. (1985). Doing something about child abuse: The need to narrow the grounds for state intervention. *Harvard Journal of Law and Public Policy*, *8*, 539-589.

Boat, B., & Everson, M. (1988). Use of anatomically correct dolls among professionals in sexual abuse evaluations. *Child Abuse and Neglect*, *12*, 171-179.

Burgess, A. W., & Holstrom, L. L. (1978). Interviewing young victims. In A. W. Burgess, A. N. Groth, L. L. Holstrom, & S. M. Sgroi (Eds.). *Sexual assault of children and adolescents*. Lexington, MA: Lexington Books.

Christiansen, J. (1987). The testimony of child witnesses: Fact, fantasy, and the influence of pretrial interviews. *Washington Law Review*, *62*, 705-721.

DeLipsey, J. M., & James, S. K. (1988). Videotaping the sexually abused child: The Texas experience, 1983-1987. In S. M. Sgroi (Ed.), *Vulnerable populations*. Lexington, Massachusetts: Lexington Books.

Dent, H. R. (1982). The effects of interviewing strategies on the results of interviews with child witnesses. In A. T. Trankell (Ed.), *Reconstructing the past*. Deventer, The Netherlands: Kluwer.

deYoung, M. (1986). A conceptual model for judging the truthfulness of a young child's allegation of sexual abuse. *American Journal of Orthopsychiatry*, *56*, 550-559.

deYoung, M. (1987). Disclosing sexual abuse: The impact of developmental variables. *Child Welfare*, *66*(3), 217-223.

Dubowitz, H. (1988). Child abuse programs and pediatric residency training. *Pediatrics*, *82*, 477-480.

Eth, S. (1988). The child victim as witness in sexual abuse proceedings. *Psychiatry*, *51*(2), 221-233.

Everson, M., & Boat, B. (1989). False allegations of sexual abuse by children and adolescents. *Journal of the American Academy of Child and Adolescent Psychiatry*, *28*(2), 230-235.

Faller, K. (1984). Is the child victim of sexual abuse telling the truth? *Child Abuse and Neglect*, *8*, 473-481.

Faller, K. (1988). Criteria for judging the credibility of children's statements about their sexual abuse. *Child Welfare*, *67*(5), 389-401.

Faller, K. (1988). *Child sexual abuse*. New York: Columbia University Press.

Farr, V., & Yuille, J. (1988). Assessing credibility. *Preventing Sexual Abuse*, *1*(1), 8-13.

Gabriel, R. M. (1985). Anatomically correct dolls in the diagnosis of sexual abuse of children. *The Journal of the Melanie Klein Society*, *3*, 40-51.

Gardner, R. (1991). *Sex abuse hysteria: Salem witch trials revisited*. Cresskill, New Jersey: Creative Therapeutics.

Goodman, G., & Helgeson, V. (1985). Child sexual assault: Children's memory and the law. *University of Miami Law Review, 40*, 181-208.

Goodwin, Sahd, D., & Rada, R. (1978). Incest hoax: False accusations, false denials. *Bulletin of the American Academy of Psychiatric Law, 6*, 269-276.

Haugaard, J., & Reppucci, N. D. (1988). *The sexual abuse of children*. San Francisco: Jossey-Bass.

Haynes-Seman, C., & Krugman, R. D. (1989). Sexualized attention: Normal interaction or precursor to sexual abuse? *American Journal of Orthopsychiatry, 59*(2), 238-245.

Hechler, D. (1988). *The battle and the backlash*. Lexington, Massachusetts: Lexington Books.

Hibbard, R. A., Roghmann, K., & Hoekelman, R. (1987). Genitalia in children's drawings: An association with sexual abuse. *Pediatrics, 79*(1), 129-137.

Humphrey, H. (1985). *Report on Scott County investigations*. St. Paul, MN: Attorney General's Office.

In re Amber B., 191 Cal. App. 3d 682, 236 Cal. Rptr. 623 (1st Dist. 1987).

Jampole, L., & Weber, M. K. (1987). An assessment of the behavior of sexually abused and nonsexually abused children with anatomically correct dolls. *Child Abuse and Neglect, 11*, 187-192.

Jones, D., & McGraw, J. (1987). Reliable and fictitious accounts of sexual abuse to children. *Journal of Interpersonal Violence, 2*, 27-45.

Jones, D., & McQuistron, M. (1985). *Interviewing the sexually abused child*. Denver, CO: Kempe Foundation.

Jordan, J., Harvey, J., & Weary, G. (1988). Attributional biases in clinical decision making. In D. Turk & P. Salovey (Eds.), *Reasoning, inference, and judgement in clinical psychology*. New York: Free Press.

King, M. A., & Yuille, J. C. (1987). Suggestibility and the child witness. In S. J. Ceci, M. P. Toglia, & D. F. Ross (Eds.), *Children's eyewitness memory*. New York: Springer-Verlag, 24-35.

MacFarlane, K. (1986). Child sexual abuse allegations in divorce proceedings. In K. MacFarlane & J. Waterman (Eds.), *Sexual abuse of young children*. New York: Guilford Press.

MacFarlane, K., & Krebs, S. (1986). Techniques for interviewing and evidence gathering. In K. MacFarlane & J. Waterman (Eds.), *Sexual abuse of young children*. New York: Guilford Press.

Meiselman, K. (1990). *Resolving the trauma of incest*. San Francisco: Jossey-Bass Publishers.

Melton, G., & Limber, S. (1989). Psychologists' involvement in cases of child maltreatment. *American Psychologist, 44*(9), 1225-1233.

Mrazek, D. A. (1980). The child psychiatric examination of the sexually abused child. *Child Abuse and Neglect, 4*, 275-284.

Myers, J.E.B. (1987). *Child witness and the law*. New York: John Wiley.

Myers, J.E.B. (1988). Child witness and the law. Supplement. New York: John Wiley.

Myers, J.E.B. (1989). Protecting children from sexual abuse: What does the future hold? *Journal of Contemporary Law, 15,* 31-50.

Myers, J.E.B., Bays, J., Becker, J., Berliner, L., Corwin, D., & Saywitz, K. (1989). Expert testimony in child sexual abuse litigation. *Nebraska Law Review, 68,* 1-145.

Myers, J.E.B., & White, S. (1989). Dolls in court? *The Advisor, 2,* 5-6.

Nurcombe, B. (1986). The child as witness: Competency and credibility. *Journal of the American Academy of Child Psychiatry, 25,* 473-480.

Quinn, K., White, S., & Santilli, G. (1987). *Influences of an interviewer's behaviors in child sexual abuse investigations.* Unpublished manuscript. Cleveland, Ohio: School of Medicine, Case Western Reserve University.

Quinn, K. (1989). Resolved: Child sex abuse is overdiagnosed: Affirmative. *Journal of the American Academy of Child and Adolescent Psychiatry, 28,* 789-790.

Raskin, D., & Yuille, J. (1989). Problems in evaluating interviews of children in sexual abuse cases. In S. Ceci, D. F. Ross, & M. P. Toglia (Eds.), *Children take the stand: Adult perceptions of children's testimony.* New York: Springer-Verlag.

Russell, M. (1987). *Public child welfare job requirements.* Maine: National Child Welfare Resource Center for Management and Administration.

Sauzier, M. (1989). Disclosure of sexual abuse. *Psychiatric Clinics of North America, 12*(2), 455-469.

Schuman, D. C. (1984). *False allegations of physical and sexual abuse.* Paper presented at the Annual Conference of the American Academy of Psychiatry and the Law, Nassau, Bahamas.

Select Committee on Children, Youth, and Families. (1990). *No place to call home: Discarded children in America.* Washington, D.C.: U.S. Government Printing Office.

Sgroi, S. M., Porter, F. S., & Blick, L. C. (1982). Validation of child sexual abuse. In S. M. Sgroi (Ed.), *Handbook of clinical intervention in child sexual abuse,* Lexington, Mass: Lexington Books.

Sivan, A., Schor, D., Koeppl, G., & Noble, L. (1988). Interaction of normal children with anatomical dolls. *Child Abuse and Neglect, 12,* 295-303.

Summit, R. (1983). The child sexual abuse accommodation syndrome. *Child Abuse and Neglect, 7,* 177-193.

Terr, L. (1986). The child psychiatrist and the child witness: Traveling companions by necessity, if not by design. *Journal of the American Academy of Child Psychiatry, 25,* 462-472.

Turk, D., Salovey, P., & Prentice, D. (1988). Psychotherapy: An information-processing perspective. In D. Turk & P. Salovey (Eds.), *Reasoning, inference, and judgement in clinical psychology.* New York: Free Press.

Wakefield, H., & Underwager, R. (Eds.), (1988). *Accusations of child sexual abuse.* Springfield, IL: Charles C Thomas.

White, S., & Santilli, G. (1988). A review of clinical practices and research data on anatomical dolls. *Journal of Interpersonal Violence, 3*(4), 430-442.

White, S., Santilli, G., & Quinn, K. (1988). Child evaluator's roles in child sexual abuse assessments. In E. B. Nicholson (Ed.), *Sexual abuse allegations in custody and visitation cases*. Washington, DC: American Bar Association.

White, S., Strom, G. A., Santilli, G., & Halpin, B. M. (1986). Interviewing young sexual abuse victims with anatomically correct dolls. *Child Abuse and Neglect, 10*, 519-529.

White, S., & Quinn, K. (1987). *Problematic interview techniques in child sexual abuse investigations*. Unpublished manuscript. Cleveland: School of Medicine, Case Western Reserve University.

White, S., & Quinn, K. (1988). Investigatory independence in child sexual abuse evaluations: Conceptual considerations. *Bulletin of the American Academy of Psychiatry and Law, 16*(3), 269-278.

Wong, D. (1987). False allegations of child abuse: The other side of the tragedy. *Pediatric Nursing, 13*, 329-333.

Yates, A. (1987). Should young children testify in cases of sexual abuse? *American Journal of Psychiatry, 144*, 476-480.

Yates, A., & Musty, T. (1988). Preschool children's erroneous allegations of sexual molestation. *American Journal of Psychiatry, 145*, 989-992.

Yates, A., & Terr, L. (1988). Debate forum: Anatomically correct dolls: Should they be used as a basis for expert testimony? *Journal of the American Academy of Child and Adolescent Psychiatry, 27*, 254-257.

Was There Really Child Sexual Abuse or Is There Another Explanation?

Kevin B. McGovern

ABSTRACT. This paper discusses the diagnostic errors that can occur in investigations of child sexual abuse. The author suggests that in our haste to protect children from abuse, investigators are forming conclusions before adequate information is available or alternative theories have been considered.

Sexual abuse between adults and children does frequently occur in our society. Most sexual abuse occurs between people who know each other. However, as child sexual abuse cases are more carefully examined, professionals will more frequently observe that some suspicions and allegations are ill-founded. These distorted perceptions have been caused by a misunderstanding of the dynamics that occur among people. Professionals and the general public should never jump to conclusions. Each case must be carefully evaluated so that reliable investigations, positive clinical services and social interventions are provided in order to prevent any ill harm from occurring to anyone — even the accused.

During an initial evaluation, investigators, case workers and trained clinicians are prone to make errors based on their own subjective biases, distorted and/or limited information conveyed to them, and their clinical training. These crucial factors can influence their perceptions regarding allegations of child sexual abuse.

These diagnostic problems are found in numerous disciplines including but not limited to: law, law enforcement, medicine, social work, psychology and education. This paper will discuss a number of diagnostic errors that can occur during the interdisciplinary evaluation of allegations of child sexual abuse. In most cases four primary groups, law enforcement,

Kevin B. McGovern is affiliated with the University of Oregon Health Science Center. Reprint requests should be sent to him at Alternatives to Sexual Abuse, Suite 214, 1225 N.W. Murray Road, Portland, OR 97229.

115

social services, mental health and medicine will become involved in these investigations and clinical assessments. This paper will focus on a number of problems that can lead to catastrophic results.

LAW ENFORCEMENT AND SOCIAL SERVICES

There are numerous human and unintentional errors that can occur during a police investigation and/or clinical evaluation. Until recently, most child abuse cases were treated through social agencies and mental health care programs and hospitals, where child abuse was seen as part of a constellation of human problems. In most jurisdictions, these cases were not criminally prosecuted. Health care providers, physicians, nurses, counselors, and others attempted to resolve these problems through therapeutic consultations and counseling. In these situations, police officers were not usually involved in the initial detection interviews and/or related investigatory procedures. Perpetrators were treated within the confines of a treatment facility. Only in rare cases would the police be asked to intervene.

Throughout the United States there has been a major policy change. Now, these incidents of child sexual abuse are being prosecuted in many jurisdictions. Although sexual abuse has always been a crime, many cases went unprosecuted, especially when the incestual behaviors involved family or extended family members. However, police officers and prosecuting attorneys are now focusing on these problems. In some jurisdictions, perpetrators are sent to prison.

As these political and social changes occur, law enforcement agents and case workers are more frequently becoming involved in complicated cases regarding allegations of child sexual abuse. Although many of these individuals have some initial course work in psychology and child development, and interviewing techniques, the majority of them have not been trained in clinical intervention. Consequently, many respond to allegations of child sexual abuse through trial and error. Police agencies and social services programs have gigantic case loads that clamor for immediate intervention and assistance. Many programs do not have the funds, resources and/or abilities to spend the time necessary to resolve the intricacies of these problems and concerns. In addition, some of these individuals are trained to provide immediate protection and/or assistance for their clients. For the police officer, immediate relief can mean intervention that occurs swiftly and effectively. After the initial investigation occurs and a statement is made, there is an immediate need to detain, prosecute, and incarcerate the alleged perpetrator once the time, date, and place has been substantiated by the alleged victim.

Social services employees often operate within the same frame of reference. They must quickly resolve serious intrafamilial problems between alleged victims and their perpetrators. Without intervention, they fear that the child will continue to be abused. This fear causes high levels of anxiety and a need for immediate intervention. Both agencies, the police and social services, do not always have the time, ability, and staff to provide long-term and comprehensive evaluations. Their investigative procedures need to be more carefully scrutinized! In some cases, there have been documented incidences of children being encouraged and/or coached to say things that could be classified as perceptual distortions, biases and/or misleading summaries of what, in fact, did not occur. Some alleged victims are told they will face a number of dire consequences until they tell the truth; such as, being placed in foster care, being placed in jail, or not being able to see their loved ones for a long period of time.

Some clinicians, case workers and police officers have ignored a number of basic fundamental principles regarding child psychology. Prior to the current need for immediate arrests and convictions of perpetrators of child sexual abuse, clinicians used to recognize the need for both comprehensive and long-term evaluations. Prior to the recent and profound increased rated of reporting, clinicians would spend significant amounts of time developing rapport with the victim, family members, and significant others. These evaluations occurred before any type of intervention occurred that might cause long-term and irreversible damaging effects upon a family environment. When these clinicians were pressed for immediate answers and/or diagnostic impressions, they often concluded that they had only reached the conclusion that more data, information, and work was needed.

THE MEDICAL PROFESSION

The same problem of misdiagnosis can occur during medical examinations. During these evaluations of alleged child sexual abuse, the pediatrician and/or family doctor is often provided with limited information regarding the sexual abuse by an irate parent or a child's advocate. For example, during the recent assessment of a 5 year old female, the doctor was provided with erroneous information by a parent. This woman had a history of psychiatric problems including a history of previous psychiatric hospitalizations. She was accompanied by a naive, inexperienced case worker to this doctor's office. The doctor in this case was told by the uninformed case worker that a psychiatrist had discovered a history of child sexual abuse, that the alleged abuser, the father, had a drinking problem, and he had an adversive sexual relationship with his wife. The physician was also informed that dad had taken multiple baths with his young daughter; that he would spend many hours in the child's room with the door closed and that dad and his daughter had several big secrets.

During the physical examination, there was some evidence of soreness and a red labia. These symptoms were consistent with several plausible explanations. In this case, the doctor did not take a detailed medical history which would have revealed that a number of bathing practices led to the child's complaints and current medical condition. A second examination by another pediatrician revealed these other problems.

Pediatricians and family doctors do not routinely examine little girls' genitals unless there has been a specific complaint. How many doctors usually examine the vaginae, anuses, testicles, scrotums, and genitalia of children who have not been abused? If doctors have not examined the genitalia of children who are not reporting any signs of sexual abuse, how can accurate comparisons be made? And will doctors with busy community responsibilities, with patients in the hospital, and with an overflowing crowd of patients in their waiting room search for other plausible explanations, such as other forms of physical trauma? Or, a disgruntled mentally disturbed patient? Or a spouse who is fighting custody?

A young, developing child experiences an array of traumas throughout his or her life. They fall, poke themselves, scratch themselves, and, in some situations, are hit or impaled by blunt objects. Recently, a young girl was running across a picnic bench. When she fell, she landed straddle-legged on the picnic table. Vaginal bleeding occurred. A hematoma and bruise were evident. There may have been some scarring and/or tissue damage from this wound. What if this child is examined 3 years later because she has drawn a picture of a penis at school and says, "Dad has touched me here." If, during the examination, scar tissue is discovered what does that mean? Does this mean the child was sexually abused?

Some children fear the reactions of their parents. In these situations, they do not report these traumas to an adult. Or, on the other hand, an adult learns about the trauma and tells the child he or she is overreacting. They are told to be tough and act like soldiers. Or, the trauma is never reported to the parents after the child has been seen by another doctor. In one such case, a little girl was visiting her grandmother in the southwest. She experienced a genital trauma, it was treated by the family doctor, and it was not reported to the mother. In the past, the mom had accused the mother-in-law of being negligent. This non-sexual trauma caused damage to the inner lips of the vulva and to the hymen. What if this child is examined 3 years later during a heated custody evaluation? What will the physical evidence show?

When the family doctor examines this child, will he or she consider what other types of trauma and/or physical aberrations could lead to the tearing of a hymen or scarring of the labia? Are all female children born with their hymen intact? Or, were there deformities at birth?

As this little girl boarded the plane, she promised Grandma that she would not tell her mother about this problem that occurred several weeks before. In several years, would a doctor find evidence of scarring and a disfigured hymen? Would a social worker, psychologist, and pediatrician then say that this same child is a victim of sexual abuse because of her depression, strange drawings and vaginal swelling? Will the professionals misinterpret the information that was provided and the misleading evidence they evaluated?

What would happen if the same child was sent to ten different physicians, with five physicians being given a history of possible child sexual abuse and five physicians being given a history of an integrated family with past medical trauma experienced while falling on a sharp object? Would that information influence the diagnosis and prognosis of the examining physician? Obviously, these are questions that need to be carefully reviewed.

These physicians may not see the same type of trauma or may argue regarding the etiology of this trauma. Can most physicians clearly identify the etiology of this type of injury when they have not examined children from various walks of life, various age ranges, and various cultural backgrounds? How can comparisons be made if most doctors are not routinely examining the genitalia of all of their patients? Or, while in medical school, they do not acquire this type of training.

Parental Pressure—Contaminating Factors

Health care providers can be provided with biased stories of distorted perceptions by their patients especially in heated custody cases. They are often asked by their patients to make complimentary and supporting statements that may strengthen their position in court. For example, in one case, a mother continued to ask her pediatrician whether or not the trauma could possibly be caused by sexual abuse. Finally, under duress, pressure, and pre-occupied with a busy schedule, the doctor said: "It could be." "It could be" was then interpreted as if it was a fact! The parent then took this statement out of context to a counselor, who then heard the words:

"The trauma was caused by sexual abuse." The counselor did not talk to the physician about the physical exam, the child's past medical history, the questions that were asked by the doctor and the conclusions that were made. In addition, the caseworker did not discuss with the physician other plausible explanations of how this trauma may have occurred! In fact, there were at least ten other possibilities that could have explained the child's current behavior and medical concerns.

The evaluating physician must carefully consider how medical evidence is obtained, interpreted and communicated to others in these cases. Just because a doctor says the infections may be consistent with the diagnosis of sexual abuse, does not mean that the child was sexually abused. The diagnosis can be consistent with several other conditions, such as poor hygienic care, self-stimulation, past traumas or other problems. "Suspicion of sexual abuse" does not mean that sexual abuse has occurred! The accurate diagnosis of sexual abuse is based on many factors, including the information given to the doctor, the experience level of the doctor, the integrity of the doctor, and the prejudicial biases of the doctor. Some parents and social agencies select doctors who are known advocates. These professionals more frequently find the causation of a trauma, infection, sore, or scrape to be sexual abuse. These professionals should ask themselves the following questions: Have I examined an equal number of nonabused children or children where allegations have not arisen? Have I examined the anatomy of "normal" children during various stages of development? Have I looked for other explanations that would rule out child sexual abuse? Are there other compelling explanations for this physical trauma? Finally, was I even trained to perform this type of evaluation?

Physicians should not discuss their initial impressions with a parent until a comprehensive analysis of the complaint has been completed. The physician should say: "Margaret, I have examined your child. I am going to study my findings carefully. I first need to discuss these findings with others, a consortium that reviews these cases. There are many reasons why a child might have these symptoms. They include bedwetting, diaper rash, allergies, dermatological concerns, self-stimulation, rubbing on objects, and physical trauma. Before any conclusions are drawn, we need to conduct other tests in order to determine whether or not these factors are responsible for the child's symptoms. During further testing we will use a colposcope and take a number of pictures of the trauma. I want to have these pictures enlarged and reviewed by two other pediatricians at this office." At that point, the doctor then has the ethical and professional responsibility to search for other explanations for this medical condition.

A parent can leave a doctor's office with distorted perceptions of what was said. Consequently, the physician must be extremely careful in what they are communicating to their patient. The parent unfortunately, can return home with an unclear impression of what has been said. The patient may have heard that the child's physical problem was caused by sexual abuse. When in fact, the doctor said: "There are many possible explanations—one possibly is sexual abuse."

Mental Health

Just as physicians can be misguided by distorted and biased perceptions and information, other clinicians, namely case workers, psychologists, psychiatrists, nurses, teachers, social workers and counselors can also be misinformed regarding initial allegations regarding child sexual abuse. In some cases, the concerned parents, loved one, advocate, relative, or other resource person may be providing a distorted analysis of what really occurred. Although the informant appears to be legitimate, the explanations of what may have occurred could be a distorted series of facts. Prior to the initial screening interview, the child may have been influenced by a number of suggestive and contaminating factors, which would influence the perceptions of the initial investigator. Clinicians need to verify initial information provided in a screening interview. In some cases, the child may have been told by the accompanying parent that he or she must tell the examiner exactly what he or she was told to tell the examiner during a series of interviews prior to the initial appointment. The child is also told to tell the intake counselor that he or she has not discussed these problems with anyone prior to this first meeting. Obviously, these previous statements can influence and/or impair the basic communication occurring between the alleged victim and the intake worker.

Since children are influenced by multiple social factors, adequate rapport needs to occur before delicate questions are asked between the intake counselor and the child. Unfortunately, many clinicians want to immediately verify the allegations of molestation and do not develop adequate rapport with their clients. This is one of the major mistakes made during initial evaluations. The second major error is believing that the initial information provided by a parent, loved one, or adult is accurate, reliable and valid.

In addition to learning more about the child and his/her perceptions, the interviewing counselor should study the personality characteristics of the complainant. As we know, people are influenced by their past social history, psychological development, and an array of other environmental factors. As we continue to study child sexual abuse, clinicians may find that people with certain personality characteristics and traits will more frequently distort reality and create unrealistic allegations.

These personality characteristics may include alcohol and drug abuse, histrionic personality, antisocial characteristics, chronic post-traumatic stress, and a history of sexual abuse. Individuals with these personality characteristics may have a greater propensity or tendency to provide examiners with unreliable information. In addition to these personality characteristics, the examiner needs to carefully look at what secondary gains can be obtained through these allegations, including financial incentives, retaliation, resolving past marital discord, revenge, punishment, reliving a previous post-traumatic stress, vindication, compliance, and a host of other factors. It is just as important to examine these factors as it is to carefully study how the allegations of child sexual abuse evolved.

The clinician should always develop adequate rapport with a child and their family while these allegations are being reviewed! Although parents, loved ones, and guardians can encourage children to make certain statements during an initial intake, it is more difficult for them to control their children's behavior when a therapist uses fifteen sessions to interview a child and other family members. As these sessions continue, two major things occur: The child starts developing rapport with the counselor and a trusting relationship begins between these two people. In this situation the child may be more willing to explore other explanations for these allegations directly or indirectly through symbolism, drawings, play therapy, and/or verbal conversation.

While a child is developing rapport with a clinician through hours of consultation, more realistic and valid observations can be obtained through these examinations. As the clinician continues to interface and interact with this child, he or she will learn more about the child's dreams, perceptions, verbalizations, mannerisms, behaviors, drawings, and other related activities. During this extensive evaluation, the clinician will also have an opportunity to observe how a parent, and/or loved one interacts with that child. In other words, are they overprotective or suspicious? Do they come to the meeting with alcohol on their breath. Or are they prompt, courteous, polite, or disheveled, angry, suspicious, or paranoid? These are variables that need to be examined by clinicians. Unfortunately, in many jurisdictions, the basic concept of comprehensive, integrated and intense evaluations has been lost, forgotten or never utilized! People want fast answers to difficult and complicated questions.

Just as physicians may make comments which misinform or confuse a parent, clinicians can make the same mistakes. Clinicians need to be very careful about the types of information they provide a parent especially after an initial interview! Unfortunately, the clinician's practice is often governed by a demanding schedule and a parent's desire for immediate validation. Fifteen years ago, Federal Express, Fax, portable computers with airline schedules, one hour photo services, microwave ovens and instant car loans did not exist. Our cultures are mesmerized by an "instant" world. Unfortunately, people want to know the answers to complicated and complex questions through peripheral, superficial, and at times, unprofessional evaluations. The complaining parent needs to recognize that evaluations examining allegations of child sexual abuse must be conducted over a period of time where pertinent, reliable, and valid information can be obtained.

A Case Illustration

In the following pages, an actual case which displays a number of serious problems regarding allegations of sexual abuse will be presented. In this case, these allegations stemmed from a situation where a concerned babysitter believed that two children were being sexually abused by a male perpetrator. Her concerns were initially sparked by a popular TV program that she watched. While viewing this show, she listened to a number of professionals describing the common characteristics of the known perpetrator and a number of symptoms that would be seen in a child who was sexually abused by a parent.

Missy, the well-intentioned babysitter, had been watching several young children at her make-shift day care center. Since the inception of the center, she primarily cared for infants and younger toddlers ranging in age from 4 months to 6 years. Recently, she had been concerned about two children's social behavior when they were left with her on offsetting Monday mornings. On several Mondays, she noticed an increase in anxiety, restlessness, and other related behavioral symptoms, such as irritability, lack of concentration, and an overall feeling of discomfort. On one Monday morning, one of the two children, Becky, complained about irritation around her "po-po." While changing her diapers, Missy noticed an irritation or sore with accompanying inflammation. She then began to ask this young child whether or not Daddy had been poking her there during their most recent visitation. This child indicated that Daddy had touched her there and she cried when he pushed on her sore spot. Missy also asked Becky's brother, Clem, a number of questions related to child care and potential parental abuse. When Becky's mother arrived at the day care center later that day, Missy described her discomfort in what she had seen and observed. Eventually, Children's Services Division was called, and a lengthy, thorough and comprehensive investigation occurred. Although there were some behaviors and signs consistent with potential inappropriate behavior, the young girl's father was eventually cleared of any misbehavior after hours of interrogation, investigation, and expensive interventions by a series of professionals and attorneys. It is estimated that over $30,000 was spent on this case.

Why was this case different? In the first place, the mother's reaction must be examined. Although the mother listened to the concerns of the well-intentioned babysitter, she did not jump to conclusions. After taking her children to the family pediatrician, she heard that there were symptoms consistent with the possibility of child sexual abuse and several other explanations that would be more realistic and believable. After these symptoms were examined by the physician, a social service agency was contacted by the hospital. The intake worker suggested that sexual abuse may have occurred and that a comprehensive study was needed. This study was to be completed by Social Services the following day. However, prior to this intervention, these children were taken to a child psychologist, who wanted the mother to authorize an extensive evaluation which would rule out other explanations for the redness, soreness, inflammation of the labia and the statement made by the child that her Daddy had hurt her "owie" or "po-po." The psychologist video tape recorded this initial and subsequent meetings.

On the following day, the intake worker for this social agency was alarmed that the children had been seen by an independent therapist. From her point of view, this evaluation should not have been coordinated since only their agency was qualified to coordinate such evaluations. The mother was encouraged not to return to this biased psychologist for any further consultations. Some innuendoes were made regarding the mother's psychological need to protect the ex-husband. The mother was told that maybe she had been aware of this abuse and was unwilling to take a protective role with her children.

After receiving a brief lecture regarding enablers and other psychologically impaired parents, the mother decided to meet with an attorney to discuss some of the inconsistencies that were occurring. This same attorney had represented her during the divorce and custody settlement. The attorney was familiar with the quality and thoroughness of the psychological evaluations coordinated by the psychologist who had already met with the children. This attorney had also encouraged a number of psychological evaluations to be reviewed by the Court. After contacting the psychologist who had met with the child the preceding day, and having reviewed the previous reports, the attorney was even more concerned about the allegations and how the babysitter and social services may have misinterpreted the child's initial statement. During the custody dispute, the psychological reports had been quite positive regarding the parenting abilities of both parents. Neither parent was diagnosed as being impaired with any major psychological problems and/or inequities. The topic of sexual abuse had been previously discussed with both children.

Becky and Clem again met with the consulting psychologist the following day. During these interviews, the psychologist did not ask leading questions. Instead, the psychologist asked for an overview of what normally occurred between the father and children during visitation. Becky also discussed the irritation, her hygienic concerns, and how Dad cared for the children when they were staying at his apartment.

On the following day, Social Services again contacted Mrs. X and reminded her that her children were in a precarious situation. The Social Service agent implied that the physical exam revealed symptoms consistent with sexual abuse and that it was not unusual for most fathers to sexually abuse their children after an aggravated separation, divorce, and custody fight. The social agent continued to remind the mother that these children could not be meeting with the perpetrator until their investigation was completed. The social worker added that many angry divorced men resolve their frustrations by sexually abusing their own kids.

On the following day, the children were asked leading questions regarding inappropriate touching and related behavior by this case worker and a police officer. These interviews were video taped. When comparisons were made between the two approaches, there was a major difference in the methodology employed by the clinical psychologist and the Social Services worker and police officer. For example, the clinical psychologist wanted to develop rapport with the children and obtain an in-depth understanding of their psychological characteristics. On the other hand, the Social Services agent wanted to immediately establish that sexual abuse had occurred. Becky was given the anatomical dolls and told that she must show how Daddy abused her by putting his hand on her po-po!

What more was needed? The doctor's report stated that symptoms were consistent with sexual abuse. However, the social worker did not want to admit that it was also consistent with numerous other possible explanations. Although the behavioral symptoms seen in the children by the babysitter were consistent with sexual abuse, they were also consistent with numerous other explanations.

The anxiety displayed by the children on Monday mornings at the make-shift day care center was a stress reaction to the fact that Mother and

Dad were not going to reunite. On Monday morning, they would plead with their father to reunite with their mother. When he told them this was impossible, the children would become quite upset, agitated, cry, and be quite unhappy with the continued inability of their parents to reunite. The distressful behavior seen by the babysitter had nothing to do with sexual abuse. It was a grief reaction! In fact, these psychological symptoms — stress, confusion, tears, agitation and a loss of appetite were common reactions to a divorce and the statement that "we cannot reunite." Reunification would not occur. The children were upset.

In the ensuing weeks, a series of difficult meetings, phone calls and memos were passed among a variety of professionals, including investigators, attorneys, case workers, supervisors, district attorneys, physicians, and a few relatives. Before long, neighbors, friends, relatives, and others were beginning to state their particular biases. As the allegations were tossed from one agency to another, the father could not even talk to his own children. Instead, he was told that a temporary restraining order had been issued by a guardian ad litem assigned to this case. He was not allowed to have any contact with his children and/or former wife. Any contact would be seen as an indicator of his guilt. In this case, the father decided to obtain legal assistance from his divorce attorney. An ensuing number of meetings then occurred between his attorney, Social Services, his ex-wife's attorney, and the child psychologist who had met with the children and their mother several weeks before.

In the midst of this interdisciplinary battle, the consulting psychologist continued to reiterate the need for an extensive evaluation that would either verify or refute these allegations. Although the child continued to say that Daddy had touched her "po-po," that she had seen his penis, and that the two of them had laid in bed together rubbing against each other, the psychologist continued to look for other explanations! Could it be that the father had placed Desenex or some other type of medicinal preparation on her labia? Could it be that in the middle of the night the child awoke from a nightmare, and climbed into bed with her father while he was half-asleep? Could it be in the middle of the night that she rubbed up against him because she was cold? Could it be that he did have an erection?

In this case, the young child had been touched for medicinal reasons. The young child had seen her father's genitalia, and the young child had rubbed against his penis while sleeping in bed with him. Those facts, by themselves do not, in any way, shape, or form, indicate that the father was a sexual abuser or planned to engage in any inappropriate sexual behavior with the child.

CONCLUSION

Clinicians, police officers, social workers and others involved in sexual abuse investigations should not jump to conclusions. They should objectively study the facts. They should ask: Are there other explanations that are consistent with these symptoms, yet inconsistent with allegations of child sexual abuse. Unless other reasonable explanations are examined, clinicians will find distorted and inaccurate evidence of child sexual abuse in many cases. These conclusions would be highly unreliable and extremely unfair.

All professionals from an array of disciplines are being challenged by this complex social disease. As with any social ills, we all want an immediate cure! However, society cannot condone irrational reactions and approaches to a serious social problem. We cannot expect an overnight solution for this complicated problem — allegations of sexual abuse. Instead, we must look for sensible solutions that interface the working policies of the various agencies and professions evaluating this perplexing problem. Obviously, clinicians need to be sensitive to the concerns of the investigating officer. On the other hand, Social Service counselors and law enforcement agents also must be cognizant of the long-term and intricate research that has already been completed in the area of child psychiatry and psychology. These long-term studies and treatment policies clearly identify the need for an extensive, unbiased and professional evaluation regarding allegations of child sexual abuse. We cannot afford superficial and biased evaluations.

Is It (or Is It Not) Sexual Abuse?
The Medical Examiner's Dilemma

Joyce A. Adams

ABSTRACT. Because of the increasing incidence of reports of child sexual abuse, medical personnel examining children who have complaints related to the anogenital area may consider sexual abuse as the most likely cause for these complaints. This article will discuss the differential diagnosis of several anogenital signs and symptoms that may commonly have an explanation unrelated to sexual abuse. The importance of a history from the child is emphasized.

Ten years ago if a mother brought her two year old daughter to her physician with a statement that the child complained of pain when she urinated, the physician's first thought would probably have been: "Does she have a bladder infection?" Today there is a good chance that his or her first thought would be "Could this be sexual abuse?" especially if the child complained after a weekend visitation at Daddy's house.

The recognition by the lay press, the public, and the medical community that child sexual abuse is a problem of staggering proportions has led to an atmosphere of near hysteria regarding abuse in many communities. One child protection worker I met called it "molesteria." Are we over-interpreting statements by young children and/or misinterpreting physical signs as representing possible sexual abuse? Has the pendulum swung too far the other way, from a denial of the possibility of sexual abuse and a lack of awareness of the prevalence of the problem, to over-reporting? As a pediatrician involved for the past seven years in the examination of children for evidence of sexual abuse, I would like to share some observations and review the current "state of the art" with respect to medical findings in childhood sexual abuse.

Joyce A. Adams is affiliated with Valley Medical Center, 445 South Cedar Avenue, Fresno, CA 93702.

129

PREVALENCE

There is no question that the sexual abuse of children is a widespread phenomenon, with estimates of prevalence in childhood ranging from 5% (Siegel, Sorenson, Golding, & Burnam, 1987) to near 35% (McFarlane, 1986) of the general population. The variation in prevalence rates is due to differences in definition, in how the data are collected, and from whom. A survey of 795 undergraduate students in New England by anonymous questionnaire (Finkelhor, 1979) found that 1 in 5 females (19%) and 1 in 10 males (9%) reported that they had been victims of sexual abuse before the age of 18 years. When in-depth interviews are conducted concerning past episodes of abuse, more positive responses are obtained than when questionnaires are administered, and younger respondents (16-18 years old) report more childhood abuse than adults, thus suggesting some reporting bias. It is likely that the true incidence of child sexual abuse is between the figures cited for reported sexual abuse cases and those obtained by surveying adults.

THE MEDICAL EXAMINATION

The goal of the medical exam is to diagnose and treat medical diseases or injuries, care for the emotional needs of the patient and finally to collect appropriate medical and legal information. A child may be referred for an examination to look for signs of possible sexual abuse when there are one or more of the following indicators:

1. A statement from the child that he or she has been sexually abused.
2. Behavioral changes noted by the parents that may include: excessive masturbation, sexual acting-out with other children or adults, extreme disruption in sleep or eating patterns, school problems, withdrawal, depression, aggressive behaviors, or other indicators of psychological distress in the absence of any clear reasons for such distress.
3. Exposure to an individual who is suspected or known to be a molester of children.
4. Certain medical signs or symptoms including: redness of the genital or rectal area, painful urination, complaints of pain in the genital or rectal area, blood on the underwear or diaper, vaginal discharge, or vaginal itching.

When the parent or guardian brings the child for an examination, there is often an expectation that the examiner will be able to tell whether or not there has been any sexual abuse. Child protection workers or law enforcement officers may request an examination before deciding how much of an investigation should be conducted. Unfortunately, the answer to the question "Has something happened?" is rarely a clear cut "yes" or "no." There are several reasons for this uncertainty. When the abuse described by the child involves touching or rubbing of the genitalia, oral-genital contact, or even anal and vaginal penetration, there may be no injury to the tissues, and consequently, no physical signs on examination. A normal examination in a child with suspected abuse does not rule out the possibility that the abuse has, in fact, occurred.

When a child is being examined within a few days (up to 4 or 5 days) of the alleged assault, a full evidential examination may be done to look for semen, adult pubic hairs, blood and signs of trauma if trauma (e.g., penetration) is alleged or suspected by history or exam. In most cases, however, the disclosure of abuse comes weeks or months after the last episode, long after minor injuries have healed and legal evidence has been washed away.

Another explanation for the finding of a normal examination on a child who describes penetration is that a young girl may not have any concept of what "in" means. "He stuck his private in my pee pee" could mean the abuser rubbed his penis between her labia (outer lips of the vulva) without actually penetrating beyond the hymen. This type of abuse usually leaves no sign on physical examination, unless the abuse has been repeated multiple times.

Disclosure vs. No History

My response to the question: "Has something happened?" is usually another question: "What does the child say?" A clear, unprompted, consistent, detailed account of molestation given by a child should be considered strong evidence that abuse has occurred, regardless of whether the physical examination is normal or abnormal. Young children *may* sometimes exaggerate or misinterpret touching they find unpleasant. "Daddy hurt me," from a 3-year-old could mean Daddy spanked her or wiped her bottom too vigorously. If further details are not forthcoming, and there are no physical or behavioral changes suspicious for abuse, the child's statement may be considered insufficient to substantiate an allegation of abuse.

False allegations of sexual abuse do occur. In a paper reviewing all reports of possible sexual abuse made to the Denver Department of Social Services in 1983 (Jones & McGraw, 1987), 34 of 439 allegations (8%) were determined to be fictitious accounts of abuse given by either the child or the parents. Children may also mis-identify the alleged abuser, either to protect the real abuser, or because their recall of events and faces is inaccurate (Benedek & Schetky, 1987).

When the child is either too young or developmentally disabled and, therefore, unable to give a history of sexual abuse, the physical examination may become a key factor in whether or not a case is pursued. The history from the caretaker of behavioral changes and/or suspicious symptoms, as listed earlier, should also be taken into consideration when determining the likelihood of abuse.

Frequency of Physical Findings

As medical examiners began to review the literature on cases of suspected abuse, we are beginning to learn more regarding physical findings seen in these children. These studies vary as to the type of patients examined, when the examination was done in relation to the alleged molestation, the age range of patients, the type of examination performed, and the definition of physical findings. While one study showed "signs of genital injury" in 17% of the children examined (Scherzer & Lala, 1980), another found that 77% of the children had signs of infection, penetration, genital trauma or non-genital trauma (Rimsza & Niggemann, 1982). Physical evidence of sexual abuse was reported in 95 of 140 boys (68%) seen for possible sexual abuse at one center (Spencer & Dunklee, 1986). Another study reported genital injuries in 5% and anal abnormalities in 29% of 189 boys examined for suspicion of sexual abuse (Reinhart, 1987). Emans, Woods, Flagg, and Freeman (1987), found abnormalities in 37% of 119 sexually abused girls, with the majority of patients having normal examinations. The variability in these studies reflects differences in the populations studied, definitions and examination techniques, interpretations of the findings by the examiners, and the time seen after allegations of abuse.

There is agreement among examiners that the presence of sperm or semen can be considered conclusive evidence of sexual abuse. Muram (1989) categorizes findings seen in sexually abused children as follows:

1. Normal appearing genitalia.
2. Nonspecific findings: Findings which could have been caused by sexual abuse, but could also have other causes.
3. Specific findings: Recent or healed lacerations of the hymen or vaginal mucosa, enlarged hymenal opening greater than one centimeter, bite marks, or the presence of one or more sexually transmitted diseases.
4. Definitive findings: Any presence of sperm or semen on body, clothes or at scene of alleged abuse.

When a child gives a clear history of sexual abuse and the physical examination reveals evidence of injury, scars, semen, or sexually transmitted diseases, the case is fairly straightforward, but these cases are rare. What happens when the physical examination findings are non-specific or questionable, or when there is no clear history of abuse, which is most often the situation? I will discuss non-specific findings first, then discuss some of the controversy regarding the determination of normal versus suspicious findings on anogenital examination.

Non-Specific Findings

The following signs or symptoms may raise the concern of sexual abuse, but other cases should be investigated completely, in the absence of a history of abuse.

Painful urination. Painful urination with or without redness of the tissues around the hymen, is most commonly caused by urinary tract infection and local irritation. A urine culture should always be obtained to rule out a bladder infection, and in a child with the sudden onset of burning on urination, a urinary tract infection should be strongly suspected. This irritation may be brought on by one or more of the following habits:

• Use of bubble baths
• Shampooing the child's hair in the bathtub, then letting the child sit in the soapy water
• Use of nylon underpants and/or tights
• Use of colored or perfumed toilet tissue
• Giving large amounts of vitamins, especially vitamin C
• Drinking large amounts of carbonated beverages
• Washing genital area with perfumed soaps
• Applying creams, perfumes or powders to genital area

Redness or severe skin rash in the genital area. Redness may be caused by local irritation, as mentioned before, or by chronic skin conditions such as eczema, seborrhea, or lichen sclerosis (Altcheck, 1984). These skin conditions can sometimes cause very severe rashes in the genital area which may be mis-interpreted as being caused by abuse (Jenny, Kirby, & Fuquay, 1989). A recent report also describes changes in the appearance of the genitalia which seemed to have been caused by excessive cleaning or the inappropriate application of various creams and ointments (Herman-Giddens & Bernson, 1989).

Vaginal discharge. There are many causes of vaginal discharge in prepubertal children and in adolescents. An excellent description of these causes is given by Altcheck (1984). A child with a persistent vaginal discharge needs to be examined, and cultures should be obtained to look for the presence of sexually transmitted, as well as non-sexually transmitted, infections, and for foreign bodies.

The presence of a sexually transmitted disease in a prepubertal child should raise the suspicion of sexual abuse (Hammerschlag, 1989). Table 1 lists seven of these infections, as well as special considerations which may be important in interpreting culture results in children. Positive cultures for *Neisseria gonorrhea* always require confirmatory testing (Whittington, Rice, Biddle, & Knapp, 1989), and the presence of *Chlamydia trachomatis* must be confirmed by cultures, not by indirect screening methods (Hammerschlag, Rettig, & Shields, 1988). However, a child over the age of 2 years who presents with vaginal discharge or discharge from the penis should have cultures obtained for all sexually transmitted diseases. If gonorrhea, chlamydia, or trichomonas (in girls) infections are confirmed, this should be considered strong evidence of sexual contact.

Many other types of bacteria can cause vaginitis in children, including those associated with respiratory infections and gastrointestinal infections. A routine culture of the discharge should always be obtained to detect the presence of these organisms. Two children were referred to Valley Medical Center recently for possible sexual abuse because of vaginal discharge. Both girls had positive vaginal cultures for *Shigella* following an episode of diarrhea and fever. This is a bacteria which may be spread from the anus to the vaginal area by wiping. Both children denied any history of abuse and had normal genital examinations.

Blood on the panties or diaper. When blood is found by the caretaker on a child's diaper or underwear, the child is usually brought to medical attention. The possibility that the bleeding could be a result of sexual abuse should always be considered, and a careful history and physical examination must be performed. The blood could be coming from the rectum, the urethra (opening to bladder) or the vagina. The type of bleeding, the history, the examination findings, and laboratory tests can help the physician localize the source of bleeding.

a. *Rectal bleeding*: The most common cause of blood in or on the bowel movements of an infant is an anal fissure. These are superficial breaks in the skin around the anus which may be caused by irritation of the skin due to rashes or diarrhea, or the passing of large, hard bowel movements. Sometimes the fissures may be difficult to see because the infant resists the spreading of the buttocks. They also seem to heal very quickly. Other common causes of blood in the stool include allergy to cow's milk, gastritis, intestinal infections with viruses, bacteria or parasites, and other types of intestinal diseases or malformations (Sheldon, 1979). If there is bruising around the anus or a history of alleged sexual abuse given by the child, the bleeding takes on a different significance.

b. *Bleeding from the urethra* may be visible on examination, or suspected if a urine specimen shows a large number of red blood cells. In girls, a condition called urethral prolapse (Emans & Goldstein, 1982), may cause bleeding which seems to come from the vagina. The bladder opening protrudes and the tissues bleed. Blood in the urine of boys or girls may indicate the presence of a bladder infection, and a urine culture should always be obtained. Hematuria (blood in the urine) may also be caused by an irritation of the tip of the penis in a male infant (usually in diapers), kidney stones, other types of kidney disease, the presence of a foreign body, or by trauma.

c. *Vaginal bleeding* in a child over nine years of age with signs of pubertal development may represent a first menstrual period. Menstrual bleeding without any other signs of puberty is occasionally seen, and may occur in a child younger than eight years. Other causes of vaginal bleeding include vaginal foreign bodies, vaginal infections, tumors, generalized bleeding problems, and a skin condition called lichen sclerosis, mentioned previously (Emans & Goldstein, 1982, p. 53-57). Accidental injuries to the perineal area are relatively common, and should present with a clear history (Muram, 1986). These are usually straddle-type injuries where the child falls on some firm object while her legs are separated, resulting in small tears which bleed profusely. As with all injuries in children, the type of injury should fit with the explanation of how the accident occurred. A story which seems bizarre or unlikely, or which changes in the retelling, should raise the suspicion of sexual abuse, and further history is required.

Labial adhesions. Labial adhesions are seen in abused and non-abused children (McCann, Voris, & Simon, 1988). This condition is postulated to occur when there has been some irritation of the skin in the vulvar region, causing the edges of the labia minora (inner lips of the vulva) to stick together. When there is an attempt to spread the labia, the area of agglutinated tissue may appear as a white line in the midline. Although some sexually abused children have labial adhesions as a result of rubbing and abrasion of the vulvar skin, not all children with labial adhesions have

TABLE 1

Significance of Sexually Transmitted Diseases in Children

Organism/Disease	Significance		
	Presence should raise suspicion of sexual abuse?	Presence may be explained by other factors?	
1. Neisseria gonorrhea	Yes (Must have confirmatory sting)	Only if infection is limited to the eyes.	
2. Chlamydia trachomatis	Yes (Must use culture, not indirect methods)	Yes, if child is less than 2 yrs., infection could have been acquired at delivery.	
3. Syphilis	Yes	If found in infant with congenital infection.	
4. Trichomonas	Yes	Non-sexual transmission unlikely.	
5. Condyloma acuminata (Human papilloma virus)	Usually	Yes, if child less than 1 or 2 yrs. of age, may have been acquired at delivery. Mother may have had virus but no lesions. Transmission by close physical contact has been postulated to occur.	
6. Herpes Simplex	Yes, if genital lesions present	Yes, if child had mouth sores 2-5 days before genital sores appeared. In babies, may be acquired at delivery.	
7. Gardenerella vaginalis (Bacterial vaginosis)	Not necessarily, but may be consistent with abuse	Yes. Organism may be present in non-abused children.	

Information in the table condensed from Hammerschlag (1988) and Beck-Sague and Alexander (1987).

been sexually abused. An analogy might be that although physically abused children may have bruises, not all children with bruises have been abused. In all cases, a careful history and physical examination needs to be performed.

Unusual lesions. Unusual lesions of the genital and perianal region may raise the suspicion of abuse. Lichen sclerosis, a skin condition mentioned previously, causes an ulcerated, scarred appearance to the skin. An unusual congenital anomaly described as a perineal groove (Gellis, Feingold, Shaw, & DeWitt, 1977), has been mistaken for trauma with resulting scar formation (Adams & Horton, 1989). Congenital variations of the perineum and anus have not been fully documented.

What Is Normal?

The major dilemma facing the physician or nurse practitioner who is asked to examine a child for possible sexual abuse is one of determining whether the findings on this particular child are normal, suspicious, abnormal but not necessarily related to abuse, or abnormal and consistent with sexual abuse.

What kind of information is available to help the examiner in making this assessment? Until very recently, there has been a frustrating lack of data and few guidelines.

An early article by Woodling and Kossoris (1981), described anogenital findings in acute and chronic molestation, but no photographs or drawings were presented to illustrate the findings which were described. Terms such as "enlarged hymenal opening," "rounded hymenal remnants" and "gapping anus" were used to describe anogenital findings said to be suspicious for abuse, but the various techniques for examination and obtaining measurements were not described in detail.

How big should be hymenal opening be in girls of different ages? How should the measurements be obtained? What factors may cause variation in the measurements? What does "anal gapping" mean? How much is too much? Is this seen in non-abused children? The answers to some of these questions are beginning to appear in the medical literature, but others remain unanswered.

Measurements of the diameter of the hymenal opening have been used by some investigators as a criteria for suspecting abuse (Cantwell, 1983; White & Ingram, 1989). Because there are different configurations of the hymen (Pokorny, 1987), different methods of visualizing the hymen (McCann, Voris, Simon, & Wells, 1990), and different techniques of measuring the opening (Adams, Phillips, & Ahmad, 1989), the validity of these measurements has been questioned. The child's state of relaxation during the examination also seems to be an important factor, although this has not been well studied. An excellent commentary and review of the use of these measurements appeared in a recent journal (Paradise, 1989).

A major dilemma facing the medical examiner who obtains measurements of the hymenal opening is the lack of valid, reliable standards for measurements in normal children. One published study (Emans, Woods, Flagg, & Freeman, 1987), reported measurements of the hymenal opening in a group of children with no history of abuse. Expected sizes in children of different ages have also been reported (Cowell, 1981), and these figures have been helpful to examiners also. The first detailed description of genital anatomy, including measurements, in non-abused prepubertal children will appear in the near future (McCann, Wells, Simon, & Voris, 1990). More data needs to be gathered, to establish a range of normal diameter in children of different ages, specifying expected variations due to hymenal type, examination method, measurement technique, and state of relaxation.

Anal findings in children with suspected abuse have generated considerable controversy. Examiners have noted the following findings in children giving a history of anal penetration: anal gapping, reflex anal dilatation, hyperpigmentation of anal skin, abnormal anal skin folds, redness of the skin, venous congestion (a purplish discoloration), anal fissures, anal scars, and "funneling." The key question at this point is this: does the presence of one or more of these anal findings indicate that sexual abuse may have occurred? Two important articles, appearing back-to-back in the same issue of a child abuse journal, demonstrate the complexity of this medico-legal question (McCann, Voris, Simon, & Wells, 1989; Hobbs & Wynne, 1989). Many of the findings described by Hobbs and Wynne as being suspicious or confirmatory of sexual abuse were found by McCann and his colleagues to be present in large numbers of children with no known history or other indicators of abuse. Table 2 lists some of these findings and their frequency. Although this study does need to be replicated, these findings should cause medical examiners to be very cautious about "diagnosing" sexual abuse in a child based on isolated physical signs.

One factor which has been important in the interpretation of changes in anogenital anatomy has been the introduction of the colposcope. The colposcope is a magnifying device traditionally used by gynecologists to examine the tissues of the cervix. It has been reported (Teixeira, 1980) to be useful in detecting evidence of minor trauma to the hymen, and in detecting subtle changes in genital anatomy in sexually abused children (Wood-

TABLE 2

Frequency of Perianal Findings in a
Population of Non-abused Children*

Findings	Subjects with Findings/ Subjects Observed	% of Subjects with Positive Findings
Anal dilatation	130/267	49%
Intermittent anal dilatation	81/130	62%
Erythema	68/168	41%
Pigmentation	74/251	30%
Venous congestion by end of examination	83/113	73%
Skin tags	18/164	11%

*Data condensed from McCann, Voris, Simon, & Wells (1989).

ling & Heger, 1986). Other investigators have found that the use of the colposcope does not increase the rate of diagnosis of genital findings in sexually abused children (Muram & Elias, 1989). The use of colposcopic photographs does, however, allow for consultation among examiners on difficult cases, as well as documentation of findings for legal purposes. A recently published color atlas of colposcopic photographs (Chadwick, Berkowitz, Kerns, McCann, Reinhart, & Strickland, 1989) has been very useful to examiners who are asked to determine whether a particular finding is normal or abnormal. As the authors mention, this atlas will require an update as research continues in the interpretation of anogenital findings.

CONCLUSIONS

The examination of prepubertal children for physical signs of sexual abuse is really a new specialty. Studies describing the appearance of the genitalia in non-abused children will be published in the near future, and this data will be extremely helpful for examiners in the field of child sexual abuse. Because child sexual abuse is common, it is essential for health care professionals to maintain a high index of suspicion when findings on a child suggest the possibility of abuse. Here are a few suggestions for the examiner:

1. A child with burning on urination, redness in the genital or rectal area, vaginal discharge, or blood on the panties or diaper *could* be having these symptoms as a result of sexual abuse, but all other causes should be investigated thoroughly.
2. A child who gives a clear history of being sexually molested has probably been sexually molested. Most likely the child will have a completely normal examination. This will be true unless force was used and the examination is performed within a few days of the abusive incident, or unless the molestation involved repeated penetration over a long period of time.
3. When signs consistent with sexual abuse are found in a child, a confidential interview by a skilled professional should be performed to determine whether there is a reasonable suspicion that the child has been sexually abused. Photographs and/or drawings should be made, and consultation with other examiners should be considered if the findings are questionable. A report to Protective Services is still mandated.
4. While research in developing standards for normal anatomy continues, children continue to be sexually abused. They continue to need an advocate who can provide a gentle and thorough examination, good documentation, and court testimony when necessary, based on the current level of medical knowledge.

A word to non-medical workers in the field of child sexual abuse: try to understand what medical examiners can and cannot do. We usually cannot rule-out sexual abuse. We can rarely state without hesitation that a child has indeed been sexually abused. An assessment of whether sexual abuse has or has not occurred must still rely heavily upon a history from the child, the presence or absence of behavioral changes, a family evaluation, and sometimes a psychological evaluation. We can perform careful examinations of a child's genitalia and state our opinion as to whether the findings are consistent with the history given by the child, or possibly consistent with other non-abusive causes.

Most academic medical centers and many community hospitals or clinics now have experienced physicians or nurse practitioners available to examine children in cases of suspected sexual abuse. Explore the resources available in your own community. Although we may not be able to give you a clear ''yes'' or ''no'' as to whether a particular child has been sexually abused, we are willing to be a part of the team to provide comprehensive evaluations, treatment, counseling and support to families undergoing the trauma of an investigation for possible child sexual abuse.

REFERENCES

Adams, J. A., & Horton, M. (1989). Is it sexual abuse? Confusion caused by a congenital anomaly of the genitalia. *Clinical Pediatrics, 28,* 146-148.

Adams, J. A., Phillips, P., & Ahmad, M. (1990). The usefulness of colposcopic photographs in the evaluation of suspected child sexual abuse. *Adolescent and Pediatric Gynecology, 3,* 75-82.

Altcheck, A. (1984). Common problems in pediatric gynecology. *Comprehensive Therapy, 10,* 19-28.

Beck-Sague, C., & Alexander, E. R. (1987). Sexually transmitted diseases in children and adolescents. *Infectious Disease Clinics of North America, 1,* 227-304.

Benedek, E. P., & Schetky, D. H. (1987). Problems in validating allegations of sexual abuse. Part I: Factors affecting recall of events. *Journal of the American Academy of Child and Adolescent Psychiatry, 26,* 912-915.

Cantwell, H. (1983). Vaginal inspection as it relates to child sexual abuse in girls under thirteen. *Child Abuse and Neglect, 7,* 171-176.

Chadwick, D. L., Berkowitz, C. D., Kerns, D., McCann, J., Reinhart, M., & Strickland, S. (1989). *Color atlas of child sexual abuse.* Chicago: Medical Publishers, Inc.

Cowell, C. A. (1981). Gynecologic examination of infants, children and young adolescents. *Pediatric Clinics of North America, 28,* 247-266.

Emans, S. J., & Goldstein, D. P. (1982). *Pediatric and adolescent gynecology.* (2nd Ed). Boston: Little, Brown and Co.

Emans, S. J., Woods, E. R., Flagg, N. T., & Freeman, A. (1987). Genital findings in sexually abused, symptomatic and asymptomatic girls. *Pediatrics, 79,* 778-785.

Finkelhor, D. (1979). Sexual socialization in America: High risk for sexual abuse. In J. M. Samson (Ed.), *Childhood and sexuality.* Montreal: Editions Etudes Vivantes.

Gellis, S. S., Feingold, M., Shaw, A., & DeWitt, G. W. (1977). Perineal groove-picture of the month. *American Journal of Diseases of Children, 131,* 921-922.

Hammerschlag, M. R. (1988). Sexually transmitted diseases in sexually abused children. *Annals of Pediatric Infectious Diseases, 3,* 1-18.

Hammerschlag, M. R., Rettig, P. J., & Shields, M. E. (1988). False positive results with the use of chlamydia antigen detection tests in the evaluation of suspected sexual abuse in children. *Pediatric Infectious Diseases, 7,* 11-23.

Herman-Giddens, M. E., & Bernson, N. L. (1989). Harmful genital care practices in children. A type of child abuse. *Journal of the American Medical Association, 261,* 577-579.

Hobbs, C. J., & Wynne, J. M. (1989). Sexual abuse of English boys and girls: The importance of anal examination. *Child Abuse and Neglect, 13,* 195-210.

Jenny, C., Kirby, P., & Fuquay, D. (1989). Genital lichen sclerosis mistaken for child sexual abuse. *Pediatrics, 83,* 597-599.

Jones, D., & McGraw, J. M. (1987). Reliable and fictitious accounts of sexual abuse to children. *Journal of Interpersonal Violence, 2,* 27-45.

McCann, J., Voris, J., & Simon, M. (1988). Labial adhesions and posterior four-chette injuries in childhood sexual abuse. *American Journal of Diseases of Children, 142,* 659-663.

McCann, J., Voris, J., Simon, M., & Wells, R. (1989). Perianal findings in prepubertal children selected for non-abuse: A descriptive study. *Child Abuse and Neglect, 13,* 179-193.

McCann, J., Voris, J., Simon, M., & Wells, R. (1990). Comparison of genital examination techniques in prepubertal females. *Pediatrics, 85,* 182-187.

McCann, J., Wells, R., Simon, M., & Voris, J. (1990). Genital findings in pre-pubertal females selected for non-abuse: A descriptive study. *Pediatrics, 86* (page citation pending).

McFarlane, K., & Waterman, J. (1986). *Sexual abuse of young children.* New York: The Guilford Press.

Muram, D. (1986). Genital tract injuries in the prepubertal child. *Pediatric Annals, 15,* 616-620.

Muram, D., & Elias, S. (1989). Child sexual abuse—Genital tract findings in prepubertal girls-II. Comparison of colposcopic and unaided examinations. *Journal of Obstetrics and Gynecology, 160,* 333-335.

Paradise, J. E. (1989). Predictive accuracy and the diagnosis of sexual abuse: A big issue about a little tissue. *Child Abuse and Neglect, 13,* 169-176.

Pokorny, S. F. (1987). Configuration of the prepubertal hymen. *American Journal of Obstetrics and Gynecology, 157,* 950-956.

Reinhart, M. A. (1987). Sexually abused boys. *Child Abuse and Neglect, 11,* 229-235.

Rimsza, M. E., & Niggemann, E. H. (1982). Medical evaluation of sexually abused children—A review of 311 cases. *Pediatrics, 69,* 8-14.

Scherzer, L. N., & Lala, P. (1980). Sexual offenses committed against children. *Clinical Pediatrics, 19,* 679-685.

Sheldon, S. H. (1979). *Pediatric differential diagnosis: A problem-oriented approach.* New York: Raven Press.

Siegel, J. M., Sorenson, S. B., Golding, J. M., & Burnam, M. A. (1987). The prevalence of childhood sexual assault: The Los Angeles epidemiologic catchment area project. *American Journal of Epidemiology, 126,* 1141-1153.

Spencer, M. J., & Dunklee, P. (1986). Sexual abuse of boys. *Pediatrics, 78,* 133-138.

Teixeira, R. (1980). Hymenal colposcopic examination in sexual offenses. *American Journal of Forensic Medical Pathology*, 2, 209-214.

White, S. T., & Ingram, D. L. (1989). Vaginal introital diameter in the evaluation of sexual abuse. *Child Abuse and Neglect*, *13*, 217-224.

Whittington, B. A., Rice, R. J., Biddle, J. W., & Knapp, J. S. (1988). Incorrect identification of Neisseria gonorrheae from infants and children. *Pediatric Infectious Diseases*, *7*, 3-10.

Woodling, B., & Kossoris, P. (1981). Sexual abuse: Rape, molestation and incest. *Pediatric Clinics of North America*, *28*, 481-499.

Woodling, B. A., & Heger, A. (1986). The use of the colposcope in the diagnosis of sexual abuse in the pediatric age group. *Child Abuse and Neglect*, *10*, 111-114.

False and Unsubstantiated Sexual Abuse Allegations: Clinical Issues

Kathleen May Quinn

ABSTRACT. Since the "discovery" of sexual abuse in the late 1970s there has been a steady rise of sexual abuse allegations. The rate of false positives in sexual abuse allegations has been estimated to be 2-8%. More than 65% of all current reports of suspected child maltreatment (physical and sexual) are assessed to be unsubstantiated. This paper discusses the clinical, cultural, and legal causes and presentations of false positive, false negative, and unsubstantiated allegations of sexual abuse.

The "discovery" of sexual abuse by both professionals and the public has resulted in increased knowledge of its natural history, techniques of investigation and treatment as well as prevention. However, as in physical abuse there are competing trends of over and under reporting of sexual abuse and large numbers of unsubstantiated cases (Besharov, 1985). For example, sixty five percent of all reports of child maltreatment (both physical and sexual) have been reported to be "unfounded," that is unsubstantiated (National Center on Child Abuse and Neglect, 1978). An urban county Department of Human Services recently reported 21-47% of all sexual abuse complaints as "unsubstantiated" (Galloway, Haverick, & Hall-Ellis, 1986). It is imperative to distinguish a false or "fictitious" sexual abuse allegation from an allegation which is unsubstantiated (Jones & McGraw, 1987). Corwin, Berliner, Goodman, Goodwin, and White

---

Kathleen May Quinn is affiliated with the Department of Psychiatry, Case Western Reserve University School of Medicine, Cleveland, OH 44106. Reprint requests should be sent to Cleveland Metro Health Center, 3395 Scranton Road, Cleveland, OH 44109. An earlier version of this paper was read at the 1986 meeting of the American Academy of Child Psychiatry, Los Angeles.

145

(1987) define an unsubstantiated case as one which the investigator cannot be confident of the allegation due to insufficient or inconsistent evidence. Such a finding does not necessarily mean that the allegation is false. The very nature of sexual abuse, especially in the young child, consisting of fondling, late disclosures and frequent recantations, contributes to the pool of unsubstantiated cases. This paper discusses the historical, societal, legal and psychological reasons which contribute to these trends of under- and over-reporting, to false negative and false positive cases, as well as to the large numbers of unsubstantiated cases.

ASSESSING SEXUAL ABUSE COMPLAINTS

Evaluations of sexual abuse allegations require meticulous investigation and analysis of the data gathered (Sgroi, 1982; Mrazek, 1981; White, Santilli, & Quinn, 1988), knowledge of the development of memory, and current data on children's vulnerability to suggestion (Goodman, 1984; King & Yuille, 1987). Included in the differential diagnosis of each allegation should be consideration of factors within the child, the person bringing the complaint, the family or the professional systems which may lead to false positive or false negative conclusions concerning the allegation. A false positive assessment of a complaint may needlessly sever family relationships and ruin reputations; a false negative may cause the child and others to be reexposed to victimization.

Estimates of false positive allegations range from 2-8% (Cantwell, 1981; Goodwin, Sahd, & Rada, 1978; Horwitz, Salt, Gomes-Schwartz, & Sanzia, 1984; Jones, 1987) in reported populations drawn from social service departments or voluntary general hospital based programs. Recently several authors have described small samples of false positive allegations arising in disputes over custody and visitation ranging from 36-75% of such referrals (Green, 1986; Benedek & Schetky, 1985; Brant & Sink, 1984). More recent work suggests that the rate of false positive sex abuse allegations in domestic relations cases is 20-22% (Pearson, 1986; Jones & Seig, 1988). Although large numbers of reported abuse (physical and sexual) are subsequently classified as "unsubstantiated," multiple factors including low standards for mandatory reporting (Besharov, 1985), inadequate investigations as well as false negative allegations appear to contribute to the "unsubstantiated" complaints.

ALLEGATIONS IN THE APPARENT ABSENCE OF ABUSE

The Overanxious Child/Overanxious Parent

A child with multiple fears may make statements which initially suggest some form of abuse. Careful reconstruction of a child's history may make an actual diagnosis possible such as Overanxious Disorder, Separation Anxiety Disorder or Avoidant Disorder (American Psychiatric Association, 1987). These anxiety disorders of childhood may be manifested by longstanding unrealistic worries, intolerance of separations, nightmares involving themes of separation, and avoidant behaviors which may be misinterpreted as behavioral indicators of abuse. Such children are particularly stressed by actual marital separations and multiple transitions from household to household during visitations and may present as one example of the false allegations arising in custody and visitation disputes.

Other children who have not been previously symptomatic may regress at the time of marital discord and separation presenting as anxious and oppositional at the time of scheduled access to a noncustodial parent (Chase, 1983; Berkman, 1984). MacFarlane describes, "it is . . . common to see a situation where a mother has overreacted to something that a child has said or done, or has read meaning into something that a less impassioned observer might not. This may represent a type of heightened vigilance that comes from the fear of sharing a child with or allowing the child to stay with a man who, for whatever reasons, she has decided not to live with any more. It may stem from her personal knowledge of her ex-husband's sexual practices or abuses of power with her, or it may possibly stem from her own memories of molestation as a child" (MacFarlane, 1986, p. 127). The interplay between the child's and custodial parent's fears may result in increasing symptoms in the child and/or interpretation of the noncustodial parent's actions as abusive. The resulting allegation is not the result of intentional deceit but is instead an example of overreaction and misperception in which both custodial parent and the child develop a shared belief that abuse has occurred and/or could occur during contact with the other parent (Sink, 1988).

Careful assessment may also elicit parenting practices which heighten such a child's anxiety although such acts would not generally be considered "abusive." For example, one clearly overanxious child with a long history of preoccupation with illness, injury, functional somatic complaints and inability to relax and unrealistic worry stated her father "tickled her in the wrong places." Investigation documented the chronic symptoms noted above long before her parents' separation. The father, a jovial, physically affectionate male, acknowledged that he enjoyed "roughhousing" with all his children but has been unaware of the distress it caused his youngest daughter. Both parents endorsed each other's positive and responsible parenting. A meeting between this daughter and her father included both a confrontation concerning her distress and guidelines for their ongoing visits which included no tickling. The girl requested to always go with siblings and her father concurred. Visitation proceeded without incident or new allegations on a one year follow-up.

Changing Family Dynamics

Alterations in family practices concerning privacy, nudity, toileting or bathing, or changes in perceptions of these practices in separating or divorcing families may also result in a false allegation of abuse. For example, a family practice of parents sleeping with children previously tolerated by a child or parent may begin to be experienced and/or interpreted as overstimulating or abusive after a parental separation.

Other patterns which may generate a false allegation include a noncustodial parent assuming parenting tasks previously done by the same sex parent to the discomfort of the child. In addition, a noncustodial parent may fail to appreciate a child's growing modesty and independence concerning personal hygiene. A careful psychosocial history of a family before and after a parental separation may permit the correct diagnosis of the influence of these family forces. The allegation often arises due to the concerns of an overanxious child or custodial parent as described above. Parental guidance interventions by mental health personnel may sufficiently address practices assessed to be overstimulating but not abusive.

Malingering

Malingering is the intentional production of false or grossly exaggerated physical or psychological symptoms in pursuit of a recognizable goal (American Psychiatric Association, 1987). An allegation of sexual abuse could be pursued to seek goals such as alternate placement or conscious pursuit of custody. Goodwin, Sahd, and Rada (1978) described adolescents who readily acknowledged that they had lied in order to leave a conflicted but nonabusive setting. Older latency age children and adolescents are most likely to pursue a malingered sex abuse complaint. Workers in the area of domestic relations have recently described cases which they have assessed to be examples of such conscious deception in parents fighting for custody of minor children (Benedek & Schetky, 1985; Mac-

Farlane, 1986; Green, 1986; Gardner, 1986). The children in such cases may appear "coached" or may give little in the way of a spontaneous allegation. MacFarlane (1986) describes such complaints as having several common characteristics such as lack of detail, use of adult language, lack of authenticity, and repetitiveness. Gardner (1987) has published the Sex Abuse Legitimacy Scale as an assessment tool. Jones and McGraw (1987) includes a lack of accompanying emotion to the allegation as another possible indicator of a fictitious allegation. There are, however, no indicators of false allegations of sexual abuse of children which have been research validated. Indeed, several of these indicators may have alternate explanations. For example, a seriously traumatized child may experience emotional numbing due to a post-traumatic stress disorder. A very young child may have limited language skills resulting in a lack of detail and a repetitive account.

A history of escalating allegations by the custodial parent against the noncustodial parent, chronic visitation restrictions, a late arising sexual abuse complaint, evidence of brainwashing and the absence of substantiating factors may be consistent with either a conscious or unconscious endorsement of a false allegation.

Copycat Phenomena

Large scale investigations of mass disclosures, "rap" groups, educational programs for prevention of abuse and wide media coverage of the topic have benefitted many children but appear to have also added to unsubstantiated and/or false positive allegations of abuse. For example investigations of a residential school for children and developmental centers for the retarded yielded many actual cases of abuse resulting in criminal convictions. However, investigators noted a trend that late arising complaints were more likely to be unsubstantiated even after vigorous investigation. Many school based educational programs and rap groups have been flooded with children stepping forward with allegations. Anecdotally, many teachers have been concerned that the groups in their pursuit of "self-disclosure" may generate false complaints.

Little is known of the psychology of the "copycat" phenomena. The best studied examples are of product tampering. Underlying causes of these events have included mass hysteria (Wood, 1983), imitation, hoax (Spiro, 1982), and profit (*New York Times*, 1986). Only the true imitator is classified as a copy cat hypothesized to be in pursuit of attention, fame, or excitement (Rappeport, 1982). Further study is needed to determine the relationship of these causes to false allegations of sexual abuse.

Overinterpretation of Bodily Curiosity and Knowledge

There is little formal clinical research on the development of children's concepts of sexuality. Many early writers including Kraft-Ebing and Freud described the early appearance of masturbation in development. Masturbatory fantasies of young girls are described as often including imagining themselves floating, dancing, or flying. The child may imagine themselves alone or admired or envied by onlookers (Clower, 1975). Oedipal fantasies have a diffuse romantic quality. A modern study based on questioning preschool teachers also elicited the finding that children showed a marked interest in their own genitals as noted by fondling and showing them to others. Both sexes were more interested in male genitalia. What sexual questions were posed to teachers by the children concerned primarily pregnancy and birth (Gunderson, Melas, & Skar, 1981). However, normal, unabused oedipal age (3-6) children may beg to see their mother's genitals or breasts or pursue a parent in the bathroom showering or toileting (Solnit, Call, & Feinstein, 1979). These behaviors may be misinterpreted as evidence of abuse especially in divorced or separated families. Questions such as "where did you learn that?" or "did —— put that in your head?" are likely to yield a facesaving reply by the child which may fuel an allegation. During investigatory interviewing the oedipally involved child may play out bedroom or bathroom scenes but is unlikely to show explicit sexual acts such as penetration of orifices (Yates & Musty, 1988).

Studies by Kreitler and Kreitler (1966) and Bernstein and Cowan (1975) reviewing children's development of concepts concerning conception and birth demonstrate a vagueness in the children's theories of social and physical sexual causality extending to late latency. These studies predate the trends in some families to educate using anatomically correct terms and functions, exposure to explicit media and literature materials and family practices promoting nudity and decreased privacy. These studies and current social trends demand that the assessment of a sexual abuse complaint fully explore the family's use of terminology for body parts, their attitudes and practices concerning nudity and privacy, the details of their daily living routines such as bathing, toileting and sleeping practices.

Psychopathology in Child and/or Parent

Benedek and Schetky (1985) and Green (1986) describe false allegations of sexual abuse arising in cases in which there are prominent paranoid and histrionic traits in caretakers. Clinically, investigation of such cases should include documentation of overt delusions, severe character pathology or oversexualization of multiple social interactions to support such a conclusion. Rarely, a child and caretaker will mutually share a bizarre implausible belief concerning the alleged perpetrator consistent with a folie à deux. Kaplan and Kaplan (1981) have described such a case in which a custodial parent originated a sexual abuse allegation. In paranoid family systems such beliefs may extend to all living generations. In other families the child may mouth the accusation with little explicit detail or age-inappropriate language. Some children may say they "know" or "remember" that the alleged acts took place. However, on careful gentle probing it becomes apparent that they have no independent memory of any events. Such children may give parrot-like, unvarying statements or may give vastly different and inconsistent allegations in investigatory interviews separate from the complaining parent. In many such cases new accusations will continue to be brought forward which are absurd. One 8 year old child, for example, stated her father completely undressed while she was left alone with him for several minutes in an evaluator's office while the door was open and co-workers were directly across the hall.

Jones and McGraw (1987) have recently described false allegations brought forth by either children or adults who were previously abused. These complaints described explicit sexual abuse based on their previous abuse but falsely attributed the abuse to a new "perpetrator." An unresolved post traumatic stress disorder was hypothesized to generate the new false complaint.

Actual Abuse/Wrong Perpetrator

Katan (1973) described several children in analysis who initially attributed sexual abuse to the wrong person – their fathers. More frequently, a child will accuse someone falsely when the actual perpetrator is a father, stepfather, or person in a parental role. Such false allegations are fueled by oedipal or preoedipal fantasies as in Katan's cases (rarely), or more commonly by loyalty issues or fear, or may result from improper or inadequate investigation of an allegation.

Medical Conditions Mistaken for Sexual Abuse

Physicians working in the area of physical abuse have long described conditions such as osteogenesis imperfecta, bleeding disorders, syphilis, scurvy, and congenital marks such as Mongolian spots which may be mistaken for physical abuse. Certain physical conditions may be mistaken for sexual abuse. These may include infections such as pinworm or monilia, congenital abnormalities such as hemangiomas and unusual injuries such as a bite by a wild dog (Geil & Goodwin, 1982). Other conditions such as colitis may cause rectal bleeding misinterpreted by family members as secondary to abuse. Conditions such as encopresis or enuresis which may be associated with some cases of abuse are ambiguous as behavioral indicators of abuse. Instrumentation of a nonverbal or retarded child may cause a child to perform traumatic play which may appear to be secondary to abuse but is not. Procedures such as cystoscopy, colonoscopy, enemas, rectal temperatures, or other penetrating procedures may seriously confound data which can be gathered from such children during an abuse investigation.

Contamination/Cross-Germination of Interview Data

Within the past several years workers in the area of sexual abuse have increasingly become aware of the issue of both external and internal contamination of interview material from children who have been sexually abused. A case which highlights this issue was the Scott County Case in Minnesota. When all the facts became public, the case became a prototype of what can occur with repeated questioning, lack of documentation and cross-germination of allegations between child witnesses. For example, in the Attorney General's report on the matter, it was noted some children were interviewed over 30 times by up to 10 interviewers. The lack of documentation was seen as hampering the assessment of consistency in the allegations. The practice of telling one child what another child had said was also questioned in the Attorney General's report. "In these cases the problem of cross germination exacerbated the severe credibility problems already created by excessive interviewing of the children and the absence of reports to document the allegations made by the children" (Humphrey, 1984).

Review of the Jordan case by Attorney General Humphrey also gives an example of apparent contamination of an allegation by fantasy. The first child in the case to mention homicides (which were never confirmed) was a 12 year old who had experienced sexual abuse over an extended period of time by a convicted sexual offender. After multiple interviews (approximately 23) she began to describe killings including the murder of an infant who was first sadistically sexually abused. In subsequent interviews by state and federal officials, she vividly described very different homicides including the use of different weapons. She was described as "at ease" and "extremely talkative" as she described the homicides. This case may be an example of what Jones and McGraw (1987) has described as possible clues to fabrication—the absence of emotion, especially in children who have previously been abused and are suffering from an unresolved post-traumatic stress disorder from past abuse.

Stern (1939) came to believe that although the mixing of fantasy and reality occurs in some cases (internal contamination), the falsification of testimony is most likely the result of questioning. As early as 1910 he advocated for specially trained interviewers and only one interview shortly after the incident which did not contain leading questions. Israel and other European countries have adopted these suggestions. Today, in some agencies, due to the backlash of Scott County, again only one investigatory interview is being performed to validate a complaint of sexual abuse. Unfortunately the pendulum has swung too far. A minimum of two and a maximum of three investigatory interviews are recommended to assist in assessing consistency of the report.

Structured protocols (Boat & Everson, 1986; Friedman & Morgan, 1985; White, Strom, Santilli, & Halpin, 1987) and meticulous documentation of the process of investigatory interviews will aid in the prevention of contamination. Difficult cases will continue to arise in the cases of allegations by very disturbed individuals whose allegations may be susceptible to internal contamination due to fantasy. A classic example of this occurred in the case of Breuer's patient Anna O, who on the day of her termination of treatment went into "false labor" to deliver her therapist's imaginary child (Jones, 1953). An eroticized or psychotic transference may produce such an allegation. Today, complex allegations may occur on inpatient or residential units which can not be substantiated. Often the individual bringing the allegation has been abused in the past. The aim of any investigation is to attempt to distinguish a second, new allegation from fantasy material and memories of past abuse.

UNDERDIAGNOSIS OF CHILD ABUSE

Allegations may be dismissed which eventually are confirmed to have been real. This may occur because a child cannot or will not talk and no corroborating evidence exists. Certain professionals may not understand the natural history of abuse which includes frequent late disclosures of long-term relationships (Summit, 1983) and false retractions during the suppression phase (Sgroi, 1982). Such individuals may disbelieve children instead of recognizing these features of disclosures as often typical of abuse. Other professionals may simply choose not to report a sexual abuse allegation. A 1978 study found that only 42% of physicians polled would report all cases of sexual abuse despite mandatory reporting laws (James, Womack, & Strauss, 1978). These doctors claimed they were concerned that reporting would be "harmful" to the family or that cases would be poorly handled by the mandated investigating agency. Other cases are not substantiated due to a failure to fully investigate. For example, a notation on a medical chart was found on document review which noted a vaginal discharge and irritation in a 7 year old. A complete set of cultures and introital opening measurements had not been made and no follow-up had been arranged.

Prejudice of professionals including mental health professionals, jurors, judiciary and/or investigators may cause children making credible allegations to not be believed. The study by Yarmey and Jones (1983), for example, showed that 69% of potential citizen jurors felt a child could not provide accurate testimony. There is a danger that in certain sites such as domestic relations cases that triers of facts and attorneys will simply dismiss a parent raising a concern of sexual abuse rather than listening to all the data due to the spate of sexual abuse allegations in the Court.

Problems of case management may also result in a false negative outcome. Poor preparation of a child witness or overpreparation of another may cause the resulting testimony to appear unauthentic. A choice taking a case into criminal court rather than juvenile court may result in an acquittal due to the high standard of beyond a reasonable doubt in criminal court.

Finally, a child who has embellished a true story of abuse may be discredited with the charge of contamination. Often previously abused or disturbed, these children are best served by having the full content, context, and chronology of their initial disclosure well documented. This documentation and testimony of initial examiners permits a careful review of their allegation.

CONCLUSION

As the study of sexual abuse becomes more sophisticated we are increasingly aware of clinical presentations which may lead to either false positive, false negative and unsubstantiated sexual abuse allegations. It is imperative that field workers become aware of this growing body of data. At the validation stage of each sexual abuse allegation the possibility of a false positive or negative allegation should be considered. Attention to careful planning of the investigatory process, separation of the roles of investigator and therapist, emphasis on the context and chronology of allegations, careful evaluation of the thoroughness of previous evaluators and attention to maintaining objectivity will assist in correctly diagnosing these cases.

REFERENCES

American Association for Protecting Children, Inc. (1986). *Highlights of official child neglect and abuse reporting, 1984*. Denver, CO: American Humane Association.

American Psychiatric Association. (1987). *Diagnostic and statistical manual of mental disorders*, (3rd Ed), Revised. Washington, D.C.: American Psychiatric Association.

Benedek, E.P., & Schetky, D. (1985). Allegations of sexual abuse in child custody and visitation disputes. In D.H. Schetky & E.P. Benedek (Eds.), *Emerging issues in child psychiatry and law*. New York: Bruner-Mazel.

Berkman, C.F. (1984). Psychodynamic and family issues in post-divorce child custody litigation. *Journal of the American Academy of Child and Adolescent Psychiatry, 23*, 708-712.

Bernstein, A.C., & Cowan, P.A. (1975). Children's concepts of how people get babies. *Child Development, 46*, 77-91.

Besharov, D.J. (1985). Doing something about child abuse: The need to narrow the grounds for state intervention. *Harvard Journal of Law and Public Policy, 8*, 539-589.

Boat, B., & Everson, M. (1986). *Using anatomical dolls: Guidelines for interviewing young children in sexual abuse investigations*. Chapel Hill: University of North Carolina.

Brant, R., & Sink, F. (1984). *Dilemmas in court-ordered evaluation of sexual abuse charges during custody and visitation proceedings*. Paper presented at the 31st annual meeting of the American Academy of Child Psychiatry, Toronto, Canada.

Cantwell, H. (1981). Sexual abuse of children in Denver, 1979: Reviewed with implications for pediatric interventions and possible prevention. *Child Abuse and Neglect, 5*, 75-85.

Chase, G.A. (1983). Previsitation anxiety, postvisitation depression, visitation phobia: Visitation conflicts: Preludes to child custody contests. *Conciliation Courts Review, 21*, 81-86.

Clower, V.L. (1975). Significance of masturbation in female sexual development and function. In I.M. Marcus & J.J. Francis (Eds.), *Masturbation: From infancy to senescence*. New York: International Universities Press.

Corwin, D., Berliner, L., Goodman, G., Goodwin, J., & White, S. (1987). Allegations of child sexual abuse in custody disputes — no easy answers. *Journal of Interpersonal Violence, 2*, 91-105.

Finkelhor, D. (1984). *Child sexual abuse: New theory and research*. New York: The Free Press

Friedeman, V., & Morgan, M. (1985). *Interviewing sexual abuse victims using anatomical dolls: The professional's guidebook*. Eugene, OR: Shamrock.

Galloway, B., Haverick, J., & Hall-Ellis, M. (1986). *Sexual abuse monitoring*. Unpublished document, Cuyahoga County (Ohio) Department of Human Services.

Gardner, R.A. (1986). *Child custody litigation: A guide for parents and mental health professionals*. New Jersey: Creative Therapeutics.

Gardner, R.A. (1987). *The parental alienation syndrome and the differentiation between fabricated and genuine child sex abuse*. New Jersey: Creative Therapeutics.

Geil, C., & Goodwin, J. (1982). Physical conditions that may be mistaken for sexual abuse. In J. Goodwin (Ed.), *Sexual abuse: Incest victims and their families*. Boston: John Wright.

Goodman, G.S. (1984). The child witness: Conclusions and future directions for research and legal practice. *Journal of Social Issues, 40*(2), 157-175.

Goodwin, J., Sahd, D., & Rada, R. (1978). Incest hoax: False accusations, false denials. *Bulletin of the American Academy of Psychiatry and the Law, 6*(3), 269-276.

Green, A. (1986). True and false allegations of sexual abuse in child custody disputes. *Journal of the American Academy of Child Psychiatry, 25*(4), 449-456.

Gunderson, B.H., Melas, P.S., & Skar, J.E. (1981). Sexual behavior of preschool children: Teacher's observation. In L.L. Constantine & F.M. Martinson (Eds.), *Children and sex: New findings, new perspectives*. Boston: Little Brown.

Horwitz, J., Salt, P., Gomes-Schwartz, Z., & Sanzia, M. (1984). *Unconfirmed cases of sexual abuse*. Unpublished document, Tufts-New England Medical Center, Division of Child Psychiatry, Boston.

Humphrey, H.H. (1984). *Report on Scott County investigations*. Unpublished document, Office of the Attorney General of Minnesota.

James, J., Womack, W.M., & Strauss, F. (1978). Physician reporting of sexual abuse of children. *Journal of American Medical Association, 240*, 1145-1146.

Jones, D., & McGraw. (1987). Reliable and fictitious accounts of sexual abuse to children. *Journal of Interpersonal Violence, 2*, 27-45.

Jones, D., & Seig, A. (1988). Child sexual abuse allegations in custody or visitation cases: A report of 20 cases. In E.B. Nicholson (Ed.), *Sex abuse allegations in custody and visitation cases*. Washington, D.C.: American Bar Association.

Jones, E. (1953). *The life and work of Sigmund Freud, Vol. 1*. New York: Basic Books.

Kaplan, S., & Kaplan, S. (1981). The child's accusation of sexual abuse during a divorce and custody struggle. *Hillside Journal of Clinical Psychiatry, 3*, 81-95.

Katan, A. (1973). Children who were raped. *The Psychoanalytic Study of the Child, 28*, 208-224.

King, M., & Yuille, J.C. (1987). Suggestibility and the child witness. In S.J. Ceci, M.P. Toglia, & D.F. Ross (Eds.), *Children's eyewitness memory*. New York: Springer-Verlag.

Kreitler, H., & Kreitler, S. (1966). Children's concepts of sexuality and birth. *Child Development, 37*, 363-378.

MacFarlane, K. (1986). Child sexual abuse allegations in divorce proceedings. In K. MacFarlane & L. Waterman (Eds.), *Sexual abuse of young children*. New York: The Guilford Press.

Mrazek, D.A. (1981). The child psychiatric examination of the sexually abused child. In P.B. Mrazek & C.H. Kempe (Eds.), *Sexually abused children and their families*. New York: Pergamon.

National Center on Child Abuse and Neglect (1978). *Child sexual abuse: Incest, assault and sexual exploitation*. DHHS Pub. OHDS 79-30166.

_____. 1986. Plea of guilty in drug-tampering. (1986, August). *New York Times*, p. 10.

Pearson, J. (1986). *Sexual abuse allegations project*. Association of Family and Conciliation Courts, Research Unit, Denver, CO.

Rappeport, J.R. (1982, October 29). We can blame media in copycat poisonings. *USA Today*, p. 8A.

Sgroi, S. (1982). *Handbook of clinical intervention in child sexual abuse*. Lexington, Massachusetts: Lexington Books.

Sink, F. (1988). Studies of true and false allegations: A critical review. In E.B. Nicholson (Ed.), *Sex abuse allegations in custody and visitation cases*. Washington, D.C.: American Bar Association.

Solnit, A.J., Call, J.D., & Feinstein, C.B. (1979). Psychosexual development: Five to ten years. In J.E. Noshpitz (Ed.), *Basic handbook of child psychiatry*. New York: Basic Books.

Spiro, P. (1982, December 6). Chaos by the capsule. *New Republic*, pp. 10-11.

Summit, R. (1983). The child sexual abuse accomodation syndrome. *Child Abuse and Neglect, 7*, 177-193.

White, S., Santilli, G., & Quinn, K. (1988). The role of evaluators in child sexual abuse cases. In E.B. Nicholson (Ed.), *Sex abuse allegations in custody and visitation cases*. Washington, D.C.: American Bar Association.

White, S., Strom, G.A., Santilli, G., & Halpin, B.M. (1986). Interviewing young sexual abuse victims with anatomically correct dolls. *Child Abuse and Neglect, 10*, 510-519.

White, S., Strom, G.A., Santilli, G., & Halpin, B.M. (1987). *Clinical guidelines for interviewing young children with anatomically correct dolls*. Unpublished manuscript, Case Western Reserve University School of Medicine, Cleveland, OH.

Wood, A.P. (1983). Psychological impact of the Tylenol scare. *Clinical Psychiatry News, 11*, 3.

Yarmey, A.D., & Jones, A.P.T. (1983). Is eyewitness testimony a matter of common sense? In S. Lloyd-Costock & B. R. Clifford (Eds.), *Witness evidence: Critical and empirical papers*. New York: John Wiley.

Yates, A., & Musty, T. (1988). Preschool children's erroneous allegations of sexual molestation. *American Journal of Psychiatry, 145*(8), 989-992.

SEXUAL ABUSE ALLEGATIONS IN CUSTODY/VISITATION DISPUTES

Multiple Perspectives:
Factors Related to Differential Diagnosis
of Sex Abuse and Divorce Trauma
in Children Under Six

A. Margaret Eastman
Thomas J. Moran

ABSTRACT. This paper will review research related to how children and their parents adjust to divorce and to sexual abuse, will establish criteria for assessment, and propose standards for decision-making. This paper will also set forth a framework for assessing cases involving allegations of abuse in divorce/custody conflicts that will hopefully reduce unnecessary conflict and trauma that often accompanies these disputes.

In recent years, there have been increases both in the rates of divorce (Hetherington, 1979) and in the reporting of child sexual abuse (Finkelhor, 1984). Research reveals that children are much more likely to be affected

A. Margaret Eastman and Thomas J. Moran are affiliated with the Children's Program, P.C., The Water Tower at John's Landing, 5331 S.W. Macadam Avenue, Suite 210, Portland, OR 97201.

159

emotionally by divorce when it occurs between the ages of two to five years (Wallerstein, 1984). Ironically, children between two and five years are also at highest risk to be molested (Finkelhor, 1984). Children at this vulnerable age react to each of these major stressors with a variety of often overlapping symptoms: anxieties, sleep disorders, toileting problems, sexualized behaviors, and regressive tendencies. Deciding whether the symptoms are linked to divorce trauma or to sexual abuse becomes extremely difficult and can be influenced by the observer's perspective. Parents and professionals need to work together to manage the stress, or otherwise, they can foster a climate of blame, mistrust, and paranoia which fuels conflict and prevents resolution. The child then becomes a prize, a symbol of victory and righteousness, to warring camps of parents and professionals.

A MODEL FOR INTERVENTION

The relatively independent fields of divorce and sexual abuse have undergone many conceptual changes during the past two decades. Moving away from theory and case examples, the empirical efforts of many investigators have discovered a host of discriminators and correlates of divorce and abuse. Missing, however, from the majority of these contributions is a general model which is able to account for the considerable variation surrounding these types of trauma. Our proposed model is offered in an effort to consolidate the existing theory and research.

The model emphasizes individual, developmental, and family systems approaches to assessing a child's reaction to divorce and/or sexual abuse. It places particular emphasis on the preexisting functioning of the child. For example, children who exhibited less mature, "protective mechanisms" before divorce or abuse show a slower rate and poorer quality of resolution. This model is an extension of a growing body of research that has found that events (e.g., unexplained absence of a parent) and interactions surrounding the actual divorce or sex abuse similarly affect the adjustment process. Additionally, the model sees the parents' individual functioning, the nature of the couple's interaction, and the quality of the parent-child relationship as critical contributing factors. The model defines the resolution phase as the period of time during which individual family members are able to reconcile issues and accept each other again. Obviously, there is no guarantee resolution can be obtained, or that it may be accomplished within a predictable length of time. This model acknowledges what many investigators (e.g., Hetherington, Cox, & Cox, 1982) of the longitudinal effects of these traumatic experiences have uncovered, that adjustment reactions change significantly over time.

CHILD FUNCTIONING

That developmental and personality factors play a key role in a child's adjustment to situations involving divorce and sexual abuse is only now becoming well understood. A child's emotional and behavioral response to either event is associated with his/her previous personal adjustment and developmental level of functioning. This section of the paper will bring into focus the principal literature which has evaluated the developmental consequences of divorce and sexual abuse for children. The discussion will suggest a bridge between these fields of study and offer a more systematic basis from which to evaluate children's adjustment reaction within a unified developmental perspective.

Developmental Impact of Divorce on Children Under Six

Previous investigations on divorce have discovered a number of variables influencing the speed with which a child recovers from the stress of loss and change. Young children under six are often preoccupied with being abandoned and are thus highly susceptible to the emergence of fears, particularly separation anxiety. For them, regression in sleep and toileting are normal reactions to the stress of divorce. Researchers have found that children experience symptoms of anxiety and depression, including psychosomatic complaints as part of a "natural" course of post-divorce adjustment reaction (Hetherington, 1979; Waldron, Ching & Fair, 1986; Wallerstein & Kelly, 1980a). In their study of 200 families in Hawaii, Waldron, Ching, and Fair (1986) found that almost one-third of children studied met the clinical definition of depression both at separation and at divorce. An additional 30 percent of the children reacted with anger, while another 10 percent of preschoolers showed marked signs of regression.

Wallerstein and Kelly (1980a) and Hetherington, Cox, and Cox (1982) in their longitudinal research on children's adjustment to divorce, discovered that the age of the child, the ability of the parents to put the child's needs first, the level of parental conflict, the nature of visitation, and the continuity of the child's relationship with the noncustodial parent were all crucial predictors of the child's long-range adjustment to divorce. Stolberg, Camplair, Curruer, and Wells (1987) found similar results and also discovered that children were most affected by familial variables such as marital hostility, parenting skills, and parental emotional adjustment.

Emery (1982) and Rutter (1980) have further clarified the degree to which marital discord, its persistence past the divorce, and its intensity are related to the adjustment of the child. How parents model the handling of anger and aggression, combined with their overall parenting styles is significant to the child's well being (Patterson, 1982). Behavior problems involving aggressive actions are more common among boys, and somatic complaints are more common among girls. However, Rutter (1980) discovered that children who moved from a home characterized by discord and stress to one more harmonious displayed marked reductions in their emotional disturbance.

Children exposed to extended parental conflict and/or a noninvolved father also slip academically (Guidubaldi & Perry, 1984). Though these children realign themselves and may eventually recover lost ground, the process is frequently long and painful. Hetherington, Cox, and Cox (1982) found that intellectual functioning during the initial adjustment after divorce was significantly related to paternal availability, paternal warmth, maternal and paternal control, family disorganization, exposure to conflict, and total time spent with adults. At two years post-divorce, the influence of the father's role greatly diminishes. Then the strongest predictors of academic achievement and divorce adjustment are the amount of time a child spends with adults and maternal warmth. In later years, however, paternal availability and warmth again become more strongly associated with intellectual functioning for boys.

Unfortunately, sufficient paternal access may not be adequately structured. In 90 percent of the cases of divorce involving children, custody was not contested and the children lived with their mothers. Of the remaining cases that required court decisions, custody was awarded to the mother 95 percent of the time (Koch & Lowery, 1984). The traditional pattern of every-other-weekend visitation may compound the stress for children under five. Twelve days between contacts may fuel fears of abandonment and undermine attachments for children who cannot internalize memories of a distant parent (Kelly, 1988). Further, children under three may be unable to leave a primary caretaker even for two to three days of visitation without undue separation anxiety. Strong opposition to this belief, however, has been presented. Jacobs (1986), for example, contends that children, particularly young children, are more adversely affected if parental visitation is limited. Koch and Lowery (1984) found that, whereas the amount of contact between a child and his/her noncustodial parent was related to the quality of the spousal relationship, the frequency of contact was associated with the proximity of home environments. Additionally, the positive quality of the father-child relationship was predicted by a more cooperative relationship between father and mother, not by the amount of contact with the father. Most importantly, they discovered that continued contact with their children by noncustodial fathers was the best predictor of positive child adjustment.

Developmental Impact of Sex Abuse on Children Under Six

Young children represent the second largest age group among child victims of sexual abuse (Summit, 1987). Finkelhor's (1984) data indicate that one-, two-, and three-year-olds, along with eight- to 12-year-olds, are most at risk to be sexually abused. His research also challenges another myth: that all allegations of sexual abuse surrounding children of divorce are false. His study indicated that one of the factors for putting children at highest risk to be abused is divorce. Interestingly, the other risk factors associated with sexual abuse — presence of a stepfather, maternal emotional unavailability, reduced physical affection from father, and low income — are often found in divorce situations.

Wolfe and Wolfe (1987) have classified the most common behavioral reactions seen in child sexual abuse victims. They categorize under-controlled behaviors, over-controlled behaviors, sexual behaviors, and physical complaints. Under-controlled behaviors may best be seen as externalized, acting-out behaviors like aggression, running away, and declining school performance. Fears, anxiety, social withdrawal, sadness, and depression are classified as over-controlled behaviors. Precocious or inappropriate sexual behavior, sexual language, and fear of touching or being touched are the most common sexual behaviors found in sexually abused children.

In their review of the literature, Lusk and Waterman (1986) arrived at similar and additional categories. They observed that the affective consequences of sexual abuse in children frequently includes guilt, anxiety and depression. The overt behavior problems were characterized by hostile-aggressive types of behaviors, regression, and social withdrawal. Excessive masturbation and developmentally atypical sexual knowledge and behaviors were also common in these children.

Interestingly, investigators of the consequences of sexual abuse have paid little attention to cognitive or intellectual impairment. The few studies that are available report that children who have been sexually abused are more likely to experience deficits in attention and concentration (Mac-Farlane & Waterman, 1986).

MacFarlane and Waterman (1986) underscore many of the difficulties in the assessment of and intervention with young abuse victims. They note that attempts to assess children with limited language who are eager to please adults can produce contaminated reports of abuse. For instance, leading questions by well-meaning adults ("Did your daddy . . ."; "Was he mean to you?") can plant information and underscore anxieties. Multiple interviews by parents and numerous professionals create confusion and a demand to tell something. Even children with physical evidence of abuse may shut down with all the intrusions. They seem instinctively to know that despite all the promises that "telling will make things better," something terrible will happen once the secret comes out (Summit, 1983). For children who have not been abused, such frequent questioning may create anxiety and fantasies of abuse.

ADULT FUNCTIONING

The traditional belief has been that parental adjustment and recovery from divorce or child sexual abuse occurs relatively quickly. Recently, this belief has been questioned (Wallerstein, 1984; Finkelhor, 1984; Jacobs, 1983, 1986). Such research finds that parents are typically in crisis and may experience clinical levels of depression, hostility, anxiety, and paranoia, often for a year or more. Their emotional preoccupation with the divorce, and perhaps with dating, makes them less available to parent. Visitation demands on both parents promote tension and stress; parent-parent interactions are often characterized by mistrust (Wallerstein, 1980). Investigations looking at long-term effects on parents have discovered a number of serious dysfunctions in their adjustment. Among the important considerations is the possibility of preexisting parental pathology.

Impact of Divorce on Mothers and Fathers

Johnson and Campbell in their book *The Impasses of Divorce* (1988), highlight how parent conflict about children helps parents manage intolerable feelings of loss, humiliation, and helplessness. Wallerstein and her associates (Wallerstein, 1984; Wallerstein & Kelly, 1980a, 1980b) have presented the clearest description of the adverse effects divorce has on mothers and fathers. Follow-up investigations of 60 middle-class families in the San Francisco Bay area found that approximately one-fourth of the mothers and one-fifth of the fathers were still experiencing significant life adjustment problems ten years after their divorce. Feelings of intense anger toward the former spouse persisted. Many parents lost much of the support systems that existed during the marriage, and were unable to recover or adequately redevelop new support systems. Sadness, loneliness, and sometimes, depression were major obstacles for parents. The relative degree of disruption and disorientation was significantly greater for individuals over 40 years of age, particularly women. While about half the older men remarried, not a single woman over 40 was able to find a new spouse.

Perhaps the most significant characteristic of parents struggling after a decade of divorce was the persistence of family disorganization and parenting stress. The absence of consistent structure and the energy necessary to parent results in parent-child role reversals in a number of families. It is implicitly understood that the oldest children perform an increased share of not only the physical parenting (e.g., preparation of food), but also the psychological parenting (e.g., nurturing). Children with these responsibilities are enmeshed at a level not conducive to the natural course of child development. They battle with parents for power and control. Girls may show increased anxiety, somatic complaints, and precocious sexual behaviors. Boys are more likely to react with conduct problems.

Profile of Mothers and Fathers of Sexually Abused Children

In investigating the effects of sexual abuse on children, researchers have uncovered a number of variables associated with mothers' and fathers' pre-abuse functioning. The most common profile of abusing fathers is one in which he is dominant and authoritarian (Herman & Hirschman, 1981). Alternatively, Herman and Hirschman (1981) found that mothers frequently display significant dependence and passivity and are often ineffectual. The family system in which abuse occurs often is socially isolated, possessing a restricted support network. Martial discord may be characterized by sexual disinterest in the mother (Maisch, 1973).

The fathers vary in their uses of subtle or overt coercion to involve their daughters in sexual activity. Interestingly, some investigators have found that fathers who have begun sexually abusing their daughters display relatively little affection, such as through nurturing touch (Mrazek, 1981). Mrazek has hypothesized that this may contribute to a girl's vulnerability to sexual abuse when she seeks to feel cared for and loved.

Daughters who have been sexually abused tend to engage in a complicated reversal of roles with their mothers, leaving the relationship unpredictable and frequently stressed. Herman and Hirschman (1981) reported that in their sample of abused girls, 45 percent of them assumed a range of domestic roles, including child care and cleaning. This finding was true even for preschool children.

It is common that families in which sexual abuse has taken place are quite enmeshed and view outsiders as a threat. The disengagement from the outside world often creates an insurmountable obstacle in the disclosure and treatment process for the victim.

Unique issues in divorce compound the difficulties in investigation of sexual abuse in young children. The mistrust between parents creates a climate where the divorce-related emotional symptoms the child exhibits may be exaggerated and/or blamed upon the ex-spouse. An anxious parent may go overboard to train a young child in abuse protection, creating paranoia in the child and a climate of suggestibility. New people entering the child's life as caretakers, parent partners, and "siblings" may greatly increase the opportunity for premature exposure to sexuality and/or abuse. Custodial parents who have some lingering trust and hope that their child have a normal relationship with the ex-spouse may try to deal with the child's distress by talking with the noncustodial parent. Defensiveness, mistrust, or pressures from extended family or new mates may undermine these attempts. When the child's symptoms include sexual behaviors, chaos and conflict are certainly likely to take over. In the context of these pressures and tensions, an already guilt-ridden and overwhelmed child is more likely to make false or unconvincing reports or to retract reports of abuse. The child seems instinctively to know not to overburden his/her already distressed parents.

KEY ASSESSMENT QUESTIONS

Cases which involve divorce and abuse allegations represent unique challenges for investigators and practitioners because of the frequency of ambiguous and contradictory information. The following case example provides a good example of the complexities involved in clinical assessment of families involved in divorce and abuse allegations.

Tim is a four-year-old whose father had been his primary caretaker while his mother was in medical school. Shortly after the mother launched a demanding practice, father moved into the home of his girlfriend and her seven-year-old son, Robbie. Robbie had previously been a witness to domestic violence and a victim of physical abuse by his alcoholic father. Tim admired Robbie, and the two became close. Over the first nine months of visitation between Tim and his father, there were financial conflicts between his parents. Tim became increasingly aggressive and anxious, his sleep was disturbed, and he exhibited toileting problems and became sexually provocative to children and adults. The pattern of symptom escalation correlated directly with his parents' conflicts. Nonetheless, family friends were concerned Tim had been molested. Evaluation revealed no physical evidence of abuse, but Tim made verbal reports to his pediatrician and his therapist that Robbie had played "privacy games" including oral and anal sex, which Tim guiltily admitted he enjoyed.

A long, difficult mediation process set parameters for "safe" visitation to continue between Tim, his father, and his "step" family. Just as the final court hearing to resolve the divorce was to occur, Tim returned from visitation with anal injuries. He refused to name the perpetrator or discuss the matter. His emotional status had significantly deteriorated. At this point, the angry mother suspected the father of molesting Tim, which the father denied. He displayed a marked defensiveness, and such an intense rage that he could not empathize with his son. The stage was now set for a major battle: a power struggle between parents and their experts. For Tim, the dilemma was obvious: to disclose anything about his own distress might risk a further escalation of the war. He kept quiet in hopes it would all magically disappear, but became increasingly symptomatic.

Professionals face a dilemma—how to differentiate divorce trauma from sexual abuse in a symptomatic child who cannot or will not talk. Embattled parents' perspectives become skewed by paranoia and bitterness. They are poor historians and observers of their child. Questions raised by the evaluator can have multiple and conflicting answers. For example, is the anxiety the child shows before and after visits a function of a fear of loss and further abandonment stemming from the divorce, a fear of further abuse, or a fear of escalating parental conflict? Are the nightmares and sleeping problems a normal developmental phenomenon, a stress reaction to divorce, or a sign of abuse? Is the toileting regression stress related, and, if so, to divorce? abuse? Or is it due to exposure to over-controlling parents who inadequately shield the child from their conflict? Is it related to the stress of repeated interviews by multiple "helping" professionals? Is the graphic display of sexual acts a reenactment of abuse, paranoia about abuse, a modeling of adult sexual behavior from parents "on the rebound," or a result of possibly increased sexual exposure with new "siblings," peers, or babysitters who have become important caretakers when parents are less available? Differential diagnosis is indeed difficult under these circumstances.

Clinical Protocol

What follows is a clinical guide to comprehensive assessment questions which reflect the findings of the previously reviewed research. Eventually, by establishing valid measures in each of these areas, we may arrive at a thorough data base from which to analyze these difficult cases.

Historical factors: Child-parent relationships

1. What has been the child's course of development in the social, cognitive, behavioral, physical, and emotional domains?
2. What history of psychopathology, addiction, or abuse has there been in the parents' families of origin, in the marriage, or in the parents since the divorce?
3. What patterns of attachments have existed between the parents and their own parents, between each parent and the child?
4. How were discipline and nurturing functions balanced in the parents' families and in the child's pre- and post-divorce family?

Divorce adjustment factors: Child-parent relationships

1. Who was the initiator of the divorce? What was the reaction of the non-initiator? How congruent are the couple's reasons for seeking divorce? To what extent were violence, sexual dysfunction, and/or extreme power imbalance related to the reasons for divorce?
2. To what extent have the adults managed the characteristic first year after divorce symptoms (depression, hostility, anxiety, etc.)? Have the initial stress reactions escalated into pathological conditions in either parent?
3. To what extent have the parents been able to communicate effectively surrounding the children's needs? How have they established workable parenting plans which ensure continuity of contact with each parent? To what extent has the couple's conflict escalated in ways which adversely impacts the child?
4. How has the child perceived the divorce? Has the child rebounded from the first year of stress and reoriented? Or are there underlying issues of abandonment, depression, assumption of blame, fantasies of reconciliation, projections of hostility, or skewed alliances?
5. More than one year after the divorce, has the child shown regres-

sion; emotional, developmental or academic delay; increased internalizing or externalizing symptoms; decreased problem-solving and perspective-taking abilities; or severe behavioral problems?

The crisis of abuse and disclosure

1. Prior to disclosure, has the child shown a pattern of internalized or externalized distress symptoms? Can these be correlated to exposure to a specific setting or person? Do these symptoms indicate a pattern of trauma and increased distress? Are other significant stressors (learning problems, divorce, parent pathology) not evident or insufficient to explain the degree of the child's symptomatology?
2. Do the child's symptoms have a sexual overtone: age-inappropriate sexual acting-out, precocious sexual language or knowledge, overt seductive behavior, fear of being touched?
3. Did the child make the initial disclosure? What patterns did the child display in overcoming the powerful pressures to keep the abuse silent? What consistencies were or were not evident in the child's statements? If there were retractions, what external factors may account for the child's failure to continue reporting? Were the statements characteristic of abuse patterns? Did the statements reflect fantasies or paranoia about abuse?
4. What physical evidence of abuse exists? Are the child's statements consistent with the physical symptoms of abuse? For the child with physical evidence, but no verbal report, what may be inhibiting them in reporting? What evidence of family pathology, parental conflict, external pressure, fear of retribution, or continued access to a possible perpetrator exists?
5. What is each parent's reaction to the child's reporting of abuse? Is there adequate empathy, capacity for protection action, an ability to work together in the child's behalf? Is there recognition of the stressful effect on the child of multiple interviews and "system trauma?" What opportunities have existed for abuse to occur? Are there new sitters, friends, dating partners, sibling figures that could have exposed the child to sexual activity or abuse? Who besides the "accused" divorced parent could have been involved? To what extent do both parents look at the entire spectrum of possible causes? Are one parent's accusations masking hostility and paranoia and consequently creating a fearful, alienated child?
6. What opportunities have there been for contaminated interviewing? Have parties with clear biases spoken with the child? Have leading questions been asked? Has the child been cautioned to the point of

anxiety about the risks of private part touching? When not satisfied with the results of one interview, does either parent go "professional shopping" to the detriment of the child?

Crisis resolution phase

1. To what extent can the parents put aside their individual and divorce issues to work cooperatively to help the child resolve the abuse?
2. Are parental pathologies, paranoia, and/or escalating conflicts evident? To what extent is the child affected by these? How do these interfere with the child's process of healing from the divorce and the abuse?
3. To what extent do minimization and denial persist in each parent? To what extent does projection of blame by whom on whom prevent the child's healing?
4. What degree of system involvement has occurred? Are multiple attorneys, mental health professionals, and court hearings involved? To what extent does each serve each parent's need to be angry and blame? To what extent does each serve the child's needs for protection, stability, and security?

Assessment Complexities in a Nationally Publicized Case

We had the opportunity to evaluate a nationally publicized case which illustrates the difficulty of differential diagnosis and the importance of examining multiple variables. As we looked at the development of this case, a pattern emerged of inadvertent escalation of conflict and polarized interaction among players from different perspectives. As legal/mental health involvement became more complex, well-meaning interventions inadvertently increased the trauma to the child.

History. The nature of the parents' marital relationship and the type of attachment each had with the child reveal significant data to differentiate abuse from divorce adjustment issues. The child's parents both suffered significant parental loss in their own childhoods, were "on the rebound" from dependent and adulterous first spouses, and approached the second marriage with the expectation it would meet their unfulfilled needs. Their relationship deteriorated rapidly as the pregnancy progressed. With the birth of the baby, the couple separated, and the mother turned to the baby for fulfillment. Father alternatively sought contact to help mother and child, then withdrew in frustration from conflicts with the overprotective mother. When welfare attached the father's wages for support, he claimed the right to contact and sought legal intervention.

At age two, the child was court-ordered to see her father, a virtual stranger to her. Father and daughter were to have three short visits in the company of his extended family, who would provide some measure of objective supervision and protection. Mother was worried about the possibility of abuse before father had ever seen the child.

As a developmental expert might have predicted, the child responded to "forced" separation from her mother at two years of age with significant anxiety. When visitation did occur, the mother refused to leave the father's home, and tension between the couple escalated rapidly. The child developed fears, sleep problems and emotional distress before and after the short visits. She also began masturbating.

Mother consulted with a mental health professional who frequently treated child abuse victims. The child's distress symptoms were diagnosed as suggestive of sexual abuse, although the child was not interviewed. The mother began intensive training of her two-year-old in child abuse prevention, and visitation continued. The child's anxiety increased. After four to five hours of supervised visits, the mother refused to send the child again. Protective service and mental health investigations validated the child's distress, yet could not substantiate abuse. The mother believed fiercely in her duty to protect her child from an "abusive" father and became increasingly paranoid.

Formulation. Critical examination of this case using the assessment questions suggests the diagnosis of an anxious child experiencing significant distress due to: (1) separation anxiety associated with an anxious, enmeshed attachment with mother; (2) contact with an "unknown," person (father) at a stage when significant separation anxiety is developmentally appropriate; and (3) exposure to escalating parental tensions. Her generalized regression could be viewed as indicative of abuse from one perspective and as symptomatic of parental problems from another. Gardner (1987) has recommended in such cases swift placement of the child with the other parent to prevent escalation of the "parental alienation syndrome." Some states, such as Washington (Northwest Women's Law Center, 1988), have legislated this action in hopes of diffusing the conflict and aligning the child with the falsely "accused" parent. However, this case suggests that court-imposed sanctions may not be successful, or necessarily helpful.

In this case, the mental health, protective service, and court interventions fueled a fire of conflict. The court found the mother in contempt for hiding the child, ordered her to produce the child, and jailed her for blocking visitation. A child already suffering acute maternal separation anxiety in response to having to visit an unknown father now witnessed the police taking her mother to jail. The child was taken underground before the father could be granted visitation and, at the height of media staging, reconciled with her mother over national television. Years later, the court has yet to achieve its goal of supervised visits for the father and child, and mother has become only more ardent in her charges. A martyr in her own eyes, she has been idolized on national talk shows and in women's magazines as having made the ultimate sacrifice for her child: going to jail to defy a court order.

As the child turns five, she is aligned with her mother against a frantic fantasy of the "bad" father. She makes vague and fantastic reports that he did all sorts of terrible things during the period of "supervised" visits. The child's reality is to play out mother's cause célèbre and repress her tremendous fears of abandonment. The father has become increasingly depressed and hopeless about ever having a chance to see his daughter. Rather than provide a balanced and fair level of assistance and protection, the "system" interventions have only fed the polarizations, increased the child's separation anxiety and forced her into an even more powerful alliance with the mother.

Family Number Two: Use of the Team

In this final case discussion, we will highlight the application of our assessment and propose a consolidated team of professionals to provide ongoing assessment, de-escalate conflict, reduce polarization, and help parents resolve neglected issues.

Rose and Robert's parents were married after their first year of college, their first year away from conservative, small-town families who opposed the marriage and thought their children had married too young. With the stress of graduation, moves, two abortions, two small children, and father's demanding first job, the couple did indeed grow further and further apart. Unmet needs, power struggles, and suspicions of adultery set the stage for divorce. Mother, who had been at home full-time, obtained custody, and moved in with her parents, at a distance which made it hard for father to visit frequently. Mother withheld contact, charging the father had changed. Both parents suffered depression and increased anxiety in the initial crisis year of adjustment. The children showed regression, sleep disturbance, and separation anxiety. Mother began to work, and there were three quick turnovers in child care providers due to the oldest child's (age three) excessive separation anxiety. At the same time, overnight visits began with the father.

Tension at visitation transitions was high for parents and children. Pediatric visits increased. The children returned frequently with vague bumps and bruises. Rose, who had had frequent urinary tract infections pre- and post-divorce returned with reddened labia. Her regressive symptoms increased and included nightmares, anxiety, and tantrums before and after visits. Mother aired suspicions of abuse with a pediatrician and child psychologist, who cautioned the mother against unsupervised visitation until further evaluation could be completed. The child proceeded through multiple interviews, gave no spontaneous disclosures, but began playing out the role of investigator (e.g., "was Daddy mean . . . did he hit you . . . did he touch you . . .?"). Evaluation of the father gave no indication of abuse.

In this case, a team of family members, attorneys, pediatricians, caseworkers, and psychologists was established. Their goal was to help the parents work cooperatively to establish a safe visitation plan and a healthy, ongoing relationship with each parent. Creating such a plan should both give the parents a sense of control and underscore the importance of the children's needs. The process allows parents and professionals to formulate schedules of contact, plans for monitoring of the children, strategies to ease transition times, and rules for communication; it helps the family move from the crisis of doubt to ensuring that the children's needs are met. Another benefit of such a step-by-step plan is that it allows professionals to gather ongoing assessment data. All parties are privy to assessment information and can use this for diagnostic purposes, for legal decision making, and for ongoing mediation of the family's needs.

Further evaluation of the family by the team produced a majority opinion that there was low risk of abuse and that the children were experiencing separation anxiety. The team also found that the parents' continuing depression, repressed hostility, and anxiety from the divorce were prohibiting effective communication about meeting the children's needs. This case illustrates how only one well-meaning professional "finding" of abuse can set the stage for escalating conflict over visitation and more court involvement. Even when team meetings brought the parents to the point of cooperation, extended friends and family members introduced sufficient suspicion and doubt, based on a new independent psychologist's "findings," to sabotage plans.

CONCLUSION

Our hope is that other professionals will respond to similarly challenging cases with a broad and balanced perspective and with a greater awareness of the critical roles they can play in creating either a climate for polarized conflict or a climate for productive resolution. Only by providing a team approach to resolution and by educating parents to the financial and emotional costs to themselves and to their children of protracted conflict, can we protect children and families of divorce from the shattering effects of false allegations of abuse.

REFERENCES

Emery, R. E. (1982). Interparental conflict and the children of discord and divorce. *Psychological Bulletin, 92*(2), 310-330.

Finkelhor, D. (1984). *Child sexual abuse: New theory and research.* New York: Free Press.

Gardner, R. A. (1987). *The parental alienation syndrome and the differentiation between fabricated and genuine child sexual abuse.* Creskill, N.J.: Creative Therapeutics.

Guidubaldi, J., & Perry, J. D. (1984). Divorce, socioeconomic status, and children's cognitive-social competence at school entry. *American Journal of Orthopsychiatry, 54*(3), 459-468.

Herman, J., & Hirschman, L. (1981). Families at risk for father-daughter incest. *American Journal of Psychiatry, 138,* 967-970.

Hetherington, E. M. (1979). Divorce: A child's perspective. *American Psychologist, 34*(10), 851-858.

Hetherington, E. M., Cox, M., & Cox, R. (1982). Effects of divorce on parents and children. In M. Lamb (Ed.), *Nontraditional families.* New Jersey: Lawrence-Erlbaum Associates.

Jacobs, J. W. (1984). The effects of divorce on fathers: An overview of the literature. *International Journal of Family Therapy, 6*(3), 177-191.

Johnson, J. R., & Campbell, L. G. (1988). *Impasses of divorce.* New York: Free Press.

Kelly, J. (1988). Redefining the concept of attachment in divorce. *Journal of Family Psychology, 1*(3), 329-332.

Krugman, R. D. (1987). *Identifying false and accurate cases of child sexual abuse.* Paper presented at Do Children Lie or Adults Misperceive? Portland, OR.

Koch, M., & Lowery, C. (1984). Visitation and the noncustodial father. *Journal of Divorce, 8,* 47-65.

Lusk, R., & Waterman, J. (1986). Effects of abuse on children. In K. MacFarlane & J. Waterman (Eds.), *Sexual abuse of young children.* New York: Guilford Press.

MacFarlane, K., & Waterman, J. (1986). *Sexual abuse of young children.* New York: Guilford Press.

Maisch, H. (1973). *Incest.* London: Andre Deutch.

Mrazek, P. B. (1981). The nature of incest: A review of contributing factors. In

P. B. Mrazek & C. H. Kempe (Eds.), *Sexually abused children and their families*. New York: Pergamon Press.

Northwest Women's Law Center. (1987). *The 1987 Parenting Act: Washington's innovative approach to family law*. Seattle: Northwest Women's Law Center.

Patterson, G. (1982). *Coercive family process*. Eugene, OR: Castalia.

Rutter, M. (1980). Protective factors in children's response to stress and disadvantage. In M. W. Kent & J. E. Rolf (Eds.), *Primary prevention of psychopathology: III. Promoting social competence in children*. Hanover, N.H.: University Press of New England.

Stolberg, A. L., Camplair, C., Curruer, K., & Wells, M. J. (1987). Individual, familial, and environmental detriments of children's post-divorce adjustment and maladjustment. *Journal of Divorce, 11*(1), 51-70.

Summit, R. (1983). The child sexual abuse accommodation syndrome. *Child Abuse and Neglect, 7,* 177-193.

Summit, R. (1987). *How the children are victimized by the justice system*. Paper presented at the Child Victims in the Criminal Justice System Symposium, Portland, OR.

Waldron, J. A., Ching, J.W.J., & Fair, P. H. (1986). A children's divorce clinic: Analysis of 200 cases in Hawaii. *Journal of Divorce, 9*(3), 111-121.

Wallerstein, J. S. (1980). The impact of divorce on children. *Psychiatric Clinics of North America, 3*(3), 455-468.

Wallerstein, J. S. (1984) Children of divorce: Preliminary report of a ten year follow-up of young children. *American Journal of Orthopsychiatry, 54*(3), 444-458.

Wallerstein, J. S., & Kelly, J. B. (1980a). *Surviving the breakup: How children and parents cope with divorce*. New York: Basic Books.

Wallerstein, J. S., & Kelly, J. B. (1980b). Effects of divorce on the visiting father-child relationship. *American Journal of Psychiatry, 137*(12), 1534-1539.

Wolfe, D. A., & Wolfe, V. V. (1987). The sexually abused child. In E. Mash & L. Terdal (Eds.), *Behavioral assessment of childhood* (2nd Ed.). New York.

Factors Contributing to False Allegations of Child Sexual Abuse in Custody Disputes

Arthur H. Green

ABSTRACT. This paper describes the mechanisms and psychodynamics underlying the increasingly observed phenomenon of false or unsubstantiated allegations of child sexual abuse initiated during child custody disputes. Misinterpretation of normal caretaking practices involving physical or affectionate contact between parent and child during bathing, toileting, dressing, hugging, or kissing is often at the core of the abuse allegation. This article reviews a number of possible situations involving false allegations and the impact on the children and families involved.

As reports of child sexual abuse have increased dramatically over the past few years, there has been a corresponding increase in unfounded and unsubstantiated cases of child molestation, especially where parents are involved in protracted custody battles or visitation disputes. Some parents have exploited the epidemic of child sexual abuse by initiating false allegations of sexual misconduct to promote their own interests at the expense of their child and their former spouse. These allegations easily attract the attention of the child protective agency, district attorney, or a judge and often result in the loss of visitation by the accused. However, many of these unsubstantiated allegations of child sexual abuse are made in good faith with the aim of protecting the child. These "unintentional" false allegations are usually based upon misinterpretations of ambiguous physical contact between child and spouse which may be triggered by physical or psychological symptoms in the child which are sometimes, but not necessarily, associated with sexual abuse. These symptoms are then used to "confirm" the allegation. In this article, the term "false" or "unsub-

---

Arthur H. Green is affiliated with the College of Physicians and Surgeons, Columbia University. Address reprint requests to Family Center and Therapeutic Nursery, Presbyterian Hospital BH-616, 622 West 168th Street, New York, NY 10032.

stantiated" allegation refers to the "unintentional" type unless otherwise indicated.

FALSE ALLEGATIONS OF SEXUAL ABUSE IN CUSTODY DISPUTES

Clinical Studies

Benedek and Schetky (1985) were unable to document charges of sexual abuse in 10 of 18 children during disputes over custody and visitation. This strikingly high incidence of unfounded allegations (55%) is comparable to Green's (1986) determination of 4 false allegations in 11 children (36%) reported to be molested by the non-custodial parent during custody disputes and less than Yates and Musty's report (1987) which indicated that 15 of 19 allegations of sexual abuse in custody and/or visitation cases (79%) involving preschool children could not be substantiated. Schuman (1987) states that the rate of unfounded sexual abuse reports in custody disputes ranges from 35% to 95%, depending on the sample. Brant and Sink (1984) reported that the non-custodial parent accused the custodial parent of brainwashing the child to make a false allegation of sexual abuse in three of four sexual abuse evaluations during custody disputes. While these studies are based on non-random clinical samples and cannot be used to generalize about the relative incidence of false allegations in custody disputes, they can provide valuable information on patterns and dynamics found in these cases.

Characteristics of False Allegations of Child Sexual Abuse

A common scenario encountered in cases of false allegations of child sexual abuse is as follows: A recently separated wife accuses her estranged husband of sexually abusing their child during visitation. The accusation is based upon an alleged disclosure by the child, which might be presented on audiotape. Under pressure from her mother, the child describes genital fondling or intercourse, usually with little detail. "Objective" signs, such as a vaginal or rectal irritation might be presented, but the pediatrician's report is usually negative or equivocal. The mother cites additional evidence, such as increased clinging and separation anxiety in the child just before or following the visits, and his or her stated reluctance to visit the father. There is a history of a long standing dispute between the spouses over visitation and/or custody of the child. The allegation often takes place shortly after the father is granted an increase in visitation by the court. Careful history taking often reveals that the dispute over the child began during infancy, antedating the marital friction and separation. The mother was inordinately possessive and overprotective with the baby, and sought to minimize the father's early role as a caretaker. Prior to having children, the wife was overly dependent and possessive of the husband, often accusing him of infidelity. The mother's increasing absorption with the baby was accompanied by emotional and sexual withdrawal from the husband.

If the evaluator fails to validate the sexual abuse allegation, the mother may become angered rather than relieved, and seek another professional who will document the "truth." If the court fails to confirm the allegation, and the mother has financial backing, she may initiate new proceedings in another court or locale, replace her attorneys, or file an appeal. If the court continues to vindicate the father and increases his time with the child, the mother might elect to spend time in jail for "contempt of court" rather than surrender the child to the alleged perpetrator. When legal channels are finally exhausted and numerous pediatricians and mental health professionals fail to confirm the allegations, the mother may resort, in some cases, to kidnapping the child.

Authors of false allegations rarely engage in opportunistic lying. Their sincere beliefs, however, are usually based upon misperceptions and misinterpretations of sexually innocent or ambiguous encounters between the child and spouse through an excessive reliance on defenses of denial and projection. In extreme cases, these individuals may be frankly delusional. The most frequently encountered psychiatric diagnoses are histrionic or paranoid personality disorders, or paranoid psychosis. The following types of behaviors or symptoms may be utilized to form the basis of a false allegation.

Misinterpretation of Normal Caretaking Practices

Mistrustful and/or sexually preoccupied parents might misperceive innocent bathing or toileting of the child by the estranged spouse as evidence of sexual molestation. Washing, powdering, or drying of the genital or anal area may be viewed as genital or anal fondling. In these situations, the child might respond positively to the question, "did Daddy touch your private parts?" Parents who bathe or shower with young children might be accused of having sexual intent. A father who permits a frightened child to sleep in his bed following a nightmare or sleep disturbance may be accused of sexual seduction.

Mrs. A. was concerned when her four year old daughter, Abby, began to exhibit difficulty in separating from her prior to weekend visits with her father. The parents separated when Abby was a year old. After Mrs. A. noticed a vaginal irritation in the child, she questioned her about being "touched" in her genital area by Mr. A. Abby gave a confirmatory response and the child was taken to a psychologist who reported Abby to be sexually abused, based on her interviews with mother and child. The psychologist did not ask to see Mr. A.

During the subsequent court-ordered evaluation it was discovered that Mrs. A. had offered her ex-husband a large sum of money if he would agree to reduce his visitation. It was also discovered that Mrs. A's suspicions of sexual abuse occurred several days after she witnessed a T.V. movie about father-daughter incest. Abby told the evaluator that her father hurt her vagina with a washcloth while giving her a bath. Abby related to her father in affectionate manner without any signs of fearfulness or anxiety. However, Abby was tense and frightened when separating from her mother; clinging to her teddy bear and sucking a pacifier.

Misinterpretation of Normal Sexual Behaviors in Children

Normal children of all ages, including infants and toddlers indulge in sexual activities consisting of direct or indirect genital stimulation which may be associated with erections in boys and vaginal lubrication in girls (Kinsey, Pomeroy, & Martin, 1948, 1953). Preschool children frequently engage in genital handling and fondling, sex play, sexual exploration and exhibitionistic and voyeuristic activities (Isaacs, 1933; Sears, Maccoby & Levin, 1957; Gundersen, Melas & Skar, 1981). A recent study of childrearing practices in upper middle-class families determined that 45% of 8 to 10 year old boys had touched their mother's breasts and genitals, and that 30% of girls up to age 10 had touched their father's genitals (Rosenfeld, Bailey, Siegel, & Bailey, 1986).

These types of normal sexual behavior in children may be confused with behaviors of overly eroticized and highly seductive children who have been molested, and therefore, may be misinterpreted as evidence of sexual abuse. Sexually conflicted parents who rely heavily on projective defenses may misperceive developmentally appropriate expressions of sexuality in their children.

Mrs. B. reported the sexual abuse of her four year old daughter, Cindy, to child protective services when the child told her that she touched her father's penis when they bathed together during weekend visits. Mrs. B. was also suspicious of Mr. B's sexual misconduct because Cindy started to masturbate at this time and also asked if she could touch Mrs. B's genitals.

Mr. B. admitted that he let Cindy touch his penis once or twice when she requested it when they bathed together, in order to satisfy her curiosity. He stopped the practice when she made further demands. After a preliminary investigation, Mr. B's visitation was abruptly reduced to weekly supervised contact at the protective service agency. During the evaluation, Cindy told the examiner that she wanted to see her father more often and her biggest worry is that "Daddy doesn't live with us." When asked about the "touching" incident, she admitted touching his penis after bathing; but denied being touched or fondled by him. When Mr. B. and Cindy were seen together the child was affectionate and happy to be with her father. Cindy did not display any fear or signs of abnormal sexual arousal.

Misinterpretation of Common Psychological Symptoms

Separation anxiety, regressive behavior, sleep disorders, and phobic symptoms often accompanying parental separation may be misperceived as fear of the father and offered as evidence of molestation. Indeed, these non-specific symptoms may be present in recent child victims of sexual abuse.

Confusion with Parental Sexual Overstimulation

Some parents might engage in sexually overstimulating practices such as excessive hugging, kissing, or lapsitting, inappropriate nudity, allowing the child to sleep in the parental bed, or allowing the child to view pornographic magazines or films without being aware of the adverse impact on the child. Although these parents deny sexual intent or excitement, they might derive unconscious sexual pleasure from these encounters. The impact of the sexual overstimulation, i.e., precocious interest in sexual activities and seductive behavior with peers or adults often resembles the sequelae of actual sexual molestation, which poses a real problem in differential diagnosis. However, these parents are guilty of faulty childrearing practices rather than sexual abuse. It is important, however, to realize that sexually overstimulating behaviors might be a prelude to frank genital contact by a sexual abuser. A thorough psychiatric evaluation of parent and child should help differentiate the naive overstimulating parent from the molesting parent.

Four year old Linda C. told her mother and therapist about "sucking Daddy's penis" in a gleeful and matter-of-fact manner. Linda had recently entered play therapy as a result of severe separation anxiety prior to leaving her mother's home for overnight visits with her father. Linda had been shifted back and forth between her parents since she was two years old, under a joint custody arrangement. The therapist reported Mr. C. for sexual abuse because of Linda's preoccupation with fellatio and other signs of eroticized behavior, such as frequent masturbation and precocious sexual talk. The therapist interpreted Linda's separation anxiety as a confirmation of her molestation by Mr. C.

Before their separation, Mr. and Mrs. C. operated a health club in which they both led exercise classes and gave body massages. They espoused a hedonistic philosophy which included nudity in the home and permissiveness regarding sexuality and modesty. The parents showered and bathed with Linda and Mr. C. continued to bathe with Linda after the marital separation. He permitted Linda to examine his penis at her request when in the shower, "to satisfy her normal curiosity." He wanted to educate Linda "to deal with the genitals and sexuality without shame or guilt." Mr. C. also allowed Linda to sleep in his bed when she was frightened.

Mr. C. was outspoken and not at all defensive about the nature of his relationship with Linda, and he had no insight about the sexually stimulating quality of his behavior. Linda exhibited a great deal of affection towards her father, but this was expressed in a seductive and sexualized manner. Mr. C. was unable to set limits on Linda's seductive behavior. Linda gleefully told the evaluator that she touched her father's penis in the shower without the slightest hint of guilt or embarrassment. She also denied having been touched or fondled by Mr. C.

The therapist's failure to interview Mr. C. contributed to the mistaken attribution of the child's sexualized behavior to a genuine molestation, rather than a response to a sexually overstimulating environment.

Misinterpretation of Physical Signs and Symptoms in the Child

Physical signs and symptoms such as vaginal irritation or vaginal discharge resulting from a non-specific vulvovaginitis are common in young children and may be used to initiate a report of sexual abuse. Similarly, rectal irritations or fissures may be regarded as an indicator of sodomy. The presence of these physical signs might be used to substantiate an allegation of genital or anal fondling during bathing and toileting of the child.

Intentional False Allegations

A vindictive parent, usually the mother fabricates the incest in order to punish the spouse by excluding him from further contact with the child. The false accusation is often supported by the presence of non-specific physical or psychological symptoms in the child, as previously described. The vindictive parent "brainwashes" the child by repetitively discussing the alleged molestation and deprecating the "perpetrator" in the child's presence.

Psychodynamics of False Allegations of Child Sexual Abuse

Background factors include a stress-related regression in psychological functioning, depression, and an experience of loss in the parents following the dissolution of the marriage. These are often associated with feelings of sexual privation due to the loss of a sexual partner, which may be intensified if the spouse finds another lover. The mother turns to the child for the dependency gratification no longer available from the spouse and becomes threatened by the intimacy between child and father. In such a psychological climate, a "projection-prone" mother readily projects her own sexual fantasies onto the spouse and child, while exploiting ambiguous physical or behavioral symptoms in the child as "evidence" for molestation. She subjects the child to incessant interrogations about the alleged sexual contact, and pressures him or her into accepting her misperceptions, which take on a life of their own. The mother reinforces the child's compliance by withholding love and approval if he or she denies the incest or demonstrates positive feelings towards the father. Schuman (1987) describes a "positive feedback loop" in which the child's "disclosure" under pressure is used by the mother to reconfirm the allegation. In extreme cases, a child might become completely enmeshed in the maternal delusional system, creating a "folie à deux." Women who were childhood victims of sexual abuse are also likely to sexualize ambiguous interactions between spouse and child.

During the protracted course of most false allegations, the repetitive questioning of the child regarding alleged sexual events and the frequent inspection and examinations of the genitals by mother and/or physicians may provide the accuser with vicarious sexual gratification and result in sexual overstimulation of the child.

FALSE ALLEGATIONS BY THE CHILD

Allegations Based on Fantasy

Fantasized incest is more common in pre-adolescent or adolescent girls who may project their sexual wishes onto a parent, usually the father or father substitute. These girls often exhibit hysterical personality traits, more rarely they are frankly paranoid and delusional. This phenomenon is similar to Freud's early experience with adult hysterics whose powerful oedipal fantasies altered their perceptions and reality testing so that they mistakenly believed that they had been victims of incest. The unfortunate de-emphasis of the role of actual child sexual abuse in producing psychological symptoms by Freud and his psychoanalytic followers does not invalidate his important discovery of the oedipal complex and the universality of sexual fantasies in children. Those children with severe ego impairment or children who have been sexually traumatized or overstimulated are more likely to confuse sexual fantasies with reality.

Allegations Based on Revenge or Retaliation

Older children or adolescents may falsely accuse a parent of incest because of a desire for retaliation or revenge. The underlying motivation for this type of malicious allegation is often anger over a recent punishment or deprivation, or a wish to remove the father or stepfather from the home.

THE ROLE OF THE PROFESSIONAL

Pediatricians and mental health professionals may initiate or confirm false reports of sexual abuse based on their misinterpretation of equivocal physical or behavioral symptoms. The mistake might be influenced by the persuasiveness of the accusing parent or her attorney, or might reflect the professional's own bias. Some clinicians almost always "find" sexual molestation and may be retained by the plaintiff because of this reputation. These professionals often fail to interview or even inform the alleged perpetrator when they report the case to child protective services or to the police. The accuser will cling to an evaluator's mistaken validation of a false allegation to justify further litigation even in the face of consistent negative findings by all other experts and the courts. The therapist who confirms a false allegation during his evaluation or treatment of the child introduces a major problem in the reality testing of his patient.

Assessment of Sexual Abuse Allegations in Child Custody Disputes

The evaluator of a potential case of child sexual abuse must always be aware of the possibility of a false allegation, especially in the contest of a custody dispute. The assessment should be carried out by a trained mental health professional, such as a psychiatrist, psychologist, psychiatric nurse, or social worker who has special expertise in the area of child sexual abuse. The evaluator should have knowledge of child development, child psychopathology, family dynamics, and the signs, symptoms, and sequelae of child sexual abuse, but should be equally versed in the symptoms and manifestations of false allegations. Familiarity with the typical psychopathology of incest families and sexual offenders, as well as the characteristics of parents who make false allegations is also indispensable. The clinician should be aware of his or her own feelings and biases concerning sexual behavior and sexual victimization of children, so as to minimize countertransference reactions.

Assessment of the Child

Children who describe sexual victimization are usual telling the truth, so that a child's disclosure of sexual abuse must be taken seriously. However, children do lie sometimes about sexual abuse and might support a false allegation by a parent or share a parental delusion regarding an imagined molestation. Most lying is done by actual victims of sexual abuse who deny their victimization out of fear or shame. The child will often require a longer period of evaluation than the usual child psychiatric patient, as sexually abused children and children taught to believe that they were molested are often very defensive and resistant to direct questioning. In some cases, several sessions might be necessary to establish initial rapport and trust before focusing on the sexual abuse allegations. If the child is able to talk about the sexual abuse, detailed descriptions of the events should be obtained when possible. This should include the type of molestation, its frequency, duration and location, and whether or not threats were used. The young child's perception of the incest may be elicited indirectly through play, fantasy, and dreams. Drawings are often useful in validating the sexual abuse allegations. The drawing of genitalia, precocious sexualized representations, and the exaggeration or avoidance of sexual features can be indicators of sexual abuse. However, children who are subjects of false allegations may appear to be sexually overstimulated as a result of continual questioning about alleged sexual activities. Young children who have difficulty describing the molestation might be provided with anatomically correct dolls in order to facilitate their communication. One must be careful not to use the dolls in a leading manner. Leading questions must be avoided during the interviews. The credibility of the child is weakened if he or she is unable to recall details of the alleged molestation, if the stories are varying and inconsistent, if the child uses adult sexual terminology, if the molestation is described matter-of-factly with little or no affect, and if the child is unduly suggestible. A detailed history of the child should be provided by the custodial parent prior to interviewing the child. The history should include a developmental survey, medical history including the presence of genital and anal symptoms, information about the development of sexual behavior and sexual interests, family attitudes regarding sex and modesty, and some information about the child's usual behavior and coping, to provide a contrast between pre- and post-traumatic functioning. The history should be designed to elicit the presence of the typical signs and symptoms of the child sexual abuse syndrome, such as anxiety related phenomena such as fearfulness, sleep disturbances, nightmares, somatic complaints, depressive symptoms, and extremes of precocious hypersexuality and sexual avoidance. At the same time, alternative explanations for these symptoms must be considered. These may include stress related to separation and bitter parental disputes, involvement in extreme loyalty, conflicts, exposure to sexually overstimulating behavior. Assessment of the child can usually be completed in 4 to 6 visits.

Evaluation of the Parents

A separate psychiatric examination of each parent should complement the assessment of the child. This should include a family history with information concerning a background of abuse and family violence, a sexual history, information regarding impulse control, drug and alcohol usage, cognitive and psychological functioning, and the history of the marriage, separation, and the custody/visitation dispute. The fathers should be questioned about other forms of abnormal sexual behavior, i.e., exhibitionism, rape, voyeurism, etc. which are often associated with pedophilia. Fathers should be asked for their degree of participation in child care activities such as bathing, diapering, and toileting of the child. The presence of early, pre-separation conflicts between the parents over the "control" of the child should be ascertained. The presence of hysterical, paranoid, or delusional psychopathology in the mother should alert one to the possibility of a false allegation. However, it should also be remembered that these maternal disorders may coexist with actual sexual victimization of the child. Each parent should be asked about previous psychiatric disorders and psychiatric treatment. Consent should be obtained for the release of prior records and for permission to contact therapists. Assessment of the parents should be accomplished in 3 to 4 visits each.

Observation of the Child with Each Parent

Mother-child interaction. The mother-child interaction provides a baseline for the assessment of the relationship between the child and the alleged perpetrator. One should note the degree of warmth, closeness, and support offered by the mother, and whether the mother allows the child freedom and spontaneity, or attempts to control the child's behavior. Mothers making false allegations often control the child by monitoring his or her responses through eye contact and subtle facial expressions. The child may respond by "checking" with the mother before proceeding. These mothers often encourage the child to discuss the "molestation" with the examiner before the child is ready. They are often impatient and goad the child into revealing what allegedly happened. Mothers involved in false accusations do not hesitate to deprecate the alleged perpetrator in front of the child. Disparagement of the father by the child is encouraged and reinforced. The child is also taught to fear the father, and to expect further sexual abuse, even if visits are supervised.

Father-child interaction. In cases of false allegations, there is often a striking discrepancy between the child's negative attitudes towards the father in the mother's presence and his or her affectionate and relaxed demeanor when observed alone with the father and free from the mother's influence. In cases of actual molestation, the child is likely to exhibit genuine fearfulness, anger, or discomfort during the encounter with the father, and in some cases will refuse to enter the room with him. Surprisingly successful supervised visitation with the father is compatible with a false allegation. However, one must be alert to the possibility of a benign father-child interaction in cases of "gentle" fondling of a preschool child who is unable to appreciate the inappropriate and deviant nature of this experience. A father-child evaluation session should not take place if the child is firmly opposed to such a meeting.

SEQUELAE OF FALSE ALLEGATIONS

Allegations of sexual abuse receive unprecedented publicity on television and in the newspapers, and the name of the "perpetrator" is revealed to the community. There is a presumption of guilt before the decision is rendered in court. Contact between the father and child is abruptly terminated. This may occur without any evaluation of the father or the circumstances surrounding the allegation. The ensuing publicity can destroy his professional reputation, and his personal and financial resources become focused on his defense. The child is besieged by the parents, evaluators and the court to describe sexual contact which may or may not have occurred. The child is often placed in psychotherapy for the alleged sexual victimization, and the therapist might insist that the child remain in treatment until he or she is able to describe the molestation. The child becomes confused and his sense of reality is compromised when he is forced to testify against a parent regarding events that did not take place. Needless to say, a previously healthy father-child relationship will be severely undermined as the child feels compelled to accommodate the mother's misperceptions. The child might feel betrayed by the mother and turn against her at the realization that he or she was misused as a witness and wrongfully alienated from the father. Mothers who repeatedly subject their children to psychiatric and physical examinations in order to uncover "new evidence" of molestation after the failure to substantiate previous allegations, or who continue to interfere with paternal visitation are liable to lose custody to the "alleged perpetrator."

SUMMARY

Any clinician evaluating potential cases of child sexual abuse should become as familiar with the phenomenon of false allegations as he or she is with the actual syndrome of child sexual abuse. The evaluator should understand the manifestations and underlying psychodynamics of false allegations and the typical characteristics of the accusing parent, the alleged perpetrator, and the child, as well as its long-term outcome and sequelae.

REFERENCES

Benedek, E., & Schetky, D. (1985). Allegations of sexual abuse in child custody and visitation disputes. In D. Schetky & E. Benedek (Eds.), *Emerging issues in child psychiatry and the law*. New York: Brunner/ Mazel.

Brant, R., & Sink, F. (1984). *Dilemmas in court-ordered evaluation of sexual abuse charges during custody and visitation proceedings*. Paper presented at the Annual Meeting of the American Academy of Child Psychiatry, Toronto.

Green, A. (1986). True and false allegations of sexual abuse in child custody disputes. *Journal of the American Academy of Child Psychiatry, 25*, 449-456.

Gundersen, B., Melas, P., & Skar, J. (1981). Sexual behavior of preschool children: Teacher's observations. In L. Constantine & F. Martinson (Eds.), *Children and sex*. Boston: Little, Brown.

Isaacs, S. (1933). *Social development in young children.* London: Routledge and Kegan Paul.

Kinsey, A., Pomeroy, W., & Martin, C. (1948). *Sexual behavior in the human male.* Philadelphia: Saunders.

Kinsey, A., Pomeroy, W., Martin, C. & Gebhardt, P. (1953). *Sexual behavior in the human female.* Philadelphia: Saunders.

Rosenfeld, A., Bailey, R., Siegel, B., & Bailey, G. (1986). Determining incestuous contact between parent and child: Frequency of children touching parent's genitals in nonclinical population. *Journal of the American Academy of Child Psychiatry, 25,* 481-484.

Schuman, D. (1987). Psychodynamics of exaggerated accusations: Positive feedback in family systems. *Psychiatric Annals, 17,* 242-247.

Sears, R., Maccoby, E., & Levin, H. (1957). *Patterns of childrearing.* New York: Harper & Row.

Yates, A., & Musty, T. (1987). *False allegations in molestations of preschool children.* Paper presented at the Annual Meeting of the American Psychiatric Association, Chicago.

Alleging Psychological Impairment of the Accuser to Defend Oneself Against a Child Abuse Allegation: A Manifestation of Wife Battering and False Accusation

Catherine C. Ayoub
Penelope F. Grace
Jan E. Paradise
Eli H. Newberger

ABSTRACT. This paper discusses a group of divorced or separated parents who are in conflict over custody and/or visitation with their children. In each case, a mother alleges that the father has been sexually or physically abusive to the couple's children, and the father alleges that the mother's own abuse during childhood produced a psychiatric disturbance that forms the basis for her pathological need to project accusations of abuse onto him. The authors found that a satisfactory analysis of the competing parental allegations and a recommendation about the children's subsequent guardianship could not be developed until they explored the hypothesis that wife battering had contributed to the family's distressing circumstances.

The thorough and dispassionate evaluation of a family conflict about child custody that involves allegations of child abuse presents a challenge for mental health, social service, and medical professionals. Patients, cli-

---

Catherine C. Ayoub, Penelope F. Grace, Jan E. Paradise, and Eli H. Newberger are affiliated with the Harvard University School of Medicine, Boston Children's Hospital. Jan E. Paradise and Penelope F. Grace are also affiliated with Boston City Hospital and Boston University School of Medicine. Address reprint requests to Catherine C. Ayoub at Boston Children's Hospital, 300 Longwood Avenue, Boston, MA 02115.

nicians, and agencies are seeking evaluations of families with such inter-related difficulties with increasing frequency. We discuss here a group of five separated or divorced couples with disputes that illustrates the complexity of assessing the authenticity of abuse allegations. The presenting characteristics are:

1. Divorced or separated parents,
2. Conflict between the parents over custody of and/or visitation with the children,
3. A mother who alleges that the father has been sexually or physically abusive to the couple's children, and
4. A father who alleges that the mother's own abuse during childhood produced a psychiatric disturbance that forms the basis for her pathological need to project accusations of abuse onto him.

In the five cases we observed, one husband alleged that his wife had abused their children and four husbands claimed that their wives had fabricated allegations of abuse against them. All the accused parents denied that they had abused or neglected their children. All the husbands claimed that seriously disturbed relationships in the wives' families of origin were the true source of the present family difficulties and that their wives' perceptions of reality had been distorted by these childhood disturbances.

In each case, we found that a satisfactory analysis of the competing parental allegations and a recommendation about the children's subsequent guardianship could not be developed until after we had explored the hypothesis that wife battering had contributed to the family's distressing circumstances. A variety of behavioral cues on the part of both parents and children raised this concern among the evaluating clinicians. Following Schecter (1989), we use the term "wife battering" in this paper to describe a "distorted power relationship between spouses" in which a husband develops and maintains a pattern of intimidation and coercive control over his wife that often includes physical force, but may also be expressed as sexual abuse, economic control, or emotional manipulation.

FAMILY ASSESSMENT METHOD

The children and families we describe were evaluated by multidisciplinary teams of professionals in a child protection specialty clinic of a children's hospital. Most families seen in the clinic have been evaluated previously, have received services from public or private child protective service agencies, and have experienced intervention by family courts. Many of the clinic's evaluations are mandated by the court in order to ensure family members' participation. Common referral questions involve visitation and custody arrangements, placement decisions, and termination of parental rights.

The evaluators include pediatricians, nurse-practitioners, social workers, and psychologists. A team of two or three evaluators is assigned to each case. In the course of evaluating the families described below, the clinic members developed a policy of assigning both male and female evaluators to cases known or deemed likely to involve wife battering.

Families are usually interviewed six to ten times. Interviews include various groupings of family members as well as individual interviews to allow the evaluators to assess relationships in the family. Whenever consent is given, interviews are conducted in a one-way mirrored room with a microphone, allowing non-participating team members to observe the interactions. As needed, evaluations include sexual abuse disclosure interviews, physical examinations of children, and psychological testing of children and adults. Records of previous evaluations of family members are routinely reviewed by the clinic team. At the conclusion of each evaluation, the evaluators confer with the children's parents and with agency representaives to present and discuss their findings and recommendations.

Of the five cases we describe, two were referred to the clinic by probate courts, one was referred by a pediatrician, one by a child protective services agency, and one was self-referred. Because of some family members' refusal or threat of refusal to cooperate during the evaluation, four of the five evaluations were ultimately ordered by the court.

DESCRIPTION OF FAMILIES

Selected characteristics of the five cases we report are summarized in Table 1. We present two cases here in greater detail to illustrate the difficult issues we encountered in evaluating these families.

Case Reports

Case A. The A family included Bob, age 40 years, Nancy, age 21 years, and their 21-month-old daughter Kristi. The family was referred to the clinic by both parents' attorneys to assess the cause of Kristi's skull fracture. Mr. A was a respected businessman in his community. Mrs. A was a secretary. A physician had identified Kristi's skull fracture by radiograph after Mrs. A brought Kristi's scalp swelling to his attention. Mrs. A noticed the swelling one day after Kristi's return from a weekend visit with her father.

Mr. A was personable and participated willingly in the evaluation. He

Table 1. Selected Characteristics of Five Families with Alleged Child Abuse and Wife Battering.

Case Number	Parents' Age (yrs), Occupation, Substance Abuse History — Father	Mother	Children: Sex, Age (yrs)	Source of Referral	Parents' Allegations — Father	Mother	History of Wife Battering; Marital Status
1	35, Business professional Alcohol, cocaine	34, Business professional None	Boy, 8 Girl, 5	Self	M vengeful, denies F access to children, insufficiently attentive to F	F's violence is source of boy's aggressive behavior at school	F beat M, threatened M with knife Recently divorced
2	30 Contractor Alcohol, "drugs"	29, Mental health aide "Drugs"	Girl, 9 Girl, 4 Girl, 3	DSS	M's allegations due to her own childhood victimization. M an incompetent parent	F sexually and physically abused girls	F beat M, marital rape Recently divorced
3	33, Carpenter Alcohol, marijuana	29, Real estate broker None	Girl, 2.5	Court	M's allegations due to her own childhood abuse. M inadequate homemaker, manipulative of "systems"	F physically and sexually abused girls	F prohibited M from driving, obtaining psychotherapy. F threatened and slapped M. Recently divorced
4	40, Business owner None	21, Secretary None	Girl, 1.8	Pediatrician	M's allegations due to her own physical abuse. M incompetent parent and homemaker	Skull fracture occurred while girl visiting F's home. Possible sexual abuse	F harassed, threatened and humiliated M Separated; divorce in process
5	47, Business owner Alcohol	41, Housewife Alcohol	Girl, 6 Boy, 3 Boy, 2	Court	M burned girl and boy with cigarettes. M incompetent, alcoholic	F abuse children. F accusing M for monetary gain	F beat M, broke her and finger Divorced 1 year before evaluation

expressed regret at his wife's psychological impairment and ascribed this to her having been abused as a child. He discussed his daughter comfortably, but never referred to her by name. The evaluators' initial impression of him was positive.

Mrs. A's subsequent account of their marriage was unanticipated. She described a man who had been kind and generous during courtship, but who after their marriage became highly coercive, required her to participate in humiliating sexual behavior, and indicted her for having an alliance with the devil.

Kristi was developmentally normal and played comfortably during sessions with both parents. By the end of the two-month evaluation, no explanation for the skull fracture had emerged. The staff recommended that mother retain full custody of the child, that visits with father be supervised, and that both parents seek psychiatric treatment.

Case B. The B family included Ted, age 35 years, Sally, age 34 years, and their children, 8-year-old Rob and 4-year-old Jenny. Both Mr. and Mrs. B held graduate school degrees and professional positions. They had separated after Mr. B allegedly abused Mrs. B verbally and threatened her physically on numerous occasions. When Mr. B held a knife to her throat, threatening to kill her and mutilate her body, Mrs. B. escaped and called the police. Mr. B. was involuntarily removed from their home. Mrs. B obtained a restraining order against her husband and refused to consider reconciliation.

During the evaluation, Mr. B presented himself as an innocent victim of circumstances. Formerly a substance abuser, he was active in a self-help organization for drug abusers which he viewed as a focal point of his life. He expressed anger at his wife for her lack of fervor about this organization. In his opinion, the marital separation had occurred because his wife's enmeshed relationship with her own father made her unable to commit herself emotionally ("enter fully into") to the marriage. He minimized his threatening behavior toward Mrs. B and explained that her stubborn unwillingness to meet him halfway provoked his angry reactions.

Mrs. B was nervous during the interviews. She was careful to separate opinions she held from information that had been corroborated by others. She indicated that she was afraid of Mr. B, but tried to present a balanced picture of the difficulties in their relationship. She viewed her husband as psychologically troubled and expressed hope that he could receive help. She did not condemn or criticize him, as he had led the evaluators to expect she would.

Collateral contacts were made with each parent's psychotherapist. Mr. B's psychotherapist attributed responsibility for the marital difficulties to

Mrs. B's "provocative behavior and unsupportive attitude." The therapist had developed this formulation without ever having seen Mrs. B. On projective testing in the clinic, Mr. B's angry feelings toward women were prominent.

Mrs. B's therapist was very focused on safety issues. She was concerned about Mrs. B's minimization of her husband's violent behavior. Although the therapist understood the value of minimization as a coping mechanism, she persisted in confronting Mrs. B with the potential danger of her situation.

Jenny could not be engaged in conversation with the evaluators, and remained withdrawn throughout the evaluation. She seemed quite attached to her mother. She repeatedly avoided contact with her father, even by telephone. In contrast, 8-year-old Rob displayed overtly angry behavior. He expressed fear of his father. He berated his mother and tried to hit her frequently. He was also distressed and angry at school, having tried to hit both classmates and teachers on a number of occasions. His relationships with his peers were generally problematic.

At the end of the evaluation, the clinic team recommended that Mrs. B retain physical and legal custody of both children, that Mr. B have supervised visits with the children, that the children continue in individual psychotherapy, and that the clinic's recommendations be reviewed during a reevaluation of the family in six months.

During the sixteen months that have elapsed since those recommendations were made, Mrs. B and the children have continued in psychotherapy. Mr. B discontinued his therapy. His only contact with his son has been by telephone. His daughter refuses to speak to him on the telephone. He has not seen his children in person because of his refusal to visit with them under the supervised conditions that the court ordered.

CLINICAL OBSERVATIONS

In each of the five cases we observed, the mother accused the child's father of abusing the child. Both sexual and physical abuse were the presenting allegations in three cases; in the other two, the allegations were of physical and emotional abuse. During the intake process for each case, neither spouse made any reference, explicitly or implicitly, to wife battering.

Identifying Information

The fathers were very productive at work and expressed comfort with their extrafamilial relationships. They pointed to their relatively high status in their communities as evidence of their credibility. All participated actively in and considered themselves very committed to highly structured social systems. Two men were very involved with their churches and espoused fundamentalist personal beliefs. A third man was very committed to Alcoholics Anonymous, and a fourth considered himself a "survivalist," although he was not a member of any organized group. The fifth man operated the small business he owned with a highly autocratic style.

All the women worked outside the home before and during their marriages. Most ended or significantly curtailed their careers after they had children.

Presenting Problems

At the beginning of the evaluations, most of the men appeared pleasant and cooperative. Outlining their wives' shortcomings and psychiatric disturbances, they presented themselves as innocent but understanding victims of misdirected accusations. The wives, according to their husbands, came from disturbed families of origin in which they had been physically or sexually victimized as children. The wives were thus projecting the anger and mistrust they felt for their childhood abusers onto their husbands by fabricating accusations against them. This explanation was offered by each husband to discredit his wife's allegation.

The wives initially appeared cooperative, anxious, and somewhat depressed. During interviews with their husbands, they volunteered little information. Several wives expressed concern that they would be unable to present their situations coherently, but in fact provided detailed anecdotes to illustrate their concerns.

Parents' Families of Origin

As the evaluations proceeded, the husbands appeared unable or unwilling to direct their attention away from their wives' problems to other important aspects of their situations. When asked to describe their own families of origin, they provided brief, superficial, idealized accounts of "happy and safe childhood[s]" or "humble and giving" parents. In three cases, the evaluators obtained information from other sources indicating that, in contrast to these fathers' statements, their families of origin had been troubled, with fathers described as harsh, authoritarian, or abusive. Four fathers had had at least one alcoholic parent.

The wives provided detailed information about their families of origin. Three wives described themselves as having been raised by single or married parents in relatively stable families and denied having been abused during childhood. The other two women reported they grew up in a families with alcoholic fathers who exercised an authoritarian style. One of these two women had been physically abused during childhood. The other, the most psychologically disturbed woman in the group, had been sexually abused during adolescence by a maternal relative and was ostracized by her family when she disclosed the abuse. This woman's husband eventually joined her parents in the alliance against her.

Parents' Views of Their Marriages

The fathers' and other informants' descriptions of their marriages displayed some notable discrepancies. Most fathers described their marriages as "average" or "normal." They portrayed themselves as patient and protective of their overemotional, immature partners. Wives were described as "flighty" or "disorganized." Three husbands explained that their wives were especially poor homemakers but that they (the husbands) had benevolently excused this shortcoming until it became intolerable. One husband pointed to his wife's psychiatric hospitalizations as evidence of her incompetence. The fifth husband, rather than excuse his wife's failures, accused her of treating him in a "goading, vengeful" fashion.

When interviewed alone, the wives described marital relationships that were initially idyllic but gradually deteriorated. All five relationships included wife battering. Three wives had been physically abused. One wife had been raped by her estranged husband. Another had been forced to participate in degrading sexual activities and afterward was accused by her husband of being "a dirty whore." Her husband also forbade her to drive a car, to seek psychotherapy, and to visit relatives and friends. Another husband insisted on purchasing his wife's clothes, her makeup, and all household items. When she suggested what was needed, he said she had poor taste and was an incompetent homemaker. If she raised the subject again, he denied that the first conversation had occurred.

Throughout their interviews, the women seemed persistently and pervasively anxious. They could not at first identify specific sources of their distress. Their affect seemed blunted when they described harassment, physical violence, and sexual assault. Several wives expressed fear that they might be "going crazy" and worried that their husband's portrayals of them might be accurate. All described vigilantly attempting to discern their husbands' unpredictable moods and to protect themselves from their husbands' anger or vindictiveness.

Parents' Descriptions of Their Children

The fathers rarely referred to their children by name. All the fathers could describe some of their children's behaviors, but they seemed unable to paint a picture of their children as separate individuals. One father, when asked about his expectations of his daughter, replied that he expected her to be just like him. When pressed for other role models he named several other men but no women. Another father presented himself as uniquely able to control his child's aggressive, contentious behavior and expressed the belief that at times he could "read the child's mind." The men appeared to view their children not as people with internal states and emotional needs, but rather as objects to be governed by others. Several fathers worried that their children would become "just like my wife" if they did not exert tight control over both.

When the evaluators asked the fathers to consider the reports that they had abused their children, they all denied the allegations but at the same time offered no specific alternative explanations. In discussing his child's disclosure, one father said, "I can't think about it. It's like jumping out the window." Others reiterated their opinions that the mother was "a liar," "crazy," "sinful," or "bad" and that her influence was solely responsible for the child's statements and behavior. One man, presented with the information that his daughter had exhibited sexualized behavior during the evaluation, remarked, "If my wife would only stop her sinful lies and come home, everything would be all right."

The mothers, in contrast, seemed more able to describe their children as having internal needs and feelings. Each of the women could identify their children's strengths and weaknesses and could acknowledge the frustrations as well as the gratifications they encountered in raising their children. All could recount detailed examples of their children's behavior and experiences. However, three women seemed at a loss about how to address their children's emotional needs. Two were overwhelmed by their children's difficulties. All the mothers expressed concern about the quality of the relationship between her children and their father. Each emphasized her fear that her husband would harm their children if further contact were permitted.

The wives actively challenged their husbands' problematic behavior when they developed concerns for their children's welfare. Several mothers began to limit their husbands' contact with the children after their husbands treated the children inappropriately or harshly. One woman reported having seen her husband fondling her child at bath time and during diaper changes. Another wife had watched her husband attempt to breast-feed their child. Three husbands had verbally and physically abused their wives while the children watched.

Evaluations of the Children

Children in two families were referred because of physical injuries — cigarette burns and a skull fracture — characteristic of physical abuse. Children from two other families were referred for suspected sexual abuse. Two boys behaved very aggressively with both their mothers and their peers and had been identified as troubled at school.

On evaluation, the children whose mothers were severely emotionally distressed and were not currently living with them seemed most emotionally impaired. These children were living with their fathers at the beginning of the assessment. The children in one of these families were transferred to foster care shortly after the evaluation began. In a third family, older children who had lived with both parents until recently were also in significant distress. The two young children who lived only with their mothers after the age of 18 months seemed developmentally and emotionally normal.

On the basis of information gathered during semi-structured interviews, the clinic evaluators concluded that children in three families had been sexually abused. During interviews, children in two families were variously depressed, hypervigilant, physically violent, and highly impulsive. These children said they were afraid to be left alone with their fathers. Pediatricians assessing the children's physical injuries concluded that they were inflicted, not accidental.

At the end of the evaluation, all the children over two years of age were referred for psychotherapy. Three children in one family were later psychiatrically hospitalized.

Recommendations of the Evaluators

In each of the cases we describe, the evaluators recommended that the mother retain or be awarded sole physical custody of their children and that both parents retain the children's legal custody. In two cases, maternal custody was recommended despite the evaluators' recognition that the mothers' substantial social, economic and emotional difficulties were likely to compromise their ability to care for their troubled children. The alternatives, paternal custody and foster care, seemed even less desirable. Interim foster care had been recommended for the children in these two cases during the course of the evaluations when their emotional distress had become incapacitating, the caretaking parents seemed unable to meet the children's acute needs, and the evaluators felt that the children's safety was in question. The evaluators made efforts to strengthen these mothers' home situations by referring them to women's advocates, recommending that the court mandate adequate child support, and helping to arrange for housing. For each of the children, regular, professionally supervised visits with their fathers were recommended. Individual psychotherapy was recommended for all of the parents.

DISCUSSION

In the cases we describe here, men discredit their spouses by invoking a psychological explanation for allegations of child abuse, thus deflecting attention away from their own abusive behavior. We will present a theoretical explanation of the dynamics of these families that may facilitate clinicians' ability to recognize similar cases and to formulate productive approaches for treatment.

We propose that structural-developmental theory (Kegan, 1982; Selman, 1980; Gilligan, 1982) provides a particularly useful framework for understanding the behavior of both the husbands and the wives in the families we have presented. The structural-developmental group of neo-Piagetian theories holds that distinct aspects of mental organization can be identified and followed as they become differentiated over a person's life span. Kegan (1982) proposes that a single evolving "deep structure" gives rise to a series of differing mental structures, each with a unique organizing principle that determines how the person "makes meaning of his world." A variety of life experiences can foster, distort, or detain an individual's progression through these stages of making meaning.

A Theoretical Explication of the Men's Behavior

The men in these families appear to have had limited insight about their own emotions and those of others. Although they recognized that other people have feelings that differ from their own, they were not able to hold both their own and another person's point of view simultaneously. They were thus unable to empathize. Because of this incapacity, they could not reliably predict others' responses to situations or interpret others' emotional needs. This led to their perception that the reactions of others are unstable and often hostile. An individual functioning at this level of developmental organization sees others in terms of whether or not they meet his needs, fulfill his wishes, pursue his interests, and affirm his competence. Thus, inside the family, basic rules of conduct are cast aside by the husbands in order to meet these emotional needs. The cliche that a man is "king of his castle" is taken to the extreme.

The men we describe share the universal human need to appear publicly competent and successful to associates and community. In their pursuit of publicly acknowledged competence, they depended heavily on well-defined external structures such as religious and self-help groups to help regulate their behavior in this realm. They were aware that coercive behavior is not acceptable in the public domain. Since to these men a person is only guilty if he is caught violating social rules, they were careful to appear compliant with societal rules in public. Appearance is paramount.

The inclination of men like those we describe to use violence is intensified by their inability to empathize and their need to intimidate others in order to make them conform to their own expectations. Instead of processing competing needs internally and experiencing internal conflict, these men project conflicts onto their intimate companions and perceive them as antagonistic holders of competing points of view. To maintain emotional homeostasis, an individual at this developmental stage must control or at least be able to predict the behavior of other people, particularly his intimate companions. The impossibility of this task intensifies the anxiety he experiences in his relationships with both his wife and his children. His perceived lack or loss of control exacerbates his desire for control and reinforces his inclination to use coercion.

The men in our series can be divided into two groups based on their degree of success at controlling family members and their ability to manage their overwhelming internal needs. The first group of men are those whose ability to maintain homeostasis was more limited. These men had volatile and unpredictable mood swings, used less effective defense mechanisms to control expression of their feelings, and seemed particularly brittle. They expressed rage publicly, became suddenly violent on occasion, and used alcohol and illicit drugs more regularly than did the second group. These behaviors may have been an attempt to ward off anxiety or to suppress sudden unwanted overflows of emotion. Their relatively ungoverned feelings also intruded into the public arena, where they were less accomplished than the men who managed their distress more successfully. Theoretically, this group has considerable difficulty with more primitive impulses that may have gone unchecked in prior stages of development. Interestingly, during the evaluation, two men in this group indirectly acknowledged feeling sad or distressed through stories and references to others.

The second group of men maintained tighter control over their impulses and projected personas that differed dramatically from the figures described by their spouses. They were not reported to have been inappropriate in public. Their separation of their public and private realities was so profound that they maintained calm demeanors throughout the clinic's probing investigations. Their comments seemed distant, even placid, as they described their lives in generalized, idealistic terms. They portrayed themselves as benevolent dictators, innocent victims of the emotional outbursts of others. They were intelligent and successful but lacked empathy, demanding that their intimate relationships either be ideal or be destroyed.

The violence and coercion this group of men employed seemed more premeditated and sadistic. They engaged in subtle but constant efforts to belittle their intimate partners. If their violent behavior was made public, it was minimized or denied. Because the facade presented by these men is so convincing, it can be difficult to recognize the true nature of their relationships with their partners and children.

Both groups of men viewed their children as objects that should be completely under their control and beholden to them. A child with thoughts or actions incongruent with these fathers' notions of correctness is perceived as threatening; such a child may be at serious risk of abuse. The children received confusing and unpredictable messages from their fathers, whose reality was distorted in an effort to maintain their emotional balance. The anxiety and hypervigilance we observed in several of the older children who had had more unsupervised contact with their fathers may be partially attributable to such problematic interactions.

A Theoretical Explication of the Women's Behavior

We believe that constructive-developmental theory is also useful for understanding the behavior of the women we describe in terms of the ways they make meaning of their emotional worlds. The women in these families viewed relationships interpersonally, demonstrating a stage of development that commonly begins during the teenage years and extends into young adulthood (Kegan, 1982). There is evidence to support the hypothesis that women acquire "interpersonalism" at a younger age (Selman, 1980) and maintain this view of relationships longer (Gilligan, 1982) than do men. The women seemed capable of perceiving another person's point of view and of distinguishing it from their own. A corollary of this capability was their presumption, unfortunately an incorrect one, that their husbands had the same capability. Although interpersonalism is a necessary element of mature adult development, it is a characteristic that may have made these women more vulnerable than they otherwise would have been to accepting responsibility for the violence their husbands directed against them.

These women also appeared to have had a strong need for approval from and intimacy with others, much like adolescents who seek out peer groups for a sense of belonging. The women did not "have" their relationships with their husbands; rather, they "were" those relationships. Their intimate relationships defined their inner selves.

Because of their interlocking needs, the men and women became infatuated with each other. In the romantic phase of their relationships, the women misinterpreted the men's controlling behavior as intense interest, attentiveness, and caring. Ironically, as the women became more committed to the relationships, their husbands began to criticize them more strongly for not conforming to their rigid, idealized models of "a good wife." Because of their overdependence on external validation, the women accepted responsibility for their ostensible failures and, as a result, for their husbands' dissatisfaction. To varying degrees, the women empathically "understand" that their husbands "have to" threaten, coerce, and injure them because their (the wives') behavior does not live up to the standards both partners had mutually established. They internalize and, to varying degrees, assume principal responsibility for what is now presented as a marital conflict.

Child Abuse Escalates the Crisis

The wives' empathy was central to the tragedy that next developed when children upset the precarious balance that had been established. When children arrived, the wives assumed additional responsibilities as their children's parents and protectors. The mothers' empathy with their children's needs pushed them toward confrontation with their husbands when the children became targets of their fathers' overwhelming needs or anger. The mothers then decided to take action on behalf of their children that they had not taken for themselves.

However, after making a decision to separate from their husbands precisely because of their concern for their children's welfare, the wives' inevitable feelings of loss were exacerbated by the helplessness they experienced when the marital separation necessitated visiting arrangements that ironically exposed the children to the fathers without the protection of their mothers' presence. The degree of the mothers' success or failure in negotiating with the child protection and legal bureaucracies had an additional impact on their sense of personal worth. It is thus understandable that the women who received little support in negotiating with the system were characterized by insecurity, anxiety, minimization, and depression.

Effect on the Children

The intense conflict between the parents in these five families put enormous demands on the children who strained to reconcile their parents' competing viewpoints. The children were at risk of emotional or physical abuse whenever they failed to meet their fathers' needs or expectations. The fathers' distortions of reality and inability to comprehend the children's developmental needs further impaired the father-child relationships. The mothers in these families, in turn, tried to appease their husbands and often minimized the abuse they experienced in the hope that things would improve. The children perceived the attentions they received from both parents as simultaneously loving and troubling. Some children wished for reunification of their families, while others remained frightened of the abusive parent. All of the older children were fearful about the family conflict and chaos that the situation had engendered.

RECOMMENDATIONS FOR FAMILY EVALUATORS

The framework provided by structural-developmental theory can enhance clinicians' ability to better understand the interpersonal dynamics in families like those we describe. This knowledge can be used to develop interventions based on a detailed formulation of each family member's weaknesses, strengths, and capacity for change.

Based on our observations of these five cases, we recommend the following with regard to similar families:

(1) Clinicians should analyze the relationship between the parents, keeping alert to the possibility that wife battering is an element of the relationship. Because battering relationships are often difficult to assess, the recommendations listed below may serve to enhance their identification.

(2) Mandatory rather than voluntary evaluation should be arranged to ensure evaluators' access to family members and pertinent records. Although some evaluators prefer not to review previous records relevant to a case, we believe that clinicians should review existing information as completely as possible to enhance understanding of the history of the case, to learn what other observers have concluded, and to have a context for interpreting information from family members. Records that merit review include protective services reports, court documents, summaries of therapy, and school and hospital records.

(3) Both female and male evaluators should participate in assessments. In view of the intensity of the feelings generated by cases of alleged child

abuse, it is important to highlight the risk that an evaluator may develop an unwarranted sense of alliance with or skepticism toward one or another of the adults being evaluated. This must be acknowledged and resolved before any decisions about the case can be rendered. When two or three clinicians, including at least one man and one woman, are responsible for each evaluation, more than one professional can interview each family member, decreasing the possibility that an inappropriate alliance might develop between a single interviewer and one family member. Conferences that include all members of the clinical team can also provide an opportunity to enhance objectivity, share insights, and identify questions for further examination.

(4) Parents should be interviewed separately and if possible on different days. Clinicians who evaluate adults who have made threats or been violent must give careful consideration to ensuring the safety of both family members and themselves. We encountered several cases in which a father waited until his wife and children had finished their appointments and confronted them in the lobby or the parking lot. One mother was so anxious and fearful because her husband was in the building that she and her daughter spent most of a session after father's exit doing little more than holding each other and rocking. Joint interviewing, when planned, should be arranged so that no client or clinician is placed at risk of injury.

(5) Children should be evaluated carefully, not only for signs of abuse, but also for more subtle forms of emotional distress. Allegations involving children should be taken seriously. Their assessments must be done with great patience and care. A number of the children in this sample were seen in supportive, non-directive sessions for some time before they were able to begin to share information about life at home. Direct and forceful questioning of reluctant children must be avoided. Children should be observed when possible during interactions with each parent.

(6) Conferences throughout the evaluation should include all interviewers so that conflicting reports by family members can be identified and evaluated. Members of the clinical team must maintain a neutral stance throughout the evaluation. Negotiating an understanding about the questions to be addressed and the course of the evaluation with each of the parents allows the team to hear each parent and child's story without any family member feeling at an unfair disadvantage.

(7) A "debriefing" conference should be offered to each parent at the end of the evaluation. Such a conference affords the clinicians an opportunity to present the team's findings and recommendations in detail, to provide clarifications, and to answer questions. In the case of the wives, this

time was used to validate their perceptions as real and not "crazy" and to encourage them to seek safety for themselves and their children. For the men, the reality of their behavior and the team's unwillingness to sanction it was made clear. As these cases illustrate, an adequate resolution of the family crisis could not be established, until the possibility of wife battering was considered.

CONCLUSION

There is no substitute for careful, comprehensive evaluation in cases involving allegations of child maltreatment. Evaluators must be willing to examine the entire context of family dynamics. When the focus of an evaluation is primarily on whether or not abuse occurred, important information may be missed. As these cases illustrate, an adequate resolution of the family crisis could not be established, until the possibility of wife battering was considered.

REFERENCES

Gilligan, C. (1982). *In a different voice.* Cambridge: Harvard University Press.
Kegan, R. (1982). *The evolving self.* Cambridge, MA: Harvard University Press.
Schecter, S. (1989, March). *Treatment and advocacy of battered women: Principles and distinctions.* Paper presented at the Fifth Annual Conference on Abuse and Victimization in Life-Span Perspective, Boston, MA.
Selman, R. (1980). *The growth of interpersonal understanding: Clinical and developmental analysis.* New York: Academic Press.

ALLEGATIONS OF MALTREATMENT IN FAMILY FOSTER HOMES

Maltreatment in Family Foster Homes: Dynamics and Dimensions

Emily Jean McFadden
Patricia Ryan

ABSTRACT. This article discusses the dynamics and dimensions of child maltreatment in family foster care. The topics considered include the nature and incidence of child maltreatment in foster care, family factors and system factors that lead to maltreatment, characteristics of foster children at risk for maltreatment, and reasons for false allegations against foster families.

Family foster care is in a state of crisis. Increased numbers of children in care coupled with a decrease in the number of foster family homes (General Accounting Office, 1989) results in a serious shortage of adequate placements for children as reflected in increased reports of maltreatment of children in family foster care. Although substantial numbers of homes are licensed or approved each year, retention rates for new families are low. In some areas fewer than 50% remain licensed for a year or more.

Emily Jean McFadden and Patricia Ryan are affiliated with the Institute for the Study of Children and Families, Eastern Michigan University, Ypsilanti, MI 48197.

As more experienced foster parents leave the system, they are not being replaced. There are many reasons for the shortage of homes and low retention rates. Few foster parents receive training to handle the problems of the children placed with them. Board rates seldom cover their out-of-pocket expenses for the children. High caseloads allow little time for support services. Those families that continue to provide a home for children are often overloaded and find community resources are inadequate to meet the needs of the children in their care. As foster parents learn of allegations of abuse against other families, they fear such allegations will also be brought against them.

CHILD ABUSE IN FAMILY FOSTER CARE

During the early eighties, substantiated allegations of abuse and neglect against foster parents ranged from two to twenty-eight per thousand licensed homes in a sample of states (Ryan & McFadden, 1983). These rates have risen significantly although it is not clear whether this reflects an increase in maltreatment or merely an increase in reports as workers and the community become more sensitive to the possibility that children in family foster care may be maltreated by those who are charged with their protection. There has been a proliferation of civil and class action suits charging state and local agencies with the abuse and neglect of children injured, exploited or killed in foster homes while legal experts seek to establish constitutional grounds for the protection of children while in out-of-home care (Mushlin, 1988).

This article focuses on the dynamics and dimensions of maltreatment of children while in family foster care. It will address the following issues:

1. System factors in family foster care maltreatment,
2. Types of maltreatment,
3. Foster family dynamics leading to maltreatment,
4. Characteristics of children at risk for maltreatment, and
5. Reasons for false allegations against foster families.

The article draws upon a variety of resources in addition to the limited body of literature on maltreatment in foster care. The authors studied the quantitative and qualitative aspects of allegations of maltreatment in foster care in a sample of 164 cases drawn from five states referred to here as the AAFC study[1] (Ryan, McFadden, & Wiencek, 1987a). In addition, they have engaged in intensive training experiences focused on the prevention of maltreatment in family foster care. The National Foster Care Education

Project[2] (Ryan & McFadden, 1986) brought selected trainers from all fifty states together for week long sessions. Over 350 individuals participated in training groups focused on foster home maltreatment, sharing case studies and the practices of various agencies. The authors have also served as expert witnesses in both civil liability and class action suits involving foster care abuse. They have worked with and interviewed foster families, foster children and former foster children in North America and abroad. Although the formal data base is weak, the seriousness of the problem demands a summary of what is currently known, both as the basis for improved practice and to highlight those areas where more research is needed.

TYPES OF MALTREATMENT

The definition of what constitutes maltreatment in foster care differs from agency to agency in line with state statutes and standards. Many agencies prohibit foster parents from using punishments prevalent in the community such as spanking, withholding food or making threats. In a misguided effort to control a child's behavior, a foster parent may overuse what might otherwise be an acceptable disciplinary tool, such as confinement to a bedroom all weekend or writing "I will be good" 1,000 times. Many behaviors handled as maltreatment by the agency when the child is in foster care would not be grounds for intervention in a biological family. However, once the state has removed children from their own homes and placed them in foster care for their protection, a higher standard of care is promulgated through state licensing regulations or agency disciplinary policy.

Physical Abuse

Physical abuse of children in foster care may include any form of physical punishment ranging from a mild swat to being beaten, hit, bitten, burned or otherwise injured. The extent of injury involved may vary from no visible marks or bruises to broken bones, internal injuries, and even death.

Sexual Abuse and Exploitation

Sexual abuse and exploitation also includes a number of different behaviors from fondling, to penetration, vaginal or oral intercourse, to using youngsters in prostitution or in producing pornographic materials.

Lack of Supervision

Lack of supervision may include such diverse behaviors as those resulting in a child setting a fire or in one child victimizing another child. It is
often related to maltreatment by other children in the foster home, or
leaving children with an inappropriate caregiver. Because children in foster care have survived earlier traumas leading to their placement, they
often need more intense supervision than children who have not been maltreated. By assuming custody of a child, the agency assumes a certain
degree of legal responsibility for the child's health, safety and well-being
(Besharov, 1983). The risk of liability increases the need for close supervision. As foster parents do not know much about new children in their
home and as agencies frequently lack or fail to convey appropriate information about the child's conditions or behaviors, there is a high degree of
unpredictability of behavior.

Emotional Abuse

Emotional abuse includes such behaviors as swearing at or demeaning a
child. It also includes some behaviors unique to foster care. A foster parent who criticizes the child's original family or threatens to have the
worker remove the child is being emotionally abusive by many agencies'
standards.

Neglect

Neglect by a foster parent may be failure to provide necessary food and
clothing, or the misuse of funds designated to meet the needs of the child.
Some foster families have only minimal resources to meet their own
needs. They have difficulty when the foster care payment is late or if a
child has a need not covered by the standard rate. Neglect may be related
to unusual pressures on the family such as a serious illness in the family,
or it may stem from lack of knowledge about procedures and role responsibilities. Medical neglect or the failure to get medical attention necessary
to prevent serious illness or disability may be due to lack of resources
which accept Medicaid or to the foster family's lack of knowledge about
preventive health care and disease processes.

Unfortunately, children in foster care are sometimes subject to other
treatments which are not readily classified above. These usually involve
severe emotional trauma and sometimes physical maltreatment as well.
Examples from the AAFC study (McFadden, Ryan, & Wiencek, 1986)
include forcing a child to drink urine, locking a child out of the house in
the dark, forcing a child to sleep in an unfinished basement or having

children run a gauntlet where they are beaten by other children. One foster parent punished a child by forcing her to watch an adult light one match after another, knowing the child had survived a fire in which her sister had died.

SYSTEMIC FACTORS CONTRIBUTING TO MALTREATMENT IN FAMILY FOSTER CARE

One study of foster home maltreatment in New York City (Vera Institute of Justice, 1981) found several child welfare practice variables related to abuse including: failure of the agency to match children with the preferences and skills of the families with whom they were placed; placement of too many children in a home; absence of worker home visits or monitoring; lack of foster parent training; and failure to decertify homes which had been found deficient. Tobias (1982) found a significantly higher rate of abuse or neglect in situations where a child was placed on an emergency basis and where the home studies were of poor quality. The AAFC study (Ryan, McFadden, & Wiencek, 1988a), however, found that homes licensed as emergency homes were less likely to have allegations substantiated against them suggesting that placement of children in homes specially trained and organized for emergency placements might be able to better handle traumatized youngsters. This study also reported that allegations of abuse against a foster family were less likely to be substantiated when the child had had contact with his or her family within the past thirty days and when the worker had interviewed the child at the last licensing renewal.

Agency responsibility in preventing maltreatment of children in foster care might be divided into three categories: Certification or approval of foster families, placement of a given child with a family, and monitoring of the placement. These functions are limited in their effectiveness by the critical shortage of foster homes, huge caseloads and lack of training for agency staff as well as foster parents.

Certification

Certification, licensing or some form of approval of foster families is required by every agency. The home study is one way to determine whether a family is suited to foster care and to reject a family with a high potential for maltreating children. Typically agencies attempt to evaluate a family's experiences parenting their own children and other experiences which may influence their suitability as foster parents. Unfortunately, the process does not necessarily reject potential families which are inadequate or dysfunctional. In an era when agencies do not have enough homes and children are kept in hospitals, RTC or shelters long after they should be sent home, there is tremendous pressure to approve homes. Workers faced with keeping a child overnight in the office many not be as selective in developing new homes as they might wish to be. Although many agencies strive to maintain standards, the chronic shortage of foster homes acts as a countervailing force. Workers may feel pressured into taking shortcuts to license families. Home studies are often superficial, important information is not ascertained and critical questions are never asked. The maltreatment investigation then uncovers critical areas. These might include inappropriate arrangements for child care or the existence of extended family members who are very involved with the family but who were never included in the home study.

Case No. 1. Mrs. Q, the single parent of an adolescent daughter, had two adult sons living out of the home. One was a drug dealer, the other was in a half way house for the mentally ill. Both of these men were in and out of the home regularly, but the agency did not know of their existence until the mentally ill son was accused of beating a ten year old boy for disobeying Mrs. Q. In this case the worker did not even attempt to learn about adult children and the extent to which their current life situations might reflect either unperceived difficulties in the foster family or environmental risks for children who might be placed there. An intuitive feel for the foster mother's warmth led this worker to accept, without any probing, her statement that her sons were now on their own and had very little to do with the family.

Case No. 2. Mr. L was a divorced single father who specialized in taking school-aged boys under the age of twelve. He was noted for his devotion to the children. The agency staff was shocked when allegations of sexual abuse were filed. Only later did they learn that he never saw the children of either of his marriages, having lost custody in both divorces due to the children's allegations that he had sexually abused them. If the agency staff had followed a practice common to adoption, they would have contacted all children living out of the home as part of the home study. If like many states, they had required fingerprinting and a thorough police check, they would have discovered that Mr. L was a pedophile. Had staff been adequately trained, they might have recognized several indicators of his problem.

The criteria for evaluating a home are often difficult to operationalize. Few workers have the training and experience in family assessment to make objective determinations. Most licensing regulations list numerous tangible criteria such as number of rooms in the home or smoke detectors. These are much easier to determine than the family's ability to cope with unusual behaviors or their flexibility in parenting. Many workers rely on intuitive reactions to a family. Unfortunately, this not only leads to the licensing of inadequate families but may result in rejection of potential resources because families differ from what a worker feels is normal or good.

While licensing is a first line of defense in the prevention of foster home maltreatment, particularly the screening of applicants by police check and child abuse registry, not all abuse occurs in inadequate families who could be identified as such in advance. Often families who have done a good job in raising their own children and have provided excellent foster care to a number of children will not be able to handle the behaviors of a particular child and use more and more extreme forms of discipline. Because the agency holds these families in high regard, staff is likely to overload the family with children who are more and more difficult. After they demonstrate skill with one or more needy child, even more difficult children are placed in the family with concomitant increase in stress and pressure on the family. A family member may physically abuse a child in an attempt to discipline; an ill or chronically depressed foster parent may neglect the physical needs of a child or become verbally or emotionally abusive; or someone misreads the sexualized behaviors of a child as a sexual invitation rather than as the need for attention or affection.

Recertification

As important as the initial home study may be in screening out inappropriate applicants, the recertification process is just as important. Much of the maltreatment in foster care occurs not in inadequate families but in families stressed by the rigors of fostering, especially sequential overloading. The escalation of stress in the home should be assessed in the yearly or biennial recertification process. In an effective recertification process all members of the family, including all children placed in the home, are interviewed and observed; all changes in family composition noted and assessed; family economic resources are verified; health issues are discussed and medically verified if necessary; and the home environment is reassessed in terms of health and safety. A critical element of a thorough recertification is a complete review of all earlier family studies and recertifications in order to assess the direction and magnitude of change and family coping mechanisms.

Like all families, foster families constitute a complex and ever changing set of relationships. Foster families are even more complex than most others because children are constantly coming and leaving. This often leads to a situation of chronic grief. The family must adapt to separations from children to whom they have become very attached. Young children in the family may not understand why some children leave and others stay. They may become anxious that they will also be moved by the caseworker. Often feelings of sadness over a child's departure are not resolved before another child is placed. Without a chance to mourn, anger may be displaced, the former child idealized, and unfavorable comparisons made. In many families this chronic grief leads to feelings of fatigue and depression or somatization of affect with headaches, stomach problems or back aches. This escalation of illness and health problems often leads to maltreatment.

> Mrs. R had been fostering for over twelve years. The most recent recertification study before the maltreatment investigation noted severe problems in housekeeping. A review of earlier studies would have revealed that Mrs. R had originally been described as an "immaculate housekeeper" and as a nurturing, high energy woman. After her husband's untimely death five years ago, the quality of home care declined, with worker notes that housekeeping had been discussed. Mrs. R became particularly upset after her husband's death when twin boys were returned to their parents against her advice. Licensing records revealed Mrs. R had reported headaches which would leave her prostrate. The agency continued to place preschool children in the home despite Mrs. R's statement that she was getting "too old to chase little ones around." Following the death of Mrs. R's only daughter, the licensing worker noted her depression and the poor housekeeping. A homemaker was sent to help her clean the house. Mrs. R continued to complain of health problems and became more upset each time a child left. Finally a complaint of neglect was substantiated due to her poor housekeeping and the chronically dirty condition of the children.

A comprehensive recertification process would have noted and responded to Mr. R's downward spiral of grief, depression, health problems and poor housekeeping and recommended a change in the number or type of placements especially in light of Mrs. R's stated reservations about caring for very young children.

Decertification

When a home is decertified, workers feel disillusioned and angry with the family which no longer lives up to their expectations. Identifying with the child's pain and feeling guilty about the placement, their reaction is often punitive even when they have worked closely with the family for many years. Regardless of staff's opinion as to the authenticity of the allegations, they must investigate them. Potential liability or criminal charges further complicates any attempt for mutual problem identification and resolution. Frequently children are moved precipitously, the home is decertified or the foster family decides they will no longer foster. Regardless of the results of the investigation, a family exploited by the agency to provide protection of children faces a crisis which may last for years if help and support are not provided.

Placement

Placement of a child in a specific home is another critical point in prevention of abuse. Inappropriate placement of children is again part of the larger problem of institutional neglect. Lack of adequate resources for foster care, overburdened caseworkers, uncovered caseloads, and a chronic shortage of foster homes lead to short cuts and violations of good practice. The good will of foster parents is exploited and homes are overused, filled with difficult children until stress mounts up, causing the family to leave care because of illness, anger, burnout, marital problems. The parents pass their threshold of tolerance and maltreat a child. Because there are so few homes, foster parents' preferences and self-assessments as to the type of children they can care for are often ignored. It is not unusual for a license to be expanded to care for a wider age range of children or even for more children simply on the basis that the placement worker has been able to talk a family into taking one more child, or one who is older or younger than the family wanted. Because few foster families have received adequate training, they have difficulty resisting the worker who wants to place an inappropriate child with them simply because this is the only opening available. They do not know about, or know how to insist on getting, the resources and support they need to work with a difficult child. They easily succumb to pleas that they are the only resource and that if they refuse, this child will be sent to an institution. In this way, families are overloaded or find themselves working with children for whom they are emotionally and physically ill-prepared.

Monitoring

Monitoring the placement once a child is in care is also critical in reducing the potential for maltreatment. Most agencies require caseworker visits with the foster family at least monthly. Such visits provide the agency with crucial information about the child's development and adjustment to the foster home. Unfortunately, large caseloads and other time pressures often make it difficult for workers to make the required visits. Once a child has settled in, visits may become fewer and fewer. Agency staff want to believe that everything is going well. They are relieved when they are not called upon. It is easy to feel that foster parents are super-human beings who can heal any child. Agency awards for "Foster Parent of the Year" often reflect the illusion of the perfect family and reinforce any tendency to believe that foster parents can do the job alone, freeing workers for other tasks. Staff like foster families who never refuse to take a child no matter how difficult. They want families who will spend many hours transporting children to appointments and visits, who will work with the children's own families, who can find their own resources, who do not call on them often. They often find it easier to give foster parents superficial reassurances especially when they can not find the time to develop more substantive assistance. They expect foster parents to put fostering ahead of all other aspects of their lives. They forget or do not understand the cumulative stress of fostering.

Maltreatment in family foster care is not limited to new, inexperienced families. Dawson (1983) reports that over half of the incidents he studied were in families that had fostered for over five years and the AAFC study (Ryan, McFadden, & Wiencek, 1987b) found that the mean length of time families had fostered at the time of the substantiated incident of abuse was 4.70 years. The AAFC study also found that 50% of the families with substantiated abuse complaints had fewer than five contacts with a worker during the previous six months and that 18% had not had any contacts at all during that period.

Similarly, the stresses of fostering may affect the marriage, thus weakening the entire family's adaptive capacity.

> Mr. and Mrs. A had been considered among the agency's finest foster parents. They were a couple in their mid-forties whose adolescent children had been leaving home over the past five years. As each of the A children left, the agency placed an additional adolescent boy in the home. Mrs. A remained very involved with the youths but Mr. A gradually withdrew from family life as he became more and more unhappy with the chaotic home situation. The work-

ers were not aware of his discontent as they never talked with him or visited when he was at home. Mrs. A had made a brief reference at the time of recertification that her husband was very busy with work, but did not mention his increased drinking or the deterioration in their relationship. In neediness and frustration, she turned to one of the youths in the home, rationalizing that since he had earlier been sexually abused by a male, she was providing reassurance that he was truly heterosexual. The situation came to the attention of the agency only after Mr. A moved out.

The agency ignored the A's life cycle crisis point as their children left home and continued to place youths without helping the family reevaluate their situation. The recertification, and all of the other visits, were superficial and did not involve the foster father. Because he worked during the day, he was never present, nor did workers reach out to discover his perceptions of the family situation. Good casework support might have helped this couple deal with marital problems before the family was split and a youth abused.

Such failures are all too common and when uncovered, it is easy to point to poor casework practice. However, caseload size, little systematic training and lack of supervision are the real source of poor practice. Over half of the foster care workers in public agencies lack any social work education and few agencies provide more than superficial training for their staff. Consequently, staff turnover is very high (Ryan, McFadden, & Wiencek, 1988b). Although the normative case size is believed to be 20 cases per worker, those of most public agencies are much higher, often by several times. Workers with caseloads of 40 or more have less than 4 hours a month per case for visits, paper work, court appearances and services to natural families. Under these conditions, no amount of training or commitment will overcome the sheer lack of time. However, caseload size depends on resources and is often established by decree rather than on the basis of an analysis of what it takes to accomplish the task, in this case protecting children and providing services to them and their families.

FOSTER FAMILY DYNAMICS LEADING TO MALTREATMENT

The causes of abuse and neglect in family foster care are diverse. In some cases they are similar to those leading to abuse and neglect in other families. However, one study (Bolton, Laner, & Gai, 1981) comparing maltreatmenting foster families with abusive natural families found foster parents to be older, more affluent, and more likely to be married and that the maltreatment was more likely to be in response to a discipline situation. Foster parents may be viewed as a select group of parents since they have been licensed or in some way studied by agency staff. Yet they, like all families possess vulnerabilities which may be exacerbated by the rigors of fostering. They take on responsibilities which far exceed the demands of parenting one's own children. The foster parent encounters many stressful situations engendered by the fostering role or the agency's lack of resources. Board payments rarely cover the actual costs of the child. It is often hard to find a provider who will accept the child's Medicaid card. They frequently lack crucial information about a child's background and workers often fail to return telephone calls. They are almost always caught in conflicting expectations, "treat them just like your own" but "restrict discipline to what is allowed by agency standards"; "give them all the love you can" but "be careful how you touch them."

Lack of Training

Despite the recent emphasis on including foster parents as members of the treatment team, they are still often excluded from the decision making process. Foster parents are often isolated from each other and lack training. They are frequently expected to work with children's families without any preparation to deal with differences in values and behaviors, and have no help in dealing with their feelings about the family's abusive behavior which brought the children into care. Although foster parents may have been competent parents to their own children, they soon discover that fostering is very different from the normal parenting role. The stressors inherent in fostering can be wearing and frustrating.

As the foster family confronts the exigencies of the fostering role, they simultaneously experience the normal stresses of family living. Things change. Children start school or leave home. Foster parents reach middle age and reevaluate their situations. Their own parents may make new demands upon them. They may no longer be able to maintain their usual pace because of an illness or a death in the extended family. Unanticipated factors such as unemployment may diminish the family's resources. Often a marriage which needs room to grow is swamped under the demands of fostering.

Sexual Boundaries

Much of the sexual abuse perpetrated by foster parents occurs in homes where there is no indication whatsoever that the parents sexually abused their own children. This suggests that the incest taboo is salient and parents feel a firm restraint with their own children. However, such feelings do not necessarily apply when dealing with an unrelated child, especially adolescents. It is not always clear what triggers sexual responses on the part of foster family members. In cases of younger victims it may be related to the child's sexualized behavior while with the adolescents it may be their developing sexuality and body changes accompanying puberty. Analysis of cases in which a foster parent had sexual relations with an adolescent, suggest that the relationship appears to resemble an extra-marital affair more than the typical incest case.

Economic Resources

The AAFC study (Ryan, McFadden, & Wiencek, 1987a) found no relationship between maltreatment and a number of foster families characteristics including socio-economic status, age of parents, family size, and marital status with the exception that there was a very low incidence of sexual abuse in families headed by a single woman. However, in several cases the family's lack of economic resources appeared to play a role.

> Mrs. W was a widow who had successfully raised her own children on social security survivor benefits and had not worked outside the home. Her financial situation was tenuous at best. She needed the intensive rate received for fostering children with special needs and rarely refused a placement. A nine year old developmentally disabled girl was placed with her. The child soiled her bed and pajamas every night. Each day after the children were on the school bus, Mrs. W would walk five blocks to the laundromat to wash the dirty linen. The child's teacher complained that the child usually smelled. Mrs. W asked the agency for help but did not get a response from the worker. The school reported bruising on the child's buttocks. Mrs. W admitted she had begun hitting the child with a hairbrush each time she had an accident.

This case typifies a number of salient issues such as the foster parent's lack of resources (no washing machine), the overloading of the home with special needs children, the lack of foster parent training and support, and the risk created by the child's behavior. This foster parent had provided good care for foster children in the past and demonstrated her ability to provide for a family on meager resources. She was used to taking her washing to the laundromat but going every day was too much especially when school staff added to her pressures by intimating that she was not clean. One wonders what would have happened if the agency had provided her with a washing machine. Certainly the worker failed to discuss the child's soiling and how it should be handled.

Foster Family's Children

Too often agencies fail to prepare and train foster parents to understand that children who have been maltreated may act out with other children in the family. Because of the shortage of foster homes, workers may fail to heed the common practice dictum that children who are physically or sexually aggressive should not be placed in homes with younger children who could be potential victims.

> The M's were shocked and horrified to find their own eight year old son engaged in sexual play with a much younger child who had been placed with them. They were even more upset to find that the agency considered this behavior as an indication of neglect on their part. The investigation ruled out the suspicion that the foster father had been sexually abusing his own son. The investigating worker, however, determined that the child had been sexually abused by at least two different adolescents who had had short term placements with the family. Discouraged and disheartened, the M's left fostering so that their son could heal, and to assure that he would not be put in situations in which he might be either the victim or the victimizer.

As this case indicates, maltreatment in foster care has many victims. Although the agency has primary responsibility to the children in care, they also have a duty to protect all children. Placements that jeopardize other children make a parody of the child protective system. The damage to children in placement is not the only tragedy in these situations. All the members of the foster family must live with the consequences of the incident and its aftermath, including broken marriages, hurt or estranged children, and occasionally prison sentences. Foster families are not clients. They are members of the treatment team and should be treated accordingly. However, their work situations involve their whole families. Child welfare staff should have a strong value orientation toward preserving family life. Although it is easy to dismiss some maltreating foster families as dysfunctional and to rationalize that they would have come to grief in some other way even if they had never fostered, it must be recognized that many families suffer only because they tried to help. Rather than treating families in a punitive way, agencies must take responsibility and recognize the extent to which foster families are chronically exploited. When an allegation of abuse is made against a family, all the members will be in crisis and will need support. Although the agency charged with the protection of children and investigating the accusations cannot offer this support, they should identify other community resources to support the foster family. Whether or not they have maltreated children they need help, especially if there are other children in the family.

Liability issues are so strong that it might seem impossible to continue placing children in a home in which substantiated maltreatment has occurred unless there are compelling extenuating circumstances backed by expert opinion. However, there are many situations where a family might continue to provide good care to a child already in the home or to other children. The decision as to whether or not a family should continue to foster must be based on a number of factors including: the seriousness of the maltreatment, the extent to which the behavior might be repeated, and the support and counseling the family has had to assure that maltreatment will not be repeated with another child. Agencies need to invest in appropriate support and training for foster families so that they can continue to guide and protect the children who need them. This requires that agency staff also have appropriate training and manageable workloads.

CHARACTERISTICS OF FOSTER CHILDREN AT RISK FOR MALTREATMENT

The majority of children and youths in foster care have been physically or sexually abused, or physically and/or emotionally neglected. They have suffered separation from their family environment and often have a variety of behaviors that are difficult for caregivers. These characteristics put them at risk for further maltreatment in out of home placement. The situations that led to their placement along with the dynamics of separation combine to make the foster care experience threatening. Children and youths entering foster care bring with them a totality of experiences and perceptions of family living from the original abusive or neglectful environment. A child may have learned that the only time he gets attention is when he acts up and Daddy hits him. Thus, he assumes that all dads show attention by hitting. When placed in a foster home, he may exhibit a number of provocative behaviors from his earlier repertoire, and a mild mannered foster father will wonder why he suddenly feels like striking this child. With appropriate training, foster parents will realize the way in which the child's interactional patterns stem from their expectations and former adaptive coping techniques. They can then teach children that there are other ways of gaining attention and affection.

Sexually Abused Children

Similarly, a child who has been sexually abused in her family has learned a way of interacting with adults which was rewarded. Perhaps she received special praise or attention for being "good to Daddy" when she was fondled or performed certain kinds of touching. She may also have learned that she is important or powerful because of her ability to "keep Dad happy" or that she is "holding the family together." Typically such a child will expect that all adult males expect "special" touching and this is the way to please them. She bases her expectations of family living on her experiences in her own home. She does not yet realize that her behavior is unacceptable or that her foster father has only a benign interest in her. The child's perceptions of the foster family are colored by his or her prior experiences. These perceptions sometimes lead to "false allegations" of maltreatment.

Children who have been sexually abused have learned complex and subtle interaction patterns with adults. These include touching, stroking, gazing, appearing partially undressed, intrusive eye contact, hugging, and clinging. These are often refereed to as "seductive" behaviors, which is a misnomer. The child who exhibits such behavior is neither seducing nor asking to be seduced. Such a child is asking for attention or affection, and trying to please adults. Unfortunately, many adults misread such signs. Children who have been sexually abused or exploited are at high risk, not only for further sexual abuse, but for physical abuse because of foster parents' dismay or shock at their sexualized behavior. They may act out sexually with younger children and a foster parent may lose control in efforts to intervene and protect the smaller child. Many foster parents are uncomfortable with sexual behavior and are overcome emotionally when confronted by sexual acting out. Foster parents who have been trained in the dynamics of abuse and its sequelae are better able to deal with these behaviors and help children learn safer and more effective ways of meeting their needs.

Unfortunately, some foster parents, perhaps because they have been sexually abused themselves or because they are not getting their own psycho-sexual needs met, respond to these cues as if they were a sexual invitation. The AAFC study found that younger children who were sexually abused in foster homes were very likely to have been sexually abused previously while this was not as likely for older victims (McFadden, Ryan, & Wiencek, 1986). This should not be construed as meaning that children invite or cause sexual abuse. Rather it is an observation of the risk factors which make children more vulnerable. Current estimates are that 75% of children in care have been sexually abused in the past, although the agency may not be aware of it particularly in the case of male children. Boys are extremely reluctant to report sexual abuse (Nasjliti, 1989; Bolton, 1989) due to fears of being thought less masculine and the homophobia involved when the perpetrator is a male.

Adolescents

The adolescent, particularly the adolescent who has been previously abused, is also at risk for maltreatment in foster care. Adolescents face developmental issues around autonomy and moving away from parental authority. If they were maltreated earlier, they may have remained developmentally fixated at an earlier stage. Such youths need more structure and nurturing than do other adolescents (Ziefert, 1984). Poorly equipped to care for themselves, they often experience unintentional neglect by foster parents who don't understand their developmental lags and thus don't provide the high degree of care required. This problem is compounded by youths who appear pseudomature or self-sufficient.

Other characteristics may put children at high risk for victimization. Dawson (1983) found that special needs such as handicapping conditions contributed to maltreatment. Certainly conditions which require extra time, patience, skill, or resources on the part of the foster family increase their stress.

Children with Multiple Placements

Children and youths who have experienced multiple placements are also at high risk for maltreatment in foster homes. They may have developed behaviors which are unacceptable in most foster homes and they have learned to test foster parents with these behaviors. Children tend to blame themselves for the original separation from their parents. They believe they must be bad, unlovable, or undeserving. This negative self-perception is reinforced when a placement disrupts. Many such children are locked into a position of "I'll reject you before you reject me" or "Since I know they won't want me sooner or later, I might as well get it out before I begin to like it here." The more placements a child has had, the higher the risk that he or she will expect and provoke maltreatment.

However, the knowledge that the placement is permanent is in and of itself no guarantee of reduced risk for maltreatment. A study of foster parent adoption (Meezan & Shireman, 1985) found that some of the disruptions may have been situations in which the foster parent feared abusing the children while in other disruptions, foster parents reported they felt the agency staff had put pressure on them to adopt. Dawson (1983) found in Canada that children who were crown (permanent) wards were at greater risk for maltreatment in foster care. The AAFC study (Ryan, McFadden, & Wiencek, 1987) found several cases of substantiated abuse in homes where the foster family planned to adopt the child but the adoption had been delayed. The abuse may have stemmed from ambivalence about the adoption, the failure of the worker to monitor and support the family when everything seemed to be going well, or status indeterminacy creating stress for both the foster parents and the child.

Children's Behavior

In examining the risk factors and characteristics associated with maltreatment in family foster care, it is clear that the child's behavior has a great impact on the foster family. Relatively little research has focused on the types of behaviors that trigger physical abuse by an adult caregiver. In the AAFC study (Ryan, McFadden, & Wiencek, 1987) the most frequent behavior cited as leading to the physical abuse was wetting or soiling, including wetting the bed. The next most frequent category was general disobedience or oppositional behavior. Some of the behaviors which triggered the actual physical maltreatment were relatively trivial, such as failing to replace a toothpaste cap, while others were more serious as not stopping when hurting the cat. What seemed to upset the adult was that the child did not mind and a series of repeated instances of disobedience led to loss of control on the part of the adult. Reading such case records, one becomes aware of a mounting spiral of tension and frustration as foster parents deal with the stress of difficult children who do not respond to disciplinary techniques which have proved effective with other children. Often foster parents will solicit the aid of caseworkers but find premature reassurance or referral for psychological evaluations unhelpful in the immediate situation. In some cases foster parents complain repeatedly but get no help from the worker.

Although we can in no way blame a child for his or her maltreatment, it is clear that certain behaviors or characteristics increase the risk of victimization. Recognition of those characteristics that make a child vulnerable indicate a need for an even greater level of services, vigilance and support for the foster family. An assessment tool (McFadden, 1984) has been developed to evaluate the degree of risk for a particular child. Variables such as a history of maltreatment, various behaviors such as wetting and soiling, and various personal characteristics such as developmental delay can be evaluated and then shared with foster parents as part of the planning process to support their work with difficult children.

FALSE ALLEGATIONS

The increase in allegations against foster families adds to the anxiety and stress of all foster families. All families who foster wonder "will someone make an allegation against us? What would we do if a child makes a false allegation? Most agency staff tend to believe that children seldom lie about abuse. However, children may misconstrue or distort. In addition, reports of abuse may come from the community or from the child's family. Unfortunately, there are many people who are suspicious of foster families and their motives for fostering. School and medical personnel may be quicker to file reports against foster families than they would against the child's own family. Neighbors may resent the family for fostering and any disruption it brings to the neighborhood. Families who resent the agency's intrusion in their own lives may be overly quick in reporting imagined maltreatment to the children removed from their care. Whatever the source of the report, the child welfare agency must follow up. Foster families need to know that their behavior will be scrutinized and must be trained to keep records and report all unusual incidents.

Abuse Reports from Children

When children in care report maltreatment in foster care, investigators need to understand that while it may generally be true that children seldom lie about abuse in their own families, foster care is different. A child in care has already learned about the system and its impact. A child desperate to get back home may see an allegation against a foster family as a means to accomplish this end. A child in care may be caught in divided loyalties and try to reassure a parent by criticizing the foster family. Some children have learned that a sure way to get moved is to allege abuse.

In many cases, the child who makes a false allegation is not lying but has misinterpreted behavior. He or she may be confused by the intimacy of family living or confused about when certain events happened. Abused children may experience flashbacks or identify their current daddy with the behavior of a previous daddy.

Elena, age 7, had been sexually abused by her father under a fairly specific set of circumstances. It happened late at night after her mother was in bed asleep. He would come into her bedroom and sit on the edge of the bed, whispering and fondling her. Many times Elena would pretend to be asleep when penetration occurred or to have just wakened, feeling drowsy and confused. After placement in care, Elena had nightmares about the sexual abuse. One night as she was thrashing and crying out, her foster father sat down beside her trying to comfort her with a hug. Elena was half asleep and very frightened. To her, the presence of her foster father in the bedroom was an indication that he too wanted something sexual from her. She did not exactly remember what he had said, but she knew he had touched her. She wasn't sure what she had dreamed and what had actually happened but she told her worker that she was very afraid of her foster father, that he came into her bedroom at night like her dad used to do. He was scaring her and touching her like her dad did.

This case points out the problems when a foster parent believes he is engaged in appropriate parenting behavior but the child perceives it differently. The child is not lying. The child is truly confused by the intimacy of the behavior. Foster parents need thorough training in how to help children without further traumatizing them. Although there are materials and curricula available (McFadden, 1984, 1986; Ryan, 1984), very few agencies routinely train foster parents or staff to increase their understanding about the dynamics of abuse and how foster parents might protect themselves against unwarranted allegations. Foster parents need to know the kinds of behaviors and situations that lead to abuse and how to avoid confusing a child or being alone in situations a child might misinterpret. They need to know about the kinds of behaviors children bring into the foster home and how to develop disciplinary plans which will teach the child without hurting.

It is also important to remember that children will sometimes retract stories that are true. They may fear the unknown and what will happen to them if they are moved. They may have reacted in anger and want to protect the family once they have calmed down. They may fear the family's punitive reaction and that they will be further hurt. Retraction does not mean the allegation was not true. Any allegation is grounds for helping the family uncover and deal with problems whether primarily with the child or indicative of general family dysfunction. It is too simplistic to say that children never lie, yet children must be protected. Each situation must be carefully evaluated as to the context in which the accusations occurred, the child's placement history, experience before placement, desire to return home, perceptions of reality, chronological and developmental ages, the stresses on the foster family, and the role the child is playing in the foster family. It is helpful if the child has been seeing a therapist who can offer an opinion on the child's perception of reality and the dynamics in the foster family. Once again, the best solution is prevention. If workers are actively engaged in working with foster family around the child's adjustment to the home and the family's adjustment to the child, if support services are available and the needs of the child have been carefully matched to the strengths of the family, the likelihood of allegations, true or false, is substantially reduced.

SUMMARY

It is ironic that children removed from their families and placed in foster care for their own protection should be further subjected to maltreatment in a system which calls itself child welfare. It is also ironic that competent and dedicated foster families who give fully of themselves to help children should be suspect. Professionals must address this situation to strengthen the knowledge base, and find creative solutions which protect children while enhancing foster family life and providing prevention oriented services.

Although it is easy to focus blame on the maltreating foster family and to react with demands for more rigorous licensing and screening procedures, most maltreatment in family foster homes is an indication of the failure of the child welfare system, not the individual foster families. Workers need training in family assessment, family dynamics, child development and positive parenting skills if they are to assist foster families and protect children. They need realistic caseloads allowing them adequate time to do their jobs.

Of course, the majority of foster families do not react to increased stress and frustration by maltreating children in their care. Most leave fostering when they no longer feel they can accomplish their job. However, the resulting high turnover further increases the pressure on the remaining resources. All foster families need training and support. They need help in developing the ability to monitor their own families needs and empowerment to be selective in choosing the children with whom they will work. They need access to more resources and the support of the agency and the community if they are to continue to serve vulnerable children and their families. Maltreatment in family care could be significantly reduced if an outraged community demanded that child welfare agencies be given the resources needed to serve children well.

ENDNOTES

1. This project was funded by the National Center on Child Abuse and Neglect (90CA0975/01), 1984-85.

2. This project was funded by the National Center on Child Abuse and Neglect (NCAN 182/90 CA 898), 1981-85.

BIBLIOGRAPHY

Besharov, D. (1989). *Liability issues in child welfare work*. Washington, D.C.: American Bar Association.

Bolton, F., Laner, R., & Gai, D. (1981). For better or for worse? Foster parents and foster child in an officially reported child maltreatment population. *Child and Youth Services Review*, *3*(1-2), 37-53.

Bolton, F., Morris, L., & MacEachron, A. (1989). *Males at risk*. Newbury Park, CA: Sage.

Dawson, R. (1983). *The abuse of children in foster care*. Summary report. Ontario: Family and Children's Services of Oxford County.

General Accounting Office. (1989). *Foster parents: Recruiting and preservice training practices evaluation*. Washington, D.C.: General Accounting Office.

McFadden, E. J. (1984). *Preventing abuse in foster care*. Ypsilanti, MI: Eastern Michigan University.

McFadden, E. J. (1986). *Fostering the child who has been sexually abused*. Ypsilanti, MI: Eastern Michigan University.

McFadden, E. J., Ryan, P., & Wiencek, P. (1986). *Characteristics of the vulnerable child*. Paper presented at International Conference on Child Abuse, Sydney, Australia.

McFadden, E. J. (1989). The sexually abused child in specialized foster family care. In J. Hudson & B. Galaway (Eds.), *Specialist foster family care*. New York: The Haworth Press, Inc.

Meezan, W., & Shireman, J. (1985). *Care and commitment: Foster parent adoption decisions*. Albany, NY: State University of New York Press.

Mushlin, M. B. (1988). Unsafe havens: The case for constitutional protection of foster children from abuse and neglect. *Harvard Civil Rights: Civil Liberties Law Review*, *23*(1).

Nasjliti, M. (1980). Suffering in silence; the male incest victim. *Child Welfare*, *59*(5), 269-275.

Ryan, P. (1983). Survey on abuse and neglect in foster care. *Impact*. Ypsilanti, MI: Eastern Michigan University.

Ryan, P. (1984). *Fostering discipline*. Ypsilanti, MI: Eastern Michigan University.

Ryan, P., & McFadden, E. J. (1986). *Preventing abuse in family foster care*, Final Report. National Foster Care Education Project. Ypsilanti, MI: Eastern Michigan University.

Ryan, P., McFadden, E. J., & Wiencek, P. (1987a). *Analyzing abuse in family foster care*. Final report to the National Center on Child Abuse and Neglect. Ypsilanti, MI: Eastern Michigan University.

Ryan, P., McFadden, E. J., & Wiencek, P. (1987b). *Foster family characteristics related to maltreatment of child while in care*. Paper presented at the Family Violence Research Conference. Durham, NH.

Ryan, P., McFadden, E. J., & Wiencek, P. (1988a). *Analysis of level of agency services related to maltreatment in family foster homes*. Paper presented at North Central Sociological Association. Pittsburgh, PA.

Ryan, P., McFadden, E. J., & Wiencek, P. (1988b). *Casework services in preventing abuse in family foster care: Research results*. Paper presented at the National Symposium on Child Victimization. Anaheim, CA.

Tobias, D. (1982). *The foster care pyramid: Factors associated with the abuse and neglect of children in foster boarding homes*. New York: Human Services Administration.

Vera Institute of Justice. (1981). *Foster home child protection*. New York: Human Resource Administration.

Ziefert, M. (1984). *The abused adolescent*. In E. J. McFadden (Ed.), *Preventing abuse in foster care*. Ypsilanti, MI: Eastern Michigan University.

Child Abuse and Neglect Reports in Foster Care: The Issue for Foster Families of "False" Allegations

Rosemarie Carbino

ABSTRACT. This chapter discusses "false" allegations of child maltreatment in family foster care. What is a "false" report and who reports "falsely" is considered. Foster parent beliefs, experiences and needs are reviewed in relation to how agencies respond when abuse is alleged. Areas of needed change are proposed.

A LETTER FROM A FOSTER MOTHER

Don C, a crisis worker, called me at work to say he was at my home to take Allain and Andy as there was an allegation against me. I immediately went home to meet Don and two detectives. I tried to have them realize that it would harm the boys if removed because of their involvement in swimming classes and summer school. To no avail, I could not convince them. I asked how long before I would hear something. Don stated "probably tomorrow."

When the boys were still not back the next week, I asked the Social Services Director if the boys could be returned for their 4-H participation at the County Fair that they had worked for all year since no evidence of harm was pending, and there were only two people to interview when they returned from vacation. He refused.

A month after the boys left, our attorney called to tell me that the Director had finally requested the children's clothes. I said I would have them ready after my involvement with the Fair was over. Don

Rosemarie Carbino is affiliated with the School of Social Work, 425 Henry Hall, University of Wisconsin-Madison, Madison, WI 53706.

picked up the clothes. We got a letter three weeks later from the County Sheriff Department stating the District Attorney's office didn't find any abuse because the child "recanted and explained his motive."

Through the whole course of the investigation, no one from the Social Service Department had the common courtesy to ask my side of the story. I would think fifteen years of dedicated foster care should entitle me to the equal opportunity to tell my side of the story. No one ever asked me if any of this is true. We have never seen the boys again and we have not been called to take any new foster kids. I feel we were on somebody's blacklist.

Now the Social Services sent us a letter stating they are discontinuing our foster home license. We are filing papers to the State for an appeal hearing because we have done nothing wrong and we want our name cleared. But as soon as this is over we are quitting fostering.

As this letter illustrates, foster parents are generally unprepared for reports of child abuse or neglect involving their homes and for agency responses subsequent to receipt of a report. Foster parent experiences of these agency responses leave them in shock, isolation, and with a sense of stigma and continuing vulnerability (Carbino, 1987). Foster parents often feel unjustly accused and ill-treated by the agency during and long after the period of protective service investigation, particularly if the situation has not been handled sensitively and/or if children have been removed from the family. In situations where they view allegations involving their foster homes as "false," foster parents often find what ensues once abuse/ neglect is reported very unfair and very damaging.

Foster parent issues involving child maltreatment allegations will be dealt with here without reference to the experiences of reported biological families. Foster parent relationships to an agency are viewed as different from those of biological parents, particularly in that foster parents usually have a prior collaborative relationship with the agency, have fewer legal rights (Garson, 1986; Nadile, 1987; Woods, 1988) and pose more legal liability for the agency (Besharov, 1984; Cassens Moss, 1988). Thus, they may have different experiences following an abuse/neglect report. For foster parents, the collaborative relationship is disturbed. Also they may be dealt with less carefully than are biological parents. However, some issues and experiences of foster families may well parallel and be similar to those of other reported families.

WHAT IS A FALSE ALLEGATION IN FOSTER CARE?

In considering the problem of "false" allegations for foster families, there are difficulties in definition and language. Social agencies and foster parents use different vocabularies to talk about child maltreatment reports and their aftermath (Carbino, 1989). Agencies use the terminology embodied in child protection statutes. While the terms vary from state to state, generally there are two or three categories of possible outcomes. These are that the alleged maltreatment was founded (valid, substantiated, etc.), unfounded (not valid, not substantiated) or that it is not possible to determine the validity of the report (unable to substantiate). In the objective and neutral language of child abuse and neglect dispositions, "false" does not exist as a category. The word takes on its meaning and power depending on the experience and perspective of those who use it. In relation to child abuse allegations, it may mean a number of different things. It may mean that the reported behaviors or situations never occurred. This is generally what "false" means for foster parents whether the report was in error or was a deliberate misrepresentation. It may also mean a different experience of the act or different standards for the action between the reported and the reporter. Foster parents may not agree with the evaluation of the situation by the reporter of child maltreatment. It is possible for the same situation to be believed to be "false" by the one and "true" by the other. And it is possible for the agency charged with investigating the report to come to a third finding, that it is not possible to determine the validity of the report.

So, there is greatest agreement on what are "false" reports in foster care when both the reported foster family and the investigator believe that abuse/neglect did not occur. However, other instances may be considered to involve "false" reports, depending upon the perspective taken. In looking at the issues of false allegations for foster families, it is important to consider their views of the situation. "False" reports may include cases in which the foster family believes itself to be "innocent" while the investigation was unable to conclude whether or not maltreatment occurred.

WHO REPORTS "FALSELY"?

What accounts for "false" reports? There are actually a number of possible situations that involve the reporting of child maltreatment when no maltreatment occurred.

Reporting Standards

Since most jurisdictions define the standard for reporting of child maltreatment as "suspicion" or "reason to believe" a child is being harmed, it is inevitable that a certain portion of reports of child abuse and neglect will be unfounded. Since the criterion for requirement to report was expanded from evidence of abuse to suspicion of abuse in order to protect children more fully, it is reasonable to expect that some reports will be unfounded on this basis alone.

Reporter Misjudgment

Some reporters will be mistaken in their perception of a situation and make a report in good faith which turns out to be unfounded. The relatively high visibility of foster children in the community and public discomfort about conditions in foster care may influence such reports. For example, in one situation a foster parent told of having three neglected foster siblings placed in her home who had learned to survive their previous living situation by eating out of neighborhood garbage cans. Within a few of weeks of placement, the foster parent was horrified to learn that the children had continued this behavior in their new neighborhood and that neighbors had reported the foster home as neglectful.

Reports of child abuse/neglect may be made due to an overly cautious style of the individual reporter and/or the employing organization. The over-caution referred to here relates to the person's or organization's concern for their public image or legal liability rather than to child protection. In these instances, reports may be made on minimal information lest the organization be seen as not acting decisively. A foster parent couple writes,

> Seven months after our three year old foster daughter arrived, the social worker and an aide came to our door and took emergency custody. All we were told was that there were allegations of child abuse and they couldn't divulge the details. We were questioned by the police, then by the clinic where she had therapy . . . The two reports contradicted each other—one was "insufficient evidence" and the other was "abuse unknown." In the midst of this, her family's attorney filed a petition against the agency for placing her in an abusive situation and wrote . . . that they have 120 days in which to sue. So, everyone at (the agency) was shook as this had never happened before. There was a hearing on it and our social worker said if we didn't get in there, we may never have a chance to defend our-

selves. We hired an attorney and got the petition dismissed. Then the agency notified us they were revoking our license . . . We are still waiting for a fair hearing.

In some instances, the reporter may be accurate about the evidence that abuse has occurred, but mistaken about who has been the perpetrator. This can happen when the testimony of young children is involved, when a number of persons may have been perpetrators and/or when the reported abuse occurred long ago. Or some reporters, perhaps natural family members or neighbors, may be convinced there is abuse or neglect because their childhood experiences or their own mental condition convinces them this is so, despite the reality of the situation. These persons may well make invalid reports without intentionally lying.

Deliberate "False" Reporting

There may be some deliberate or malicious intent in reporting. In foster care reports, the reporter might be a natural family member who feels estranged from the agency and/or foster home, an angry child or youth, a neighbor, acquaintance or another foster parent with negative feelings about the foster family. Foster parents often experience these reports as malicious. A foster parent relates, "When our attorney got the materials from the Agency, it seemed our problem was stemming from a couple of vicious, malicious and slandering letters sent by a couple of fellow foster parents. Anyone reading these letters can surmise very quickly the malice and gossip in them."

An intent by foster children to change living situations may also be a motive in "false" reporting. Lacking a sense of how to accomplish their goals by other means, and often lacking any meaningful role in placement decisions, children and youth may resort to alleging abuse. This may be especially true for those who desperately wish to be out of a particular foster home and see no other means to accomplish their goal. Many foster children do not understand the purposes or processes of foster care and may believe that, if they can get out of the foster home, they will be able to go home. Some of their family members may believe the same thing, and, occasionally, a move to home actually does occur after there has been a child abuse report involving the foster family. Children and youth may also report in order to get to another, preferred, placement such as a group home that their friends are in or to achieve other desired goals. For example, in one case, a fifteen year old foster daughter who was infatuated with the 21 year old son of the foster parents, reported that he had sex with her in the belief that he would then have to marry her and she would live with him.

These, and other, motivations and situations result in reports that are not valid as determined by the investigating agency and are experienced as "false" by the foster family. But foster family members may also experience as "false" reports which are substantiated by the investigating agency. "False" as a term reflecting the perception and experience of a foster parent may differ from the terms used by the child protection agency.

Need for Humane Services

A true/false dichotomy is inappropriate as a basis for the service decisions that must be made in child protection. To begin with, because of the complicated family life situations which present themselves in child abuse and neglect work, there is often a mixed picture rather than an either-or situation. Because service to protect and support children in their families, including their foster families, should be the goal of protective service intervention, the nature of the services and resources needed in the situation is often more pertinent than whether a report is "true" or "false."

For example, a foster family in which reported abuse did not occur, but in which family interactions are not constructive for a given child, may need intensive services or a change in placement arrangements in order to be a positive resource. Foster families, in which some foster parent behavior has been determined as abuse by agency standards, may still be a positive resource for its foster children and require time-limited redirection rather than extensive service or placement changes. Both families may well need assistance in addition to deal with the stress generated by the report and by agency responses to it. Thus, concern for families who experience "false" allegations of abuse or neglect would include not only those cases where outcome disposition clearly indicates that abuse did not occur; it would also include those who believe the report to be false regardless of the case determination by CPS.

FOSTER PARENT BELIEFS AND EXPERIENCES

Beliefs

Foster parents see at close range the damaging effects of prior child abuse and neglect on foster children. They view themselves as providing good family care for children, unlike what has occurred in the child's natural family environment. Even when able to understand the natural family circumstances, foster parents are deeply troubled by what has happened to children and view child maltreatment by the natural family as harmful and wrong. Whatever the foster parents' behavior, they clearly separate themselves from "child abusers." In fact, as Ryan and McFadden (1986) suggest, they see themselves as child advocates. Foster parents, particularly through foster parent organizations, support high standards for applicant screening and licensure, support child protection intervention, and regularly request training and education on dealing with abused and neglected children.

At the same time, foster parents tend to be ill-informed about the provisions and implications of child abuse and neglect mandates and about potential agency procedures when maltreatment in foster homes is alleged. This is a result of the very inadequate preparation of foster families by agencies for this possibility. It is also a result of the tendency of foster parents to see the information which is provided as applicable to someone else, to "child abusers."

Given these perceptions, foster families are usually unprepared when a report of child abuse and neglect involves their home. Foster parents often assume, because they have been licensed and relicensed, have spent many years with the agency working with difficult children, and have received verbal recognition of their good work, that they are fully trusted by the agency and are unlikely to be reported for maltreatment of a foster child.

When they are provided with information regarding child abuse allegations against foster homes, there are many who still feel this does not refer to them. As one foster parent said, "I've been in your workshops, two times. I know other people who have been accused and I heard you say this could happen to any of us. But I still didn't believe it could happen to me! Well, now it's happened to me." Gradually more foster parents are becoming aware, through associations with other foster parents or through education workshops, that they are vulnerable to reports of child maltreatment, and that their agencies will treat them differently should this occur.

Experiences

What happens to foster families when agencies respond to reports of child maltreatment in their homes is a pattern of experiences which leave them in shock and isolation with a sense of lasting stigma. This pattern (Carbino, 1987) initially elicited from individual interviews with a small group of foster parents in one state, all of whom were found not to have abused their foster children, has been echoed in individual responses from foster parents from many states at workshops on the subject of abuse allegations in foster care.

Foster parents may experience sudden and abrupt agency intervention, cutoff of communication with the agency, interviews from social service or law enforcement persons they may not know, abrupt removals of one or more foster children although their own children were not removed, agency policies which appeared intended to protect the agency from lawsuit, long periods of "not knowing" what was happening, "no ending" to some investigations or "no clearance" once the investigation was completed. Some reported foster parents, even when the investigation findings indicate the report is not substantiated, say they have been so damaged by the experience that they will stop fostering as soon as their remaining foster children leave care.

Sudden Action

In addition, in instances where the agency feels at risk regarding further maltreatment reports or legal liability, agency behavior towards foster families may change dramatically. Agencies may fail to place more children without giving an explanation, they may revoke or fail to renew foster home licenses, or they may refuse to communicate or to jointly problem-solve, forcing foster parents either to give up or to take on an exhausting series of appeals hearings and other procedures which may drag on for months. Foster parents who believe themselves "falsely accused" and who are still committed to fostering children generally must struggle alone to attempt to regain their position as a trusted foster family within their agency.

These experiences suggest very damaging, albeit unintended, effects on all reported foster families when agencies respond to reports of abuse in foster care. These damaging effects may extend to the natural and foster children in the families, since all family members will be affected by family stress and by agency actions. In addition, while the focus here is not on the children in reported foster homes, it is important to remember that abrupt removals of children are also damaging to children, both those who go and those who remain and cannot be considered positive child protection. Removals and losses of children can profoundly affect all foster family members and intensify the stresses of the situation.

A foster mother of seven years writes:

> Before I knew what had happened I was facing allegations. By fall my home was closed and the Agency was unrelenting in its pursuit of seeking to revoke my license. They told me on a Friday that there was a problem. I requested them to send it all to me in writing, and they agreed there was time. But first thing Monday morning they

sent one caseworker to remove a little tyke that had been with me since he was a couple months old. He was then roughly 16 months. I had been through surgery with this child, I discovered early on that he was almost deaf, I discovered that he had delays, and now the Agency reacted like his life was in danger! Another baby that was to be adopted that Friday was supposed to be removed also but the caseworker refused and the baby stayed until the end of the week. Another little boy who was with me from three days old and now was 19 months was a very fragile personality, very fearful of people, and was to be adopted also. But instead of moving slowly they rushed him out overnight, and later when the adoptive parents had some bonding problems, they and the Agency tried to say it was my fault!

The Agency refused early on to reveal to me any reason for these allegations, so now I had to retain an attorney. By and large they accused me of violating confidentiality by sharing photos of my children with other foster parents at my foster parent group meetings. Second was an accusation of bottle propping! I quickly became an emotional basket case as my home was emptied and my license was on hold . . . . The agency would not budge on their position. It was now necessary for me to request a hearing. This is part of the administrative procedure you must follow when you disagree with their decisions. They do not have a grievance committee or procedure. According to the policy here you are to be granted a hearing within 10 days after asking for one. Mine was a series of stalls and delays so that it took almost 6 months for the initial hearing . . .

In January the hearing was held, it took nine hours. It took until April before I had a decision, guilty. We appealed at once and in short order I was granted a new decision, in my favor. Now the State appealed. Like a long tennis match followed almost three years, decisions and appeals were made. During this time not only was I under a terrific amount of stress, but I learned that foster parents have no rights, no support system, no one to talk to, and the licensing workers and others suddenly begin treating you like you have leprosy. I felt as though I was having a nightmare and I could not wake up and make it go away . . . .

Loss

Those foster families in which no maltreatment has occurred feel further abused by the "unfairness" of being "accused." They feel unfairly treated by abrupt and disrespectful intervention because it seems unde-

served and fails to recognize their good work. They are distressed to feel
that their credibility with the agency is in question and they lose confidence and trust in the agency and in their relationships with their workers.
They experience these as real losses and grieve these losses as well as the
losses of foster children.

A foster parent says:

> Now during all this time I was an emotional wreck. I had 4 empty
> cribs, 2 empty high chairs, toys sitting idle everywhere, 2 empty
> playpens, my beautiful pram sitting idly by the door, and a loose
> stroller and five empty car seats in the car. I do not think I have ever
> cried so long or so hard in my life.
>
> A pall settled over my home, my husband went gloomily off to
> work, muttering all the time about "gestapo tactics" and "you can't
> beat the system." My 4 year old son was terribly confused, asked
> me constantly "why are you crying, Mommy?", "where are my
> brothers and sisters?"
>
> When I tried to explain that the State had to take them away, he
> raised his small fist and shook it in a threatening fashion and vowed
> loudly that he would "get those guys for that!" I was very taken
> aback by his actions as my husband and I are very laid back, quiet
> people, we don't yell much and never threaten people.
>
> Since he used to go to the hospital with me to pick up our newborn
> babies, he came to me one day, put his small arm around my neck,
> and said in his best chipper voice, "don't worry Mommy, let's just
> go to the hospital and get another baby!" I bet I don't have to tell
> you here that that produced more tears.
>
> Our home took on the atmosphere of a place where death had
> visited. I felt no real anger, only a very, very sharp pain, from deep
> hurt, as though someone had stabbed me in my heart. I realized that
> I must struggle now with a grieving process, that this was not going
> to be solved in short order. So I now hastened to move anything and
> everything concerning the little ones into the "baby room," packed
> all the clothes into boxes and put them into the garage, still crying all
> the time. After this I closed the door to the "baby room" and was
> not to enter again . . . until more than two years had passed.

These accounts illustrate the damaging effects of some responses by
agencies when child maltreatment is reported in foster homes. These damaging responses are by no means restricted to investigation procedures,
but relate to the totality of ways an agency may respond and relate to
reported foster families. Though unintended, damage is done to foster

family life, to foster children who are intended to be protected, to agency relationships with foster parents in general, to retention and recruitment of foster homes and to foster care services delivery overall. Considerable changes are needed to redress the situation and these are possible.

To ease the damaging effects of some agency responses to maltreatment reports, services, support and resources should be provided to all reported foster families (Carbino, 1989; Sprouse, 1989). These include provision of information about the nature and likelihood of abuse reports in foster care and what agency responses can be expected, ongoing and special services to the foster family related to the abuse report crisis, support to foster families throughout the aftermath of maltreatment reports, and assistance to secure legal information, advice, and representation.

AREAS FOR POSITIVE CHANGE

Four areas of positive change are recommended here: (a) awareness of the traumatic impact on foster families of some agency responses to maltreatment allegations; (b) agency policy on dealing with reported foster families; (c) information provided to foster families; and (d) agency response to maltreatment reports, going well beyond investigation.

Agency Awareness

Most agencies are acutely aware that their foster homes are being reported for child maltreatment. Some staff know that many foster parents are concerned about this and that the handling of child maltreatment reports has an impact on the recruitment and retention of foster families. A fuller awareness is needed. Agencies need to recognize that the likelihood of abuse reports against foster families is high. Thus, agencies need to treat abuse reports as an ongoing part of the job, rather than as an unexpected crises. Awareness is also needed of the powerful traumatic impact on foster parents of the report and of agency responses. Many staff members may erroneously assume that abuse report policies which are moderate in intent are moderate in effect. As one foster parent protested after a workshop on abuse allegations in foster care, "But you haven't told them what it's like. You didn't show what a nightmare this really is."

It is important that agency staff members become more aware that it is possible to modify child protection practice in foster care and still protect children. They need to recognize that altering some practices which stress foster parents may be helpful to children by reducing their stress and minimizing further losses.

Agency Policy

Agency policies on responding to reported foster families should value and give the highest priority to child and family well-being and should cover the totality of agency responses when child abuse is reported. These would include how maintaining communication with the foster family during the investigation will be handled, when and how foster children are to remain, be removed or returned, and how support services will be provided to foster family members. Service interventions for children and parents should be individualized, in contract to blanket policies, and the needs of the entire family should be taken into account. In addition, agency policies should provide for input from foster parents in all of the service decisions that effect them. They should also make provisions for the appeal and review of those decisions and indicate how future placements and licensure will be handled. It would acknowledge and accept that in many instances of unfounded reports, cases in which the validity cannot be determined and some cases in which the report was valid, reported foster parents will view the reports as "false." It would recognize for all reported foster families the right to constructive service, the right to support, and the right to information throughout investigation, disposition and related agency action.

Information

Foster parents need a great deal of information regarding child maltreatment reports involving foster homes in order to be better prepared to cope with the experience when it happens. They need the information at several points in their fostering careers—at licensure, during training, and upon receipt of report. They need the information in several forms—in writing, in discussion with staff members, and in foster parent group meetings—in order to make it clear and meaningful.

Foster parents need information on the child abuse reporting law and its procedures with emphasis on implications for foster families, their legal rights and legal standing as foster parents, how the agency can be expected to respond from the time of receipt of report through disposition and all subsequent related actions, and what services, supports and resources are available to them (Carbino, 1989; Sprouse, 1989).

In relation to the dilemma of "false" allegations, there are some points which might be emphasized so that foster parents might feel less unjustly treated. These would include that "false" does not necessarily mean unfair. Abuse reporting laws and procedures are designed to ensure that even the suspicion of abusive situations for children will be investigated.

"False" may not be untrue. There may be real differences among the reporter, the reported and the investigator in their perceptions of a situation and in their definitions of abuse/neglect. Information on the investigation process should include what specific provisions there are for foster parent input into the investigation and for review of the disposition. If foster parents perceive the reports as "false," a sense that their views will at least be fully heard will be very helpful. Information regarding the availability of support should clarify that foster parents are entitled to support without regard to whether allegations are "false" or "true," and that those providing support will not be taking sides. Information on avenues of review or appeal of agency actions is important to foster parents, particularly when they view allegations as "false" or unfair. For all reported foster families, information on what to expect and what they can do will help decrease shock and stigma, reduce a sense of isolation and provide some ways to deal with the situation. However, information alone will be insufficient.

Agency Response

How agencies respond to reported foster families is crucial in all situations of abuse reports. All reported foster families, if suddenly subjected to processes they do not understand, to abrupt removals of foster children, to cutoff of communication with the agency, to disrespectful treatment by agency or law enforcement personnel, and/or to long periods of not knowing the outcome of their case will understandably feel mistreated. And they will have solid grounds for feeling this way. Though foster parents, and perhaps some agency staff members, feel that insensitive handling is unfair when allegations are "false," it is clear that there is no professional justification for treating any reported families badly. It may be helpful to recognize openly with foster parents both that they have experienced trauma and that it was not intended. Robin (1989) suggests that there is an obligation to apologize to foster parents when agency actions regarding abuse/neglect reports have caused pain and suffering.

States and communities can be successful in providing the resources, services and supports that will likely help to reduce trauma to reported foster families. A few state and county social service agencies have begun to provide these: (1) full information regarding abuse allegations and agency response, (2) continuing communication with designated staff and support by staff or selected foster parents through the investigation process, (3) means for input and review of investigation findings, (4) means of appeal of agency decisions. Likewise, some state or county foster parent associations provide support for reported foster parents through group or individual means and provide them information on their rights and resources.

SUMMARY

Foster parents are unprepared for child abuse allegations involving their homes and for subsequent agency responses, particularly if they view the allegations as "false." Changes are needed in agency awareness, policy and response related to abuse allegations in family foster care in order to reduce the unintended damaging effects on foster families, whether or not maltreatment is substantiated. Constructive response to all reported foster families is achievable. It is also necessary to the well-being of foster children and their families and to the maintenance of valued foster home resources.

REFERENCES

Besharov, D. J. (1984). Child welfare malpractice: Suing agencies and caseworkers for harmful practices. *Trial*, March, 56-64.

Carbino, R. (1980). *Foster parenting. An updated review of the literature*. New York: Child Welfare League of America.

Carbino, R. (1987). *I have never felt so alone in my life: Abuse allegations involving foster homes*. Paper presented at the 1987 International Foster Care Organisation Conference. Leeds, England.

Carbino, R. (1989). Child welfare issues in how social service systems respond to allegations of foster home abuse/neglect. In J. Sprouse (Ed.), *Allegations of abuse in family foster care: An examination of the impact on foster families*. King George, VA: American Foster Care Resources.

Carbino, R. (in press). Advocacy for foster families facing child abuse allegations: How foster parent organizations and social agencies are responding to the problem. *Child Welfare*.

Cassens Moss, D. (1988). Foster care lawsuits. *ABA Journal, 74*, 23-24.

Garson, P. S. (1986). Parental tort immunity and foster parents: Mayberry v. Pryor. *George Mason University Law Review, 9*(1), 197-210.

Nadile, V. S. (1987). Promoting the integrity of foster family relationships: Needed statutory protections for foster parents. *Notre Dame Law Review, 62*, 221-237.

Robin, M. (1989). The trauma of allegations of abuse and neglect for foster parents. In J. Sprouse (Ed.), *Allegations of abuse in family foster care: An examination of the impact on foster families*. King George, VA: American Foster Care Resources.

Ryan, P., & McFadden, E. J. (1986). *Preventing abuse in family foster care*.

Final Report. National Foster Care Education Project. Ypsilanti, Michigan: Eastern Michigan University.

Sprouse, J., Jr. (Ed.). (1989). *Allegations of abuse in family foster care: An examination of the impact on foster families*. King George, Virginia: American Foster Care Resources.

Woods, P. R. (1988). Foster family rights: Recommendations by the Council of Europe. *Virginia Journal of International Law, 28*(2),561-584.

Unfounded Allegations of Child Abuse in the United Kingdom: A Survey of Foster Parents' Reactions to Investigative Procedures

Carolyn Hicks
Stephen Nixon

ABSTRACT. Until recently, little attention had been paid to foster carers as potential abusers. While this paucity of research is being corrected, an additional problem has now emerged in the form of allegations of abuse against foster carers which subsequently turn out to be without foundation. This paper will report on a survey of foster parents in the United Kingdom who were investigated for child abuse and neglect. Topics discussed will include how allegations were made, how foster parents responded to allegations, and ways in which the sensitivity and efficacy of the investigations could be improved.

Child abuse is a most abhorrent crime, rightly arousing universal condemnation. However, it should be borne in mind that it is an easy accusation to make and a difficult one to disprove. When allegations of child maltreatment are made, it is essential to place the child's welfare as the priority and where this is in doubt, action must be taken. But the vulnerability of foster parents, their rights and integrity must also be considered, thus making the assessment of the alleged child abuse a delicate task indeed.

The issue of unsubstantiated accusations may appear to be a comparatively minor problem. With no child actually hurt, the major purpose of the child care agency remains intact. However, if it is accepted that foster

---

Carolyn Hicks and Stephen Nixon are affiliated with the School of Continuing Studies, University of Birmingham, Birmingham, B15 2TT, United Kingdom.

249

carers are the major resources of any fostering agency without whom only a limited child care service could be provided, then it becomes apparent that any such unfounded allegation, if it is insensitively handled, has the potential to detract from these services through the foster parents' withdrawal from the fostering system. To this end, it is important that the procedures adopted during such allegations, and the impact of these on the foster carers are scrutinized carefully in order to ascertain whether or not the practices currently adopted are optimal.

FOSTER CARE ABUSE REPORTS IN THE UNITED KINGDOM

The present report is based on a detailed survey carried out in the United Kingdom of 36 foster parents for whom allegations of child abuse were unsubstantiated. The aims of the study were three-fold:

a. To find out how allegations were made and whether there was any common procedural policy.
b. To ascertain the reactions of the foster carers both during and after the investigation.
c. To consider ways in which the investigative procedures might be improved.

How the Allegations Were Made

The results of the survey suggested that there was no consistent manner in which foster parents were informed that abuse allegations had been made against them. The way in which this information was imparted varied greatly in terms of the mode of contact, the personnel involved, the length and nature of the interview and the detail of the allegations. One factor, however, was consistent — none of the foster parents was given any prior warning that there were problems in the fostering arrangements. Without exception, the allegations were made unexpectedly so that the carers had no opportunity to prepare themselves for the shock. Given that predictability is an important aspect of stress control (Katz & Wykes, 1985), this lack of preparation of the foster carers served only to maximize their distress.

The manner in which the information was conveyed varied from a telephone call to direct face-to-face contact. Those foster parents who received the information by phone (33% of the sample) were united in their objection to this method of conveying the news, seeing it is an easy option for the information giver who neither had to witness directly the carers' responses nor support them in their reaction. In all cases, the phone call was abrupt, functional and unsupportive, leaving the foster carers bewildered and upset. The value of non-verbal cues as a modifying agent of harsh messages is well documented (Argyle, 1982) and yet on this most sensitive topic, such techniques were eliminated by the choice of communication method. While no other criminal charge would be made in this way, nor information about a terminal disease or fatal accident be delivered by phone, the need for comparable sensitivity on the topic of alleged child abuse seems to be overlooked with amazing frequency.

The remaining 66% of the sample was given the information in person, although there was a wide variation in terms of who imparted the news and how it was handled. Fifty-eight percent of the foster carers received an unexpected visit by a social worker (though not necessarily their own) who operated as an investigating officer, and who had almost total control over the content and format of the interview. It should be pointed out that the majority of foster carers in the United Kingdom have their own social worker, who is distinct from the social worker who supervises the child. The inflexibility of the interview schedule left the foster carers with a sense of impotence, because of their perceived lack of control over the situation. This further contributed to their stress.

When the foster parents own worker conducted the investigation, there was an immediate role conflict. This individual, who had previously been perceived as a support for the foster parents, had now changed roles and allegiances and was clearly, by assuming the role of investigator, operating on behalf of the child care agency. While some of the foster parents accepted this role confusion, the majority felt it to be inappropriate, partly because it removed an obvious source of support. In these cases a clear recommendation emerged for the allegation to be investigated by someone other than the foster carers' own social worker, thereby leaving loyalties undivided and a potential source of comfort and advice for the parents intact. The withdrawal of support from the family's own worker added considerably to the foster parents' stress.

In eight percent of the cases, the police conveyed the allegation, again without prior warning, and in two cases the foster parent suspected of the abuse was arrested and taken to the police station for full criminal investigation. Given all the usual connotations associated with an unexpected police visit, such an approach is likely to engender distress, antagonism and resentment—emotions far from useful to the preservation of reason and cooperation. The atmosphere of the police interrogation was reported to be cold, distant and unsupportive, creating a pervasive feeling of implied guilt from the start. Without exception, and not unreasonably, the foster parents were unanimous in their rejection of this approach.

The remainder of the sample (eleven percent) were informed of the allegations by both a police officer and a social worker again in an unexpected visit. In these interviews the agenda and approach conformed to the police investigative model. The content of the visit followed the pattern of questioning the foster carers and taking statements. The social workers tended to take on the role of an intermediary between the police and the foster carers by introducing and explaining the purpose of the visit, while the police conducted the main part of the interview. In over fifty percent of all the cases studied, the foster parents were not told the precise nature of the allegation and so did not know of what they were accused. Inevitably then, they had no means of proving their innocence.

The Reactions of the Foster Parents

The most consistently reported immediate reaction to the abuse investigation was shock and denial. Some foster parents reported powerful somatic responses, such as increased heart rate, sweating and palpitations. This was replaced by anger which was either expressed directly towards the person or organization making the accusation or indirectly towards those in a less powerful position, such as the natural child, foster child or relative. The hostility was linked to overpowering feelings of bitterness, which was particularly pronounced in those cases where the foster family's social worker had been involved in informing them of the allegation at the outset. These foster carers reported feelings of betrayal, isolation and fear, largely because the most obvious source of potential help and support had been removed.

The majority of the foster parents spent a considerable amount of time reliving those past events that might possibly have been misconstrued as abuse. In all cases, irrational conclusions were drawn concerning the action and the perpetrator perceived to be responsible, and guilt and hostility were directed at the family members blamed. The outcome of this was considerable discord within the home, and a major disruption of interpersonal relationships. In eleven percent of the cases, the foster parents separated and subsequently divorced.

The investigations were in most cases lengthy and involved, taking many weeks or months to complete. Throughout this time, the foster parents were provided with little information as to the state of the investigation, thereby leaving them in profound uncertainty. The long lapses without adequate information reinforced a sense of impotence among many foster parents and the realization that they had no control over either the duration or nature of the investigative procedure generated a high degree of anxiety which was manifested in a number of stress-related illnesses, and interpersonal problems.

The foster carers had mixed reactions when they eventually were told the allegations were determined to be unfounded. A third of the foster parents reported an overwhelming sense of relief, though in all cases this was tempered by a residual anger over the manner in which the allegations had been handled. The remaining foster carers experienced no such relief, but simply an increasing bitterness. The single factor apparently responsible for these differential responses concerned the role played by the foster carer's social worker. Where social workers were supportive and constructive, explaining the need for the investigation, providing information when available and generally showing a sense of solidarity with the foster parents, the outcome was more positive. In these cases, the foster parents were able to adopt an almost philosophical attitude to the necessity for investigating any suspicion concerning the child's welfare. However, when the family's social worker adopted personal responsibility for carrying out the investigation, the foster parents felt a deep sense of betrayal and isolation which subsequently led to their bitterness. Nonetheless, despite the different reactions, the overriding feeling of both groups was the same — that the unfounded allegations had cost them their self-esteem, integrity and respect; they had endured months of stress with limited power and resources to deal with the seemingly omnipotent authority conducting the investigation.

Inspection of the foster carers' responses revealed that those with partners typically had a more constructive response to the event than those who were single. The partner was seen as an effective support, both in terms of emotional catharsis and as an aid to rational thought. However, for some foster carers whose partner had been the accused party, doubts about their innocence began to develop. Conflict between rational thought and highly emotive reactions was experienced, which in most cases yielded to an overwhelming feeling of distrust and disbelief. In a number of these cases, the couples eventually separated even though the allegation was found to be without substance. Those foster parents without a partner experienced total isolation. Even if they had close family connections and a network of friends, many foster carers felt unable to discuss the allegation for fear of the accusation generating suspicion in the audience.

Whatever the mediating factors, in no case did the foster parents reach a stage of total resolution and acceptance of the situation. They remained transfixed in a state of destructive emotional forces which periodically overwhelmed them and rendered them unable to cope. Out of the sample studied, seventeen percent gave up fostering altogether as a result of this experience, and sixty four percent were in doubt as to whether they would continue with fostering in the future.

Summary of Findings

The investigation procedures adopted are clearly variable, with the majority being destructive and insensitive. Almost without exception, the way in which the enquiry was handled served to maximize the stress experienced by the foster parents.

The unpredictability of the event. Since no advance warning was given of problems in the fostering arrangements, there was no opportunity for the accused parties to prepare themselves psychologically for the shock of the allegation. It has been well documented that being able to predict the occurrence of a potentially stressful event typically reduces the severity of the stress (Katz & Wykes, 1985). Similarly, the uncertainty that many foster parents experienced during the lengthy investigation procedure, constituted another facet of unpredictability, which consequently increased the stress levels. Clearly, keeping the foster parents informed of the enquiry's progress can be very helpful.

The lack of perceived control over the event. All the foster parents reported a sense of helplessness and impotence throughout the investigation. This was generated by a number of factors, such as the lack of information about what they were accused of, lack of clear policies and procedures for investigating child maltreatment and no vehicle for making appeals or resolving grievances. Again, studies have clearly demonstrated that where individuals believe themselves to have some control over events (even though this belief may be erroneous), they will feel less stress (Geer & Maisel, 1972; Glass & Singer, 1972).

Evaluation of the event. People may perceive a given stressful event in a variety of ways, since the objective facts of a situation are less important than the subjective evaluation of it. Where an individual construes the stress-provoking event to have some short or long-term value then the degree of stress experienced is reduced. Situations perceived as threatening an individual's survival (such as a terminal disease) or self-worth are maximally stressful (Atkinson, Atkinson, & Hilgard, 1983). Obviously, allegations concerning child abuse are very destructive to self-esteem, and so constitute a major source of stress. Inevitably, none of the foster parents perceived the allegations and investigative procedures to have any positive consequences. However, it is conceivable that had they been warned during their training period or even at the outset of the investigation that the child care organization was under a legal obligation to investigate any concern, however minimal or unlikely, about the child's well-being, then the routine nature of the investigation might have modified the foster parents' wholly negative construction of the event and in consequence reduced their stress level.

Feelings of competence to deal with the stressful event. Individuals who have a clearly defined and rehearsed strategy for dealing with a stressful event experience less stress. Since people usually return to well-rehearsed actions in stressful situations, it is important that agencies provide guidelines on how to deal with various contingencies of being investigated for child abuse or neglect.

However, none of the foster carers had been given any prior advice as to how to deal with a situation of alleged abuse, despite their obvious vulnerability to such accusations. Nor did any of the respondents have a recommended strategy or procedure provided by the fostering agency when such situations did occur. The net consequence of this was that none of the foster carers had a coping policy, either at a pragmatic or an affective level, when the allegation was made, nor when the investigation was in operation. As a result, the majority of the sample reported feelings of inadequacy and helplessness. Clearly, had a set of formal guidelines been provided which the foster carers could have followed throughout the procedure, this might have effected a reduction in their stress levels.

Social support structures. The practical and emotional support provided by other people, whether they be friends or family, significantly reduces the level of stress experienced when an individual is faced by a traumatic event. Social supports can provide information, experience, advice and comfort. However, when the trauma is the accusation of an abhorrent crime, such as child abuse, then individuals may, understandably, be less than eager to share this problem with others for fear that they will be assumed guilty. Under these circumstances, then, what is needed is an impartial or anonymous support system, which provides unconditional, non-judgmental help and advice whenever the foster carers require it. Clearly, some voluntary counseling or listening service operated by individuals who understand the devastating nature of the event (perhaps as a result of their own similar experiences) could be established. This network could supply any foster carer who had problems in the fostering arrangements with advice, information, counseling, help or just a responsive ear (e.g., Nixon, Hicks, & Ells, 1986; Gill, 1984).

This service is all the more necessary when the overall reactions of the foster parents, throughout the whole allegation and investigation period are analyzed more closely. The initial reaction of the sample studied was one of shock and denial — a total rejection of the accusation and its implications. For some foster carers this reaction lasted just a few hours, while for others it continued over a period of several days and was accompanied by some degree of debilitation.

After a period of shock and denial, the foster parents began to experience a number of responses, which can be categorized in the following way:

a. Somatic reactions of breathlessness, choking, lack of strength and appetite, and sweating;
b. Cognitive reactions of preoccupation and obsession with the allegation, resulting in a state akin to daydreaming;
c. Behavioral reactions which involved changes in the foster carer's normal pattern of behavior, usually producing aimlessness and apathy.
d. Affective reactions of extreme hostility which were manifested toward the child, the natural parents, the social workers and related personnel and their own family. In addition, many foster parents reported a sense of guilt, irrationally blaming themselves for the situation. This "if only" syndrome of things done or said that might have formed the focus of the complaint generated an enormous amount of self-directed anger.

Following this intermediate stage, some ten percent of the foster parents moved on to a somewhat more realistic phase of acceptance of the situation. They were ultimately able to think and talk rationally about the situation and to distance themselves from it psychologically. However, more than three-quarters of the sample failed to reach this state of resolution, and remained bitter and angry. None of the sample appeared to reach a stage of sustained and complete adjustment.

Taken together, these responses can be seen to be very similar to those experienced during bereavement (e.g., Murray Parkes, 1972; Kubler-Ross, 1986; Bowlby, 1980). These authors, and others, have reported that the first response to information about a tragic event or loss is one of denial and numbness. This is followed by a period during which the individual develops his or her awareness of the event, becoming depressed, angry, disorganized and grief-stricken. The final stage is one of acceptance and resolution. Although the descriptors of these responses vary from author to author, there is considerable congruence over a number of points. First, individuals move through a number of stages in their response to bereavement before the final acceptance. However, not everyone reaches this final stage and in consequence many experience a variety of problems. These individuals need help and support. Second, the degree of grief experienced depends partially on the abruptness of the loss or tragic event; the more abrupt the event, the greater the response. Likewise, when a person is unprepared for a loss or tragic event, their grief reactions tend to be more pronounced (e.g., Worden, 1988).

Foster parents who are accused of child abuse suffer many losses — loss of self-esteem, integrity, their role as a foster carer, their marriage (in some cases), the child for whom they had been caring; loss of occupation and income, loss of trust in their partner and control over their own lives. Similar findings have been reported by PAIN (Parents Against Injustice), an organization in the United Kingdom which works with biological parents who have been falsely accused of abuse (PAIN, 1986). In addition, Jenkins and Norman (1972) have noted that many of these same reactions are found among natural parents whose children are placed into the care system. Given the commonality of the reactions, it becomes clear that the shared experiences of loss of foster and natural parents could be used to develop greater understanding between these two parties, thereby reducing some of the conflict that is inherent in their respective roles.

It is also obvious that the information concerning the event needs to be conveyed with utmost sensitivity, allowing the foster parents as much time as possible to prepare themselves psychologically for the events that follow. During this time as well as in the weeks and months following the allegation, realistic support should be provided. It is inconceivable that anyone would inform an individual of a progressive terminal disease over the phone, or fail to offer help, sympathy and support to the sufferer. While the loss of health and life on the one hand and the loss of a foster child may not be comparable in magnitude, this should not be an excuse for indelicate or harsh handling of the event. And yet, very few of the sample reported sensitivity or support from the official personnel involved in their case. Such a lack of empathetic awareness was construed by many to reflect the implied guilt assumed by the investigating parties.

Emerging Recommendations

The recommendations which emerge from this study are clear. However, while they are derived from a study of unsubstantiated accusations against foster parents, they would apply to any investigations of child abuse. These recommendations could form part of a Code of Practice for use in such investigation procedures. These recommendations are outlined on the next page.

1. There should be some advance warning that problems had been noted in the foster-care arrangements, since accusations of such gravity usually do not descend without warning. This would give the foster parents and foster child some time to prepare themselves psychologically for the events that will follow.

2. The allegations should not be investigated by the family's social worker, since this causes considerable role confusion as well as removing a potential source of support. The enquiry should be handled by an independent investigator unassociated with the fostering agency (Cavara & Ogren, 1983). In this way, impartiality can be achieved, and a residual source of potential support maintained.

3. The allegations should be made in person, with the family's social worker present.

4. The need to investigate any suspected threat to the child's welfare, as a routine procedure, should be emphasized during the foster parents' training. Where this has not been done it should be stressed at the outset of the investigation procedure and reinforced throughout. In this way, the investigation takes on a routine acceptability and becomes less stigmatizing.

5. The details of the allegation should be made clear in order that the foster parents could either explain an innocuous event that had been misinterpreted as abuse or at least know exactly of what they are accused.

6. The investigation should be completed as quickly as possible, to minimize the stress caused by uncertainty.

7. The foster parents should be kept informed at all stages of the enquiry as to its progress.

8. Absolute discretion and confidentiality should be guaranteed, since even unfounded allegations may leave doubt in the minds of those involved in the investigation. When the allegations concern an act as universally condemned as child abuse, social alienation and victimization are a likely outcome. For this reason, uniformed police should not be involved in any home visit to the foster parents.

9. Some standardized protocol for dealing with allegations should be developed and adopted throughout all child care agencies in the country. In this way, more acceptable procedures can be followed which would then provide all parties with a known format on the stages of the investigative procedure.

10. Foster parents should be warned during their training of their potential vulnerability to accusations of this kind. They should be

given guidelines as to possible courses of action should the need arise.

11. A network of independent support groups should be developed, such that the foster parents have a source of unconditional, non-judgmental support and help if they require it.

12. A clearer, more accessible route to the Local Authority Ombudsman should be made possible, so that any dissatisfaction with the allegation and investigation procedures can be referred to an independent adjudicator.

CONCLUSION

Foster parents are an undervalued resource. They typically have to act not only as surrogate parents to damaged children but also as guide, counselor, mentor, therapist, probation officer, confidante and friend. Yet they are usually given little training for these tasks. When the general public and the fostering agencies recognize the difficulties and vulnerabilities inherent in fostering and stop regarding foster carers as simply performing an act of extended parenting, then perhaps they will be given the training and support they require (Cavara & Ogren, 1983). Until that time, it behooves all fostering agencies to implement clear and optimal policies for investigating accusations of abuse.

The commitment of the child care organization and its social workers towards foster carers, as well as the child, must be strengthened in order to avoid both long term personal distress to the individuals at the center of such cases and any reduction in the availability of fostering services. However, what clearly emerges from this survey is that potentially defamatory allegations are made in a careless way with apparent disregard for their gravity. For the most part, the procedures adopted to investigate complaints of child maltreatment in family foster care contravene many of the fundamental principles of British justice. Obviously, some action to rectify this situation must be taken in order to preserve foster care as a resource to abused children.

REFERENCES

Argyle, M. (1982). Social behavior. In M. Herbert (Ed.), *Psychology for social workers*. London: Macmillan Press Ltd.

Atkinson, R. L., Atkinson, R. C., & Hilgard, E. R. (1983). *Introduction to psychology*. New York: Harcourt Brace Jovanovich.

Bowlby, J. (1980). *Attachment and loss: Loss, sadness and depression.* (Vol. III). New York: Basic Books.

Cavara, M., & Ogren, C. (1983). Protocol to investigate child abuse in foster care. *Child Abuse and Neglect, 7*(3), 287-295.

Geer, J., & Maisel, E. (1972). Evaluating the effects of the prediction control confound. *Journal of Personal and Social Psychology, 23,* 314-319.

Gil, E. (1984) Foster parents: Set up to fail. *Child Abuse and Neglect, 7*(3), 287-295.

Glass, D. C., & Singer, J. E. (1972). *Urban stress: Experiments on noise and social stressors.* New York: Academic Press.

Jenkins, S., & Norman, E. (1972). *Filial deprivation & foster care.* New York: Columbia University Press.

Katz, R., & Wykes, T. (1985). The psychological difference between temporally predictable and unpredictable stressful events: Evidence for information control theories. *Journal of Personal and Social Psychology, 23,* 314-319.

Kubler-Ross, E. (1986). *On death and dying.* London: Tavistock.

Nixon, S., Hicks, C., & Ells, S. (1986). Support for foster parents accused of child abuse. *Foster Care, 48,* 8-10.

PAIN. (1986). *Child abuse — working together.* Bishop's Stortford, United Kingdom: PAIN Publications.

Parkes, C. M. (1972). *Bereavement: Studies of grief in adult life.* New York: International Universities Press.

Worden, J. W. (1988). *Grief counselling and grief therapy.* London: Routledge.

Index

Abandonment
  definition, 42
  screening for, 67,68
Acting out, 53
ACTION for Child Protection, 77,
  79,87-88n.
Adolescents
  acting out by, 53
  false abuse allegations by, 101,
    184
  in foster care homes, 53,221,225
  sexual abuse of, 221,225
Adoption, by foster parents, 225-226
Advocacy, 40
Aid to Dependent Children, 10
Anna O., 153
Anxiety, separation-related,
  171-172,173,181
Anxiety disorders, 147

Battered child, 11
Battered Child, The (Helfert and
  Kempe), 12
"Battered Child Syndrome, The"
  (Kemp et al), 3
Behavioral indicators, of child
  abuse, 44-45,49
Bereavement, grief response,
  256-257
Bias, in child abuse assessment,
  78-79,95-97
Buckey, Peggy, 17
Buckey, Raymond, 17

Carbino, Rosemarie, 23-24
Certification, of foster care homes,
  213-217
  decertification, 21
  recertification, 215-216
Child abuse, 1-2. *See also* Sexual
  abuse
  atrocities of, 11-12
  definition, 40-41
    ambiguity of, 5-6,7,11
    of Federal Child Abuse and
      Treatment Act, 40-41
    investigation-related, 63
    screening-related, 63
  denial of, 24
  in foster care homes. *See* Foster
    care homes, child
    maltreatment in
  incidence, 7-9,13-16
  institutional, 38-39
  legislation regarding, 3,6,40-41
  as moral panic, 9-13
  psychopathological model, 3-5
  severity, 79-80
  as social problem, 2-5
  social psychology of, 5
  as valence issue, 4-5
Child abuse investigations, 35-50.
  See also Screening, of child
  abuse reports
  agency priorities, 54-55
  community-based services and,
    37-38
  effect on children, 26
  errors of, 18
  for institutional abuse, 38-39

DATE DUE
